Poker For Dummies® Cheat Sheet

W9-BMA-788

Poker Etiquette at Home

Do . . .

- ✔ **Be honest:** Don't try to short-change the pot or otherwise cheat.
- ✔ **Play quickly:** No one likes a slow player.
- ✔ **Be courteous and friendly:** No one likes a whiner.
- ✔ **Be a good winner:** Gloating and making fun of other players is a definite no-no.
- ✔ **Be a good loser:** We all lose. It happens. But show some class and don't show your temper, swear, or throw cards. Definitely don't insult the other players.
- ✔ **Let the other players know if you plan to leave early:** It's courteous to let the other players know in advance if you plan to quit early.
- ✔ **Bet in sequence:** Bet, call, or fold when it's your turn. Acting out of turn can adversely affect another player's hand.

Don't . . .

- ✔ **Give a player advice in the middle of a hand even if he asks for it:** This is a no-win proposition. Either the player who asked will be upset at you if the advice is wrong or the person who loses against the player will be mad at you.
- ✔ **Look at another player's hand, unless you have permission:** Some players strongly object to your looking at their hand.
- ✔ **Play poker with a guy named "Doyle," "Amarillo Slim," or "Harpo":** These guys are too good for your normal home game.

Money Management Tips

A poker game theoretically never ends, so keep these suggestions in mind:

- ✔ Quitting once you've won a certain amount of money will neither stop your losses in the long run if you are a losing player nor protect your profits if you are a winner.
- ✔ Poor players will lose their money no matter what they do. Good players establish an expected hourly win rate whether or not they quit after they've pocketed a certain amount of winnings.
- ✔ Playing fewer hours by quitting when you're ahead isn't always the right strategy.
- ✔ If you're playing in a good game, and you are playing your best, stay in the game unless you have other obligations.
- ✔ If you're in a bad game, get out of it now — never mind if you're winning or not.
- ✔ If you're emotionally upset, stressed out, fighting the flu, or otherwise not at your best, you're better off not playing since your maladies will ultimately take themselves out on your bankroll.

For Dummies: Bestselling Book Series for Beginners

Poker For Dummies®

Bluffing Strategies

The next time you're inclined to perform larceny at the poker table, keep these tips in mind:

- **Be aware of how many players you'll have to bluff your way through.** While one or even two players can be bluffed, don't think about trying to bluff more than two opponents unless you really have strong reasons to believe you'll succeed.

- **Understand that a bluff doesn't have to work to make it the correct decision.** After all, you're usually just risking one bet to win an entire pot full of bets. Bluffing has to work only some of the time to be the right choice. And even when you're caught, a bluff can be successful if it causes opponents to call when you are betting a strong hand.

- **Avoid bluffing players who are either experts or brain dead.** Instead, aim your bluffs at good opponents. Poor players will usually call " . . . to keep you honest," while experts are more likely to see through your chicanery.

- **Don't bluff for the sake of bluffing.** Some players will bluff just to "advertise." There's no need to do that. Bluff if you believe you have a reasonable chance to succeed. You'll get plenty of advertising value because some of your bluffs will be picked off regardless of how well you assess your chances for success.

- **Never bluff a hopeless hand when there are more cards to come.** Instead, think about semi-bluffing, which allows you to win the pot two ways: Your opponents may fold, or you might hit your draw.

- **Take the opportunity to bluff if all of your opponents check on the previous betting round.** It's even better if they've all checked on an expensive betting round. But your chances are diminished if any newly exposed cards appear to have helped one of your opponents.

- **Imply specific hands.** Bluffs that seem to represent specific hands, such as a flush or a straight, have a much better chance to succeed than bets that appear to come out of the blue.

- **Zero in on weak players.** It's much easier to bluff players who have shown weakness by checking, than to bluff those who have shown strength by betting on the preceding round.

- **Strive for a tight, aggressive image.** Play the kinds of starting hands recommended in this book. This kind of image has a much better chance of running a successful bluff than a player with a loose image. If you are seen as selective, tight, and aggressive, your opponents will not suspect a bluff when you bet. When you have a license to steal, use it.

- **Attempt a bluff occasionally when all the cards are out and you have nothing, but don't overdo it.** But if you have enough to beat a draw, save that additional bet and try to win in a showdown.

Copyright © 2000 Wiley Publishing, Inc. All rights reserved.

Item 5232-5.

For more information about Wiley Publishing, call 1-800-762-2974.

For Dummies: Bestselling Book Series for Beginners

Poker
FOR
DUMMIES®

by Richard D. Harroch and Lou Krieger

Foreword by Chris Moneymaker
Winner of the World Series of Poker

WILEY

Wiley Publishing, Inc.

Poker For Dummies®

Published by
Wiley Publishing, Inc.
111 River St.
Hoboken, NJ 07030
www.wiley.com

Copyright © 2000 by Wiley Publishing, Inc., Indianapolis, Indiana

Copyright © 2000 Text and any other Author Created Materials Copyright, Richard D. Harroch

Published simultaneously in Canada

For general information on our other products and services or to obtain technical support, please contact our Customer Care Department within the U.S. at 800-762-2974, outside the U.S. at 317-572-3993, or fax 317-572-4002.

Wiley also publishes its books in a variety of electronic formats. Some content that appears in print may not be available in electronic books.

Library of Congress Catalog Card No.: 99-69726

ISBN: 0-7645-5232-5

Manufactured in the United States of America

20 19 18 17 16 15 14 13 12

1O/TQ/QZ/QU/IN

About the Authors

Lou Krieger learned poker at the tender age of 7, while standing at his father's side during the weekly Thursday night game held at the Krieger kitchen table in the blue-collar Brooklyn neighborhood where they lived.

Lou played throughout high school and college and managed to keep his head above water only because the other players were so appallingly bad. But it wasn't until his first visit to Las Vegas that he took poker seriously, buying into a low-limit Seven Card Stud game where he managed — with a good deal of luck — to break even.

"While playing stud," he recalls, "I noticed another game that looked even more interesting. It was Texas Hold'em.

"I watched the Hold'em game for about 30 minutes, and sat down to play. One hour and $100 later, I was hooked. I didn't mind losing. It was the first time I played, and I *expected* to lose. But I didn't like feeling like a dummy so I bought and studied every poker book I could find."

"I studied; I played. I studied and played more. Before long I was winning regularly, and I haven't had a losing year since I began keeping records."

In the early 1990s Lou Krieger began writing a column called "On Strategy" for *Card Player Magazine*. He has also written two books about poker, *Hold'em Excellence: From Beginner to Winner* and *MORE Hold'em Excellence: A Winner For Life*.

When not writing about poker, Lou (who lives in Long Beach, California) can be found playing poker in the card casinos of Southern California.

Richard Harroch is an attorney with over 20 years of experience in representing start-up and emerging companies, entrepreneurs, and venture capitalists. He is listed in "Who's Who in American Law" and is a corporate partner in a major law firm in San Francisco, Orrick, Herrington & Sutcliffe LLP. He is a Phi Beta Kappa graduate of U.C. Berkeley and graduated from UCLA Law School, where he was managing editor of the *Law Review*. He has written a number of legal/business books, including *The Small Business Kit For Dummies; Start-Up and Emerging Companies: Planning, Financing and Operating the Successful Business;* and *Partnership and Joint Venture Agreements*. He also spearheaded the development of a premier legal-agreements Web site on the Internet.

He has lectured extensively before various legal and business organizations, including the American Electronics Association, the Venture Capital Institute, the California Continuing Education of the Bar, the Corporate Counsel Institute, the San Francisco Bar, and the Practicing Law Institute (PLI).

Richard has served as the Chairman of the California State Bar Committee on Partnerships, the Co-Chairman of the Corporations Committee of the San Francisco Bar (Barristers), a member of the Executive Committee of the Business Law Section of the California State Bar, and Co-Chair of the *Law Journal* annual seminar in New York on "Joint Ventures and Strategic Alliances."

Richard has experience in the following areas: start-up and emerging companies, e-commerce, corporate financings, joint ventures, strategic alliances, venture capital financings, employment agreements, initial public offerings, leases, loans, online and Internet matters, license agreements, partnerships, preferred stock, confidentiality agreements, stock options, sales contracts, securities laws, and mergers and acquisitions.

Richard has participated a number of times in the World Series of Poker in Las Vegas and is the co-author of *Gambling For Dummies*.

Authors' Acknowledgments

Books are always a collaborative effort. Never believe an author who tells you otherwise. Without the efforts of acquisitions editor Mark Butler, who believed in and nurtured this project for two years, this book would not have come to fruition.

Skilled editors are a wondrous breed, and the effort, assistance, and suggestions of senior project editor Tim Gallan, and copy editor Patricia Yuu Pan shaped this book into something we're proud of. With dedication and talent, Tim and Patricia possessed the magic to make the authors appear more literate, wittier, and eminently more readable than they really are.

We are also indebted to those who contributed their writing talent and poker know-how to this book: to poker's "Mad Genius" Mike Caro for his work on "tells" — the body language of poker — and for many of the statistical tables and tips found throughout this book; to Nolan Dalla for his biographical sketches of poker legends past and present; to Dan Paymar for his information on video poker; to Kathy Watterson for her chapter on Internet poker and for showing you, the reader, how to use your personal computer to improve your poker skills; and to Linda Johnson for her foreword.

The world of poker is far too large to individually thank each person we'd like to acknowledge here: the dealers, players, floormen, chip runners, food servers, board attendants, porters, cashiers, supervisors and managers, props, players, and railbirds, who have all graciously enhanced our experiences at the poker table. Here's a warm and heartfelt *thank you.* And thanks to friends and family members who have always encouraged our endeavors — even those involving a risk and a gamble.

Special thanks to the folks at *Card Player Magazine,* who collectively possess a bottomless reserve of poker knowledge, wisdom, and advice and are always willing to share.

Dedication

From Lou: I dedicate this book to Abby, David, and Karen, and to all the Lubchansky cousins whose grandparents sailed to America in steerage with not much more than a suitcase and immigrant dreams. Their dream afforded me the enviable luxury of living well by writing books and playing poker.

From Richard: I dedicate this book to the partners at my law firm who have played poker with me for many years. Thanks for your money, guys!

Publisher's Acknowledgments

We're proud of this book; please send us your comments through our Dummies online registration form located at www.dummies.com/register/.

Some of the people who helped bring this book to market include the following:

Acquisitions, Editorial, and Media Development

Senior Project Editor: Tim Gallan

Acquisitions Editor: Mark Butler

Copy Editor: Patricia Yuu Pan

Acquisitions Coordinator: Lisa Roule

Technical Editor: David Galt

Editorial Manager: Pam Mourouzis

Editorial Assistant: Carol Strickland

Cover Photo: FPG International LLC. © Buss, Gary

Production

Project Coordinator: Kristy Nash

Layout and Graphics: Beth Brooks, Amy Adrian, Barry Offringa, Tracy K. Oliver, Jill Piscitelli, Brent Savage

Proofreaders: Laura Albert, Corey Bowen, John Greenough, Marianne Santy, Kathleen Sparrow

Indexer: Sharon Hilgenberg

Special Help
Linda Stark, Tina Sims

Publishing and Editorial for Consumer Dummies

Diane Graves Steele, Vice President and Publisher, Consumer Dummies

Joyce Pepple, Acquisitions Director, Consumer Dummies

Kristin A. Cocks, Product Development Director, Consumer Dummies

Michael Spring, Vice President and Publisher, Travel

Brice Gosnell, Associate Publisher, Travel

Suzanne Jannetta, Editorial Director, Travel

Publishing for Technology Dummies

Andy Cummings, Vice President and Publisher, Dummies Technology/General User

Composition Services

Gerry Fahey, Vice President of Production Services

Debbie Stailey, Director of Composition Services

Contents at a Glance

Cartoons at a Glance

By Rich Tennant

"It looks like you've been playing cards instead of practicing your counting again."

page 7

"It's jacks or better to open, and the low card in your hand is wild...until my Mom walks in, and then we're playing Go Fish, got it?"

page 157

"You know, I'm not great at reading poker faces, but I think I'd bet against _his_ hand."

page 127

EDWARD SCISSORHANDS AT A CARD PARTY.

"Actually Ed, if any of us had been thinking, we'd have asked you to pass on the shuffle."

page 245

"Sure I'll play Fan Tan with you. If you match cards like you match shirts with ties, this should be an easy win."

page 223

Fax: 978-546-7747
E-mail: richtennant@the5thwave.com
World Wide Web: www.the5thwave.com

Table of Contents

· ·

Foreword

By Chris Moneymaker
Winner of the World Series of Poker

*A*lthough I had experience playing poker online and in poker rooms and casinos, I hadn't yet taken the time to really study the game of poker. Becoming a student of poker means more than putting in a lot of hours playing (which I did). It also means putting in time really studying — and that's where *Poker For Dummies* comes in.

When poker really started to boom, bookstores saw a flood of poker books. There are some good ones out there, and some truly bad ones. But even the good ones don't give you a broad enough picture of poker to allow you to quickly discover the most popular games, and the vast majority of poker books make one poor assumption — that you already know poker.

Most people have played some poker somewhere along the line, but how many have sat in a casino or poker room and really played the game for money? Reading *Poker For Dummies* can give you a good understanding of poker and how it's played everywhere — at home, in local poker rooms, and in the huge casinos and poker rooms in Nevada, Atlantic City, California, and elsewhere.

You can play poker in many different forms; it's a lot different than it was 30 or 40 years ago, when draw poker was the name of the game. These days, you find seven card stud, seven card stud high/low, Texas Hold'em, and Omaha and Omaha high/low in most poker rooms, played at all different stakes. *Poker For Dummies* can get you started on your way to mastering all these games, and it uses the light, witty style you have come to know in the *Dummies* series, holding your interest and making the process of figuring out poker fun and entertaining.

I sure wish someone had given me this book a few years ago. And in a way, I wish that Richard Harroch and Lou Krieger hadn't written it. The competition during my World Series of Poker win in 2003 was fierce, and the more people who read this book, the more good players I'll have to face each year.

I was fortunate enough to win the 2003 World Championship of Poker, and walk away with $2.5 million cash. But, as we got down to the final table, in the middle of one hand, one of the players pulled out *Poker For Dummies* and started reading it!

And now, you too can get that advantage by reading this book. Poker players often say, "it's better to be lucky than good." But with this book, and a little luck, maybe you can find yourself at the final table of the World Championship.

Poker is a fun, entertaining, and challenging game — all the same characteristics that make *Poker For Dummies* a valuable read. Give it a few hours of your time, and you may find that you can start competing with the big boys (and girls) more quickly than you think.

Introduction

. . . .

*P*oker has always been America's game, but poker is changing these days. In a big way. Ask a friend or neighbor with only a casual knowledge of the game to offer an image of poker, and one of three pictures is likely to appear:

Poker is a game played by Mississippi riverboat gamblers with pencil-thin moustaches, fast hands, and a derringer hidden up their ruffled sleeves, or it's played by gunfighters of the Old West (men like Doc Holliday, Wild Bill Hickok, and Bat Masterson). Welcome to Dodge City, pardner. Check your guns at the marshal's office and pull up a chair.

Another picture of poker comes right out of the movie, *The Sting*. Imagine 1930s Chicago mobsters, a round table, a low-hanging lamp illuminating the thick cigar smoke rising from the ash tray, guys with shoulder holsters and snub-nosed 38s, a bottle of cheap Scotch on the table, and someone the size of an NFL linebacker stationed by the peep-hole at the door.

There's a kinder, gentler version too. This is a picture of Uncle Jack and Aunt Gertie playing poker around the kitchen table for pennies, and somehow all the nieces and nephews always come away winners.

Poker has been all of these things, and more. Although your authors are far too young to have gambled with Doc Holliday or played cards with Al Capone, both are familiar with the kitchen table introduction to America's national card game.

Since the late 1980s, poker has undergone a renaissance, a greening, if you please. Today's poker is clean, light, and airy, and decidedly middle class. Like bowling and billiards before it, poker has moved out from under the seedier side of its roots and is flowering in the sunshine. No matter where you live, you probably live within a few hours drive of a public card casino. Poker is all around you. Seek and ye shall find, and these days you don't have to look very far either.

Why You Need This Book

If you've never played poker seriously before, you might wonder why you need a book about it. Why can't you just sit down at the table with a few friends, or visit that friendly casino nearby and learn as you go?

Well you can learn poker that way, but there are better ways to go about it. The school of hard knocks can be expensive, and there's no guarantee you'll ever graduate.

Poker's been around for a long time, and it's never been more popular. With the advent of personal computers, a great deal of research about the game has been done in recent years and some of the tried and true concepts have been changing. Players who don't keep their knowledge up to date will be left behind.

A reference book like *Poker For Dummies* explains the basic rules of the most popular variations of poker and provide a sound strategic approach so you can learn to play well in the shortest amount of time.

You'll undoubtedly find many poker players who have never picked up a book on the subject. Some even disdain this new breed of studious poker players. A few self-taught players are quite skilled, but the majority of them are not. And even if they've been playing for 20 years, that doesn't mean that they have not been making the same mistakes day after day, month after month, and year after year.

Until you are aware of your mistakes it's impossible to correct them. And don't think your opponents are going to point them out either. After all, poker is played for money. And if you find a leak in your opponent's game, you're going to try to exploit it for all it's worth — literally.

What We Assume about You

We expect that you could be approaching this book from a variety of backgrounds. Maybe you've never played poker before, and you don't even know what a full house is. We cover the basics in this book, so we have you covered.

Or maybe you've played poker since you were a kid, and for some reason, you always lose. So you know the rules, but you just don't know how to win. Well, this book certainly can help you. We present all kinds of tips, tricks, and strategies. It's time for you to walk away from the poker table with more money than lint in your pockets.

If you're a poker expert, you still can benefit from what we have to offer. Some of our suggestions may surprise you, and you can certainly learn from the anecdotes we've peppered throughout the book.

How to Use This Book

This book is a reference, not a tutorial. By that, we mean that you can read this book in any fashion you wish. You don't have to read it from cover to cover to understand where we're coming from. Say you know all the rules but want to find out what money management is all about. Jump to Chapter 9 and start reading. If you just want to get to know just the basics and save the advanced stuff for later, just read the first seven chapters and put the book away until you're ready to tackle the rest of the material. And if you really want to flatter us, go ahead and read the book from cover to cover. We promise that you'll enjoy the ride.

How This Book Is Organized

We try to keep the discussions in each chapters self-contained, and we group like chapters into parts. Here's what each part covers:

Part I: How to Play the Games

Poker consists of several games, and we show you how to play almost all of them. From Texas Hold'em to Seven-Card Stud to Omaha/8 Hold'em, we show you not only the nuts and bolts of how to play the games, but we also discuss effective strategies and offer methods for improving your game.

Part II: Advanced Strategy

Playing and winning poker involves much more than the luck of the draw, and this part covers two pretty important aspects of the game: bluffing and money management. Chapter 8 offers some guidelines on both performing bluffs and reading bluffs from other players. In Chapter 9, we actually use math to help you decide how to proceed when you are winning, losing, and breaking even.

Part III: Computers, Casinos, and Cardrooms

You can play poker in more places than just the smoky back room of your best friend's house. People are playing poker against computer-generated opponents, and what's more exciting is that you can now use the Internet to join games with real, live opponents from around the world. Video poker requires special strategies, which we discuss, and we also tell you what goes on in poker tournaments, including the World Series of Poker.

Part IV: More Poker Fun

This short part contains some information that didn't really fit in the previous parts. In Chapter 15, we pull together all of the poker terms, slang, and myths that you're likely to encounter. And in Chapter 16, we provide you with many resources for honing your poker skills.

Part V: The Part of Tens

Every *For Dummies* book ends with top-ten lists, and this one is no exception. We offer you ten ways to read your opponents, the ten best poker players we know of, and others.

Icons Used in This Book

A signature feature of *For Dummies* books, besides top-notch authors and the catchy yellow and black covers, is the use of icons, which are little pictures we like to throw next to pieces of important text. Here's what the icons mean:

A suggestion that can help you play better.

A note that will keep you out of trouble.

A more general concept that you shouldn't forget.

Where to Go from Here

It's up to you. Take a look at the Table of Contents and see what catches your eye. Or maybe look up a topic that interests you in the Index. Or start reading Chapter 1 and don't stop until you reach the end.

Part I
How to Play the Games

The 5th Wave   By Rich Tennant

"It looks like you've been playing cards instead of practicing your counting again."

In this part . . .

Poker consists of several games, and we show you how to play almost all of them. From Seven-Card Stud to Omaha, we show you not only the nuts and bolts of how to play the games, but we also discuss effective strategies and offer methods for improving your game.

Chapter 1

Poker Basics

• •

In This Chapter

▶ Exploring poker and the American dream

▶ Getting a feel for poker basics

▶ Looking at hand rankings

▶ Building a strong foundation for winning

▶ Getting acquainted with general rules and etiquette

▶ Recognizing different types of opponents

▶ Playing in a casino

▶ Getting into a game

▶ Differentiating between casino poker and home games

• •

If they're helpless and they can't defend themselves, you're in the right game.

—Mike Caro, noted poker authority

Poker is America's national card game, and its popularity continues to grow. From Mississippi and Michigan to New Mexico and North Dakota, you can find a game in progress everywhere. If you want to play you can find poker played on replicas of 19th century paddle wheel riverboat or on Native American tribal lands. You can play poker in two-table, no-frills cardrooms and elegant Los Angeles County megaclubs where 150 games (with betting limits ranging from $1–$2 to $200–$400) are in progress 'round the clock.

This book targets readers who are new to poker. If you've played in home games but have never played in a casino, this book can help you too. Even if you consider yourself to have a pretty good hand at the game, this book is bound to improve it.

Poker and the American Dream

Poker has always been a microcosm of all we admire about American virtue. It is part of the very fabric Americans have spent more than 220 years weaving into a national mosaic. Call it the American Dream — the belief that hard work and virtue will triumph, that anyone willing to work hard will succeed, that right makes might. It is an immigrant's song, a mantra of hope; it is an anthem for everyone.

Poker looks like such a simple game. Anyone, it seems, can play it well — though nothing, of course, is further from the truth. Learning the rules can be quick work but becoming a winning player takes considerably longer. Still, anyone willing to make the effort can become a fairly good player. You can succeed in poker the way you succeed in life: by facing it squarely, getting up earlier than the next person, and working harder and smarter than the competition.

Where Did It All Come From?

A profusion of western movies and gunfighter ballads has convinced the world that poker is a quintessentially American game, yet its roots go back hundreds of years. The Persians were said to play a poker-like game centuries ago. Germans played a bluffing game called *Pochen* as early as the sixteenth century; later, there was a French version called *Poque*. The French brought this game with them to New Orleans and its popularity spread — aided by the paddle wheelers that traveled the Mississippi.

Poque soon became known as *poker,* and the rules were modified during the Civil War to allow cards to be drawn to improve one's hand. Stud poker, still very popular today, appeared at about the same time. (See Chapters 3 and 5 for the full scoop on Stud games.)

People all over the world play poker, with hundred of versions played in home games everywhere. You can find games going on in casinos and poker rooms in most of the United States, England, Ireland, France, Holland, Austria, Germany, Finland, Australia, New Zealand, Aruba, Costa Rica, and probably a few other countries too. People play for pennies around the kitchen table and professionally for hundreds of thousands of dollars.

Poker is Good for You

Like the American Dream, poker is good for you: It enriches the soul, sharpens the intellect, heals the spirit, and when played well — nourishes the wallet.

Above all else, poker forces the player to face reality and deal with it head-on. Oh, sure, people can ignore those realities — lots of players do. They are the ones who lose consistently, and rather than face the deficiencies in their own game, persist in placing the blame on fate, on the dealer, on that particular deck of cards, or on anything else — except themselves — that's handy.

But poker can also be bad for you if you don't know the key strategies and your own shortcomings. But don't dismay. You have us to guide you through the rough waters and jump-start your poker education.

Perhaps British author and poker player Anthony Holden said it best. In *Big Deal: A Year As A Professional Poker Player* he writes: "Whether he likes it or not, a man's character is stripped bare at the poker table; if the other players read him better than he does, he has only himself to blame. Unless he is both able and prepared to see himself as others do, flaws and all, he will be a loser in cards, as in life."

Your challenge for as long as you aspire to win at poker is this: Be willing to examine and analyze your character and game. If you do this, and have even a modicum of talent, you can become a winning poker player.

Before You Put on Your Poker Face

Like a house, poker requires a foundation. Only when that foundation is solidly in place can you proceed to build on it. When all the structural elements are in place, you can then add flourishes and decorative touches. But you can't begin embellishing it until the foundation has been poured, the building framed, and all the other elements that come before it are in place. That's our purpose here: to put first things first — to give you a basic understanding of what you need before you begin to play.

Planning and discipline

Some poker players, and it's no more than a handful, really do have a genius for the game — an inexplicable, Picasso-like talent that isn't easily defined and usually has to be seen to be believed. But even in the absence of genius — and most winning players certainly are not poker savants — poker is an eminently learnable skill. Inherent ability helps, and while you need *some* talent, you really don't need all that much. After all, you don't have to be Van Cliburn to play the piano, Picasso to paint, or Michael Jordan to play basketball. What you *do* need to become a winning player are a solid plan to learn the game and discipline.

✔ **Plotting a strategy:** If you aspire to play winning poker you need a plan to learn the game. While the school of hard knocks might have sufficed as the educational institution of choice 20 or 30 years ago, most of today's better poker players have added a solid grounding in poker theory to their over-the-table experiences. You can find a slew of information to help you learn the game. Check out Chapter 16 for our learning plan and suggested books, magazines, and Web sites.

✔ **Discipline:** All the strategic knowledge in the world does not guarantee success to any poker player. Personal characteristics are equally important. Success demands a certain quality of character in addition to strategic know-how. Players lacking self-discipline, for example, have a hard time ever winning consistently regardless of how strategically sophisticated they might be. If one lacks the discipline to throw away poor starting hands, then all the knowledge in the world can't overcome this flaw.

Knowledge without discipline is merely unrealized potential. Playing with discipline is a key to avoiding losing your shirt — or your shorts.

If you can learn to play poker at a level akin to that of a journeyman musician, a work-a-day commercial artist, you will be good enough to win consistently. You don't have to be a world champion like Doyle Brunson, Phil Hellmuth, Johnny Chan, or Tom McEvoy to earn money playing poker. The skills of a good journeyman poker player enables you to supplement your income, or — better yet — earn your entire livelihood at the game. If you go on to become the very best poker player you can be, that should be more than enough to ensure that you will be a lifelong winning player.

The object of the game

The objective of poker is to win money by capturing the *pot,* which contains bets made by various players during the hand. A player wagers a bet in hopes that he has the best hand, or to give the impression that he holds a strong hand and thus convince his opponents to *fold* (abandon) their hands. Since money saved is just as valuable as money won, knowing when to release a hand that appears to be beaten is just as important as knowing when to bet. In most poker games, the top combination of five cards is the best hand.

Number of players

Any number of players, typically from two to ten, can play, depending on the game. Most casino games are set up with eight players for a seven-card game like Stud poker or Razz, and nine or ten players for Texas Hold'em.

The deck

Most forms of poker involve a standard 52-card deck. For Draw poker and Lowball, a joker, or "bug," is sometimes added to the deck. It's not a wild card *per se,* but can be used in Draw poker as an additional ace, or to complete a straight or flush. In Lowball, the joker is used as the lowest card that does not pair your hand. For example, if you held 7-6-2-A-Joker, it would be the same as if you held 7-6-3-2-A.

Poker chips

Whether you use pennies or peanuts to bet with at home, nothing beats the feel of real poker chips. Originally made of clay, chips now come in a durable composite or plastic. (The plastic ones are a bit more slippery than the composite and, thus, are more difficult to handle.)

Chips are available in a wide range of colors and patterns. The designs and "edge spots" you see on casino chips vary because of security reasons, but the colors generally follow a set of traditional dollar values:

$1	White
$5	Red
$25	Green
$100	Black
$500	Purple or Lavender

If you want to add a dose of Vegas-style playing to your home game, then try using real chips. Following is a list of the number of chips you'll need:

3 to 4 players	300 chips
5 to 6 players	400 chips
7 to 8 players	500 chips
Large games or multiple games	1,000 chips

The Basics of Play

Poker is a simple game to learn, although one can spend a lifetime trying to master it. You win money by winning *pots* — the money or chips wagered during the play of each *hand* (or round) of poker, from the first cards dealt until the showdown. A hand also refers to five cards in the possession of a player.

You win hands in one of two ways:

- ✔ **You *show down* (reveal) the best hand** at the conclusion of all the betting rounds. When two or more players are still active when all the betting rounds are done, they turn their hands face up. The pot goes to the player who holds the highest hand during this showdown.

- ✔ **All your opponents fold their hands.** No, this doesn't mean they politely clasp their fingers on the table in front of them. *Folding a hand* (or, more simply, *folding*) means that a player relinquishes his or her claim to the pot by not matching an opponent's bet.

  In this case, you may have had the best hand or you may have been bluffing — it doesn't matter. When opponents surrender their claim to the pot, it's yours.

In games like Seven-Card Stud and Texas Hold'em the best hand is a high hand. (For more detail about high hands, see the section titled, "Hand Rankings" in this chapter.) In other games, like Lowball and Razz, the best hand is a low hand. (The best possible low hand is 5-4-3-2-A; the next best is 6-4-3-2-A.)

In *split-pot games,* two winners split the pot. For example, in Seven-Card Stud, High-Low Split, Eight-or-Better (mercifully abbreviated as Seven-Stud/8) and Omaha High-Low Split, Eight-or-Better (or just Omaha/8) the best high hand *and* the best low hand split the pot (provided that someone makes a low hand composed of five unpaired cards with a rank of 8 or lower). The worst possible low hand would consist of 8-7-6-5-4. The best of all low hands is 5-4-3-2-A (known as a *wheel* or *bicycle*). While a high hand always will be made in split-pot games, there won't necessarily be a low hand. And when there's no low hand, the high hand wins the entire pot.

Most games require *ante* or *blind* bets. (See the sidebar titled, "Betting terms" in this chapter.) If antes are used, each player must post a token amount of money in order to receive cards. As for *blinds*, one or two players are required to make a bet or portion of a bet *before* the hand is dealt. This requirement rotates around the table so that each player pays his fair share.

Each time a round of cards is dealt, players have an opportunity to check, bet, fold, call, or raise. Any time a player decides to forfeit his interest in the pot, he may release his hand when it is his turn *to act* (to do something related to betting: raise, fold, check, or call). When a player folds a hand, he is not required to place any more money in the pot. If a player bets or raises and no one calls, the pot belongs to that player, the cards are collected and shuffled, and the next hand is dealt. If there are two or more players still active at the end of the hand, the best hand wins the pot.

While there are different rules for each specific version, poker really is this simple. Yet within its simplicity lies a wonderfully textured game structure that is always fascinating, frequently enjoyable, and, for some, a lifelong source of pleasure.

Hand Rankings

Seven-Card Stud and Texas Hold'em are the two most popular forms of poker in which the highest ranking hand wins. These games are played with a 52-card deck — there is no joker — composed of four *suits:* spades, hearts, diamonds, and clubs. Each suit is equal in value, and there are 13 *ranks* in each suit. The ace is the highest ranking card in a suit, followed by king, queen, jack, and 10 through 2 (or deuce), in descending order. An ace may also be used as the lowest ranking card in a 5-high straight (5-4-3-2-A), which is also called a *wheel* or *bicycle.*

Although Stud and Hold'em are played with seven cards, the best hand refers to the best five-card hand. Hand rankings are a function of probability. The rarer the hand, the more valuable it is. See Figure 1-1 for an at-a-glance look at hand ranking in descending value.

Royal flush; straight flush

A *royal flush* is simply an ace-high straight flush, and is the best possible hand in poker. There are only four of them: A♠K♠Q♠J♠10♠; A♥K♥Q♥J♥10♥; A♦K♦Q♦J♦10♦; and A♣K♣Q♣J♣10♣.

A *straight flush* is five cards of the same suit in sequence, such as 9♥8♥7♥6♥5♥ or Q♦J♦10♦9♦8♦.

Four-of-a-kind

Four-of-a-kind, or *quads,* is a five-card hand composed of all the cards of one rank, plus one unrelated card, such as J♥J♠J♦J♣5♣. The higher the rank, the better the hand. For example, four kings beats four jacks.

Full house

Three cards of one rank and a pair of another make a *full house.* The rank of the full house is determined by the three-card grouping, not the pair. A hand like 9♥9♠9♦5♦5♣ is referred to as " . . . nines full of fives."

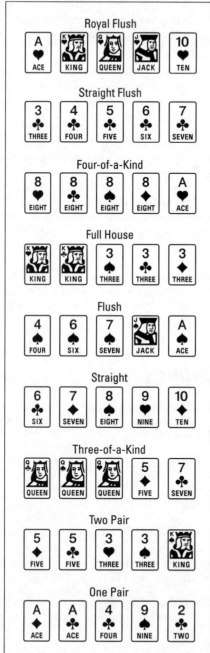

Figure 1-1: Poker hands in descending value, with royal flush as the best hand.

Flush

A *flush* is any five cards of the same suit. The cards are not in sequence. If they were in sequence, it would be a *straight flush*. If there is more than one flush, the winning hand is determined by the rank order of the highest card, or cards, in the flush. A flush composed of A♥Q♥J♥6♥5♥ is higher than A♣Q♣J♣4♣3♣.

Straight

Five sequenced cards, not all of the same suit, compose a *straight*. If more than one straight is present, the highest card in the sequence determines the winning hand. A jack-high straight J♥10♠9♦8♦7♣ will beat this 9♠8♠7♦6♠5♣ nine-high straight.

Three-of-a-kind

Three cards of the same rank, along with two unrelated cards is called *three-of-a-kind*. This hand is also referred to as *trips,* or a *set*. If you held 8♣8♥8♠K♦4♣ you could refer to it as " . . . trip 8s," or "a set of 8s."

Two pair

Two cards of one rank along with two cards of another rank and one unrelated card composes *two pair*. The higher rank determines which two pair is superior. If two players hold two pair and each has the same high pair, then the rank of the second pair determines the winner. If both players hold the same two pair, then the rank of the unrelated *side card* determines the winning hand. If the hand is identical, then the players split the pot. For example, Q♣Q♥8♠8♦4♣ queens and 8s is superior to Q♠Q♦5♣5♠K♦ queens and 5s.

One pair

One pair is simply two cards of one rank and three unrelated cards. If two players hold the same pair, then the value of the unrelated side cards determines the winning hand.

No pair

No pair consists of five unrelated cards. When no player has a pair, then the rank order of the unrelated cards determines the winning hand. For example, if Harry has A-Q-9-6-3 and Adrien has A-J-10-3-2, then Harry wins because A-Q ranks higher than A-J.

Low hands

In split-pot games, like Omaha/8, the best low hand composed of five unrelated cards with the rank of 8 or lower, captures half the pot. A hand like 7♣6♥4♠3♦A♣ beats 7♦6♣5♥3♠A♦, but will lose to 7♠4♥3♥2♣A♠.

Determining the best low hand takes a bit of practice, but if you always begin with the highest of the low cards and continue in descending order, you can't go wrong.

Betting

Without betting, poker would just be a game of luck and the best hand would always win. Betting is the key to poker, and minimizing losses when holding a poor hand while maximizing wins with good hands is what poker is all about.

Every betting interval requires a check or a bet from the first player to act. Each player to the left of the first player to act may either check or bet if no one else has bet. Whoever makes the first bet is said make the *opening bet*. If a bet has been made, other players may fold, call, or raise.

When a player folds, he loses any chips he has contributed to that pot and has no further interest in the hand. After the final betting round a showdown among the players still active in the hand determines the winner.

Different types of games call for specific kinds of betting:

- ✔ In a *fixed limit* game, no one may bet or raise more than a predetermined number of chips. This limit, however, usually varies with the round of the game. In Stud poker, betting limits usually double when the fifth card is dealt. Thus, a $10–$20 game means that the first two rounds of betting are based on limits of $10, while the last three are in increments of $20. In Texas Hold'em, with four betting rounds, betting limits usually double on the third round.

- ✔ *Spread limit* games are similar to fixed limit, but the bettors can wager any amount within the limits. A limit might be $2–$10 any time, which means that wagers can be made in any amount within those limits at any time, with the proviso that a raise must be at least the equal of the bet that preceded it.

✔ In *pot limit,* bets or raises are limited only by the amount of money in the pot at the time the wager is made. A player who raises may count her call as part of the pot. If there is $10 in the pot and someone wagers $10, a raiser may call that bet, making the pot $30 and then raise the entire pot. When she is done, the pot will contain $60.

✔ In *no limit,* a player may bet or raise any amount of chips she has in front of her at any time.

In most limit games, a bet and either three or four raises per betting round are permitted.

Betting terms

Following are some of the key terms to describe the action that occurs during a poker game:

✔ **Ante:** A token sum of money contributed by each player before the cards are dealt. Antes are used in Seven-Card Stud, Seven-Stud/8, Razz, and many other games.

✔ **Bet:** A wager of a certain amount of money by a player in a poker game. Bets can either be in *fixed limits,* such as $3 and $6, or *spread limits,* which allow a player to wager any amount within the limits at any time (such as $2–$10). *Pot limit* is another form of wagering, in which a player can bet any amount up to the sum total currently in the pot. *No-limit* poker allows contestants to wager any amount of money they have in front of them. (For more detail about betting, see the section titled "Betting" in this chapter.)

✔ **Blind bet:** A forced bet by one or more players *before* the cards are dealt. This takes the place of an ante. The requirement to post a blind bet rotates around the table from hand to hand, so that each player pays his fair share. Blind bets are common in Texas Hold'em and Omaha. In most casino games there are two blinds: a big blind and

a small blind. These blinds are considered *"live,"* which means that players who post the blind have the opportunity to raise when the action gets back around to them.

✔ **Call:** To equalize the amount wagered by putting the amount of money wagered into the pot.

✔ **Check:** A check is a bet of zero dollars. By checking, a player retains the right to call any bet made by player who acts after he does, or even to raise. But if someone's already bet when it's your turn to act, you can no longer check, and must either fold, call, or raise.

✔ **Checkraise:** To check and then raise if one of your opponents bets. This is generally done to trap players for a bet or two, when the checkraiser has a very powerful hand.

✔ **Fold:** To decide not to call a bet or raise. By folding, a player relinquishes her interest in the pot.

✔ **Raise:** To increase the amount wagered by an amount equal to your opponent's bet — or by a greater amount, if the game is spread limit, pot limit, or no-limit.

Rules of the Road

Call them rules, conventions, or poker etiquette, there are some guidelines that are common to all forms of poker, especially poker in card clubs or casinos. While you may find some minor variations from one casino to another, many card casinos are working diligently toward a uniform set of guidelines.

Going all-in

If you don't have enough to cover the bets and raises, you are said to *go all-in,* and are simply contesting that portion of the pot your money covers. Others who are active in the hand can still make wagers, but those bets constitute a side pot. At the hand's conclusion, the side pot is decided first, then the main pot. You are not eligible to win the side pot since you invested no money in it, but you can win the main pot. You can buy more chips or put more money on the table between hands.

Few things you remember from Saturday matinee westerns happen in a public cardroom. Players don't leave the game in mid-hand, go get the deed to the ranch, then use it to cover a bet. You cannot drive someone out of a pot just by betting more money than he has in front of him. The player with the limited chip supply goes all-in — by calling with the remainder of their chips. If the all-in player loses, he either buys more chips or leaves the game.

The forbidden string-raise

In a western, someone's always saying: " . . . Mighty big bet, cowboy. I'll just see your twenty," while reaching back into his stack for more chips, and with a long, lingering glance for effect, drawls " . . . and raise you forty!" As dramatic as that move may seem, you won't see that in a real poker game. Calling a bet, then reaching back for more chips and announcing a raise is called a *string raise.* It is not permitted. Rest assured someone will shout "String raise!" The dealer then informs the hopeful raiser that a string raise just occurred, and he'll have to take his raise back and simply call. Now, if someone shouts "String raise!" and another opponent says something like "That's okay. Let his raise stand," be assured your hand is in big trouble — real big trouble!

The string-raise rule prevents a player from reading the reactions of his opponents while he puts some chips in the pot, then deciding to raise if he thinks he's got the best of it.

How to raise

If you want to raise, just say "Raise." Then you can go back to your stack and count out the proper amount of chips. If you want to let your action announce your intention, you usually must put the correct amount of chips into the pot, and do it all in one motion. Otherwise . . . string raise.

No splashing

Avoid *splashing* the pot: Don't toss chips into the center of the table where they mingle with the others. Instead, stack your chips neatly on the table about 18 inches in front of you. The dealer will pull them into the pot when the action has been completed on that round of betting.

If it's your first time in a public cardroom, tell the dealer so he can help you through the mechanics of the game. After a few sessions, you will be familiar and comfortable with the majority of playing procedures. Soon you, too, will feel like a regular.

Protecting your hand; cards speak

In a casino, unlike in many home games, you are always responsible for your hand. Toss it in the *muck* (the pile of discarded cards), and your hand is fouled and cannot win. The rule in all cardrooms is that *cards speak* — your hand is worth whatever value the cards have. Dealers, however, can make mistakes. If you think yours is the best hand, turn your cards face up and announce it. Place it halfway between your chips and the pot, and hold on to it while the dealer determines the outcome.

If you're not sure whether you have the best hand or not, turn all of your cards face up at the end of the hand and allow the dealer to read your hand. If you are in a poker club or casino and there is a doubt or debate, even if the hand is over, casino security cameras can review the hands that were shown down in order to determine the winner.

Table stakes

Most games, including most casino games are *table stakes*. You cannot add chips or money to the amount in front of you during the play of the hand. If you run out of money during a hand, you can contest only that portion of the pot that your bets cover. You cannot *go light* — that is, pull more money out of your wallet — as you might do in a home game. You can, of course, always add more money to your playing stake between hands.

Time out

Anytime you are unsure of anything, the best procedure to follow is to call "Time!" This freezes the action. Then get your questions resolved prior to acting. Poker etiquette suggests that you not abuse this privilege, particularly if you are in a game where you are charged a fee for sitting at the table. Players usually want a fast, efficiently run game, with as few interruptions as possible.

Decks and dealing

Dealers — and decks — generally rotate every half-hour. In addition, players unhappy with their run of cards are prone to holler "Deck change!" Most card rooms permit a change once a deck has been in play for an entire round.

The finer points: Etiquette

Poker rules and etiquette helps speed the game along and keep it orderly. These conventions are as much a part of the game as the cards themselves. In fact, when you play casino poker for the first time, poker etiquette may take more getting used to than the game itself.

Keep in mind the following points of poker protocol:

- **Act in turn:** Each player is expected to act in turn as play proceeds clockwise around the table. If someone bets and you plan to discard your hand, wait until it is your turn to act before doing so. Not only is acting out of turn impolite, it can give a big advantage to one of your opponents. If he knows you will fold your hand, it makes it easier for him to bluff, and is unfair to the rest of the players. In poker, as in most things, it's considered polite to wait your turn.

- **Keep your cards in plain sight:** In order to maintain the integrity of the game, it is important for players to keep their cards on the table during the play of the hand. The best way to protect your hand is to keep it on the table, and look at the cards by shielding them with your hands while lifting a corner of each card to peek at it. In a game like Texas Hold'em, where players have only two cards in front of them, it is customary to leave them on the table after looking and to place a chip on top of them. This alerts the dealer that your hand is still in play.

- **Avoid discussing hands in play:** Discussing your hand with others, even if you have released it and are no longer contesting that pot, may provide information that would give another player an unfair advantage. If you want to discuss a hand with a neighbor, wait until the hand is concluded.

✔ **Practice toking:** We're not blowing smoke here, but *toking* (poker parlance for *tipping*) the dealer is customary when you win a pot. In poker casinos, tokes constitute a significant part of each dealer's income. The size of the pot and the game's betting limits generally determine the amount of the toke. If you're new to casino poker, take your toking cue from the other players at the table. In games with betting limits of $10–$20 or higher, a dollar is a typical toke for all but the smallest pots. In smaller games, tokes of fifty cents are the rule.

What Will Your Opponents Be Like?

The kinds of players sitting at your table in a poker parlor will vary with the limits you play. If you play in low-limit games, you are not going to find either last year's World Series of Poker winner, the eight toughest card players in your hometown, or any legends of the game. While there are many ways to classify players as you try to build a book on your opponents, the easiest way is to group your opponents into three types: casual recreational players, regulars, and professionals.

Casual recreational players

Casual recreational players love the game, but when push comes to shove, they are not that concerned about winning or losing. They play for the fun of it. It is simply a hobby, and no matter how much they lose, it is less expensive than keeping horses, restoring classic automobiles, or a hundred other hobbies that devour money. Naturally, you'd love to play exclusively with recreational players. If you can't beat a table full of these players, you just might want to find something else to do in your spare time. No one, however, will come right out and admit to being a casual recreational player. If someone does, watch out. He probably is not, and you're forewarned: Take heed when he fires a raise at you.

Cardroom regulars

Regulars come in a wide variety. This includes retirees, homemakers, students, people with no fixed job hours, dealers who are playing before or after their shift, and almost anyone else you can imagine. Some regulars have independent sources of income and often play in big games. Take it for a fact that all the regulars you encounter have more playing experience than you do. Even if you are a stronger player but are just making the transition from home games to casino poker, they will have the best of it for a while. After all, they are in playing shape. You, on the other hand, are in spring training and will need some time to adjust to this entirely new environment.

Regulars and casual recreational players constitute the majority of poker devotees. Some are good. Most aren't. But they're in action on a regular basis.

Professionals

You find professionals and semi-professionals in most of the larger games. Generally speaking, you don't encounter these players at limits below $10–$20. While a pro would have an easier time of it at lower betting limits, she just can't earn a living in a $2–$4 game. In these lower limit games, you'll be competing with regulars and recreational players, not professionals. But when you graduate to the higher limits you can expect to encounter some players who earn all or part of their living playing poker.

Proposition players

Proposition players, or props, play on their own money but are paid a salary by the club to help start or prop up games. You'll typically find them late at night when the club is trying to keep games going, and early in the morning when it's trying to start up a new game.

A prop's life can be tough. Playing in short-handed games, or games struggling to get off the ground isn't always a bed of roses. The minute a live player wants his seat, the prop is pulled from it — often when the game is just starting to bear fruit. Props typically play better than most regulars do, but not as well as top players do. Their defining characteristic is that they tend to be conservative.

Many cardroom newcomers panic at the thought of a prop in their game. Since the casino pays the prop, players often believe he has a big advantage. Not true. They play their own money, and as long as they're reliable and maintain a playing bankroll the card club cares not a whit whether they win or lose. I suspect that given a choice, any cardroom would prefer to employ a weak player as a prop, rather than a strong one, simply because the weaker player is a bigger draw. In fact, the ideal prop would be a poor player with a winning personality and an unlimited bankroll.

Playing in a Casino

Casino poker differs from typical home games. While kitchen-table poker may be long on camaraderie and unusual variants of the game, there are many reasons to play in a public cardroom. The most important factor may be that there is always a game. In fact, you frequently have a choice of games, which are often available 24 hours a day, seven days a week.

Another major advantage, especially in the very large poker clubs in urban locations, is the safety of public cardrooms. These venues offer professional dealers, floorpersons, and video security the equal of any Las Vegas casino to ensure that games are run squarely. Because people walk around cardrooms with large sums of money, there are more security guards than you'd find in most banks. Parking lots are brightly lit, well-patrolled, and free of strong-arm crime. Since most large clubs offer check cashing, safe deposit boxes, and ATM machines, there's no need to walk around with large sums of money in your pocket. You can also take advantage of the *players banks* available at many large clubs. While you can't write checks against it, a players bank is like a conventional bank account except that it's in a casino. You can deposit money and withdraw cash when you need it.

In a public cardroom there's never any pressure to stay. Nobody minds if you quit the game a winner. Someone else is usually waiting for your seat. You do, however, have to pay to play. It costs more to play in a casino than a home game where all you have to do is split the cost of food and drinks.

Casinos, however, offer a variety of games. If you don't feel like playing Texas Hold'em you can play Stud, Lowball, or Omaha High-Low Split. If weak players are at your table, you can punish them continuously. Weak players in home games eventually become ex-players if they can't win some of the time.

You'll find the pace of a casino game to be much faster than most home games. Dealers in a casino try to maintain a quick pace. If you are playing in a game with a time collection, you are paying the same fee per half-hour of play regardless of how many hands are dealt. Consequently, dealers act efficiently and players are expected to make prompt decisions.

Things you've probably done in home games just won't happen in a card room. No one ever fishes through the discards. The dealer handles the deck. You play your cards without the help of a neighbor.

More reasons to play casino poker

Casino playing certainly has its advantages over home games — you get variety, increased safety, and playing efficiency. If you've never played casino poker before and are thinking about giving it a shot, here are more reasons why you should:

✔ Even the toughest of games have a social aspect: rich, poor, young, old, students,

business execs, movie stars, homemakers; people of every race, color, and creed — you'll meet them all in a casino card game.

✔ Become skilled at the game and you have a hobby that pays. Golf, tennis, and boating all cost money, but thousands of people all across America earn money at poker.

How to get in a game

When you enter a cardroom, you may see a white board full of players' initials. These initials are listed under games that are available. For example, if you walk into a large casino you might find seven players ahead of you waiting for a $2–$4 Hold'em game. Just give your initials to the board attendant and indicate the games you want to be listed for. You might say: "My initials are ABC. Put me up for the $2–$4, $3–$6, and $5–$10 Hold'em, the $5–$10 Stud, and the $4–$8 Omaha High-Low Split games."

That's all there is to it. It's as easy as taking a number at Ben and Jerry's. Your initials will go up on the board for each game you request, and you'll be called as seats become available. If the board for a particular game is so long that the club can start another, the attendant will announce that game and call the players in the order they are listed. When you hear your initials, go to the table and grab a vacant seat. You're in the game.

Some cardrooms don't use a board. Just give your initials or first name to the attendant and tell him the games you want to play. In small cardrooms, where there are only one or two tables, ask the dealer if a seat is available or if there is a waiting list for the game.

Buying chips

When you first sit in the game either the floorperson or dealer will ask you how much you want in chips. Each game has a minimum buy-in. Give the floorperson your money and you'll get your chips. Large casinos have chip attendants. One of them will take your money, announce to the table that "Seat five (or whatever seat you occupy) is playing $200 behind." That means you bought in for $200, and the casino is in the process of fetching your chips. You can play that hand, even though your chips have not yet arrived. The dealer will either lend you some chips or keep count of how much you owe the pot. Your chips should arrive about the time that the first hand is played to its conclusion.

Shuffling and dealing

You may never have noticed, but the shuffle procedure in a casino is much more rigorous than it is in a game with amateur dealers. Home game players are usually unfamiliar with the mechanics of a good shuffle, and many lack the manual dexterity to perform one. Well-trained casino dealers assemble the deck so the cards face the players, frequently preceding that by scrambling the cards on the table. This is followed by a four-step procedure of shuffle, shuffle, riffle, and shuffle. Finally, the dealer cuts the deck and deals. The procedure is efficient, quick, and designed so that no cards are flashed in the process.

How Casino Poker Differs from Home Games

If you've watched a few games in a card club while waiting for a seat, you'll notice that players do not play as many hands as they do in home games. While there is seldom a spoken agreement to play every hand in a home game, because of the chummy atmosphere, many players simply play lots of hands. That's not the case in a casino. Players are more selective. Still, the biggest mistakes most players make is playing too many hands and calling on early betting rounds when they should have folded.

Tighter than home games

Low-limit cardroom games, while tighter than comparable home games, are still much too loose. In tight games, the players with the stronger hands tend to enter the pots, while in a looser game, more players enter more pots than they really should. If you simply play better starting cards than your opponents do in these low-limit games, you will usually be a *favorite* (favored to win money in the long run).

However, you won't be a favorite in any game right off the mark. Since it will take you some time to get familiar with cardroom play, give serious consideration to starting in very small-limit games. You'll probably be *paying for lessons* the first five or ten times you play in a public cardroom, and there is no reason to make these lessons any more expensive than they need be.

If you come from a home game into a public cardroom, especially the fun-to-play, jam-it-up kind of home game, you quickly realize that you can't play every hand, or even many hands, for that matter! You need standards. This is true for all forms of poker.

Players are more selective

Bobby Baldwin, former World Champion of Poker and now president of the Bellagio Hotel in Las Vegas, reflected on his early days at the table: "I was floating around, trying to figure out which hands were playable, which hands called for a raise, which hands should be thrown out. Without standards, he said, "you have to use 90 percent of your concentration deciding each time what to do with a given hand. All that mental energy should be devoted to studying your opponents and trying to decipher the small things which made this hand slightly different from familiar hands you've seen in the past."

Poker Advice from Johnny Moss

"In order to learn any game, you have to find the best players and play with them."

"In an otherwise even contest, the man with the best concentration will almost always win."

"If you're afraid to lose your money, you can't play to win."

"Nobody wins all the time, so when you lose, you need to learn what you can from it, then let it go. Forget it."

(From *Johnny Moss: Champion of Champions*, by Don Jenkins.)

Baldwin's advice is succinct. "Never sit in a game without having a preconceived set of guidelines [starting standards] telling you what your minimum calling hands and raising hands should be."

After all, you don't have to play every hand you're dealt. Folding weak hands that will prove to be unprofitable in the long run, is — like discretion — the better part of valor. Each form of poker has its own set of good hands, and you'll find out what they are as you work your way through this book. For now, it's enough to remember that you should fold more hands than you play.

Games are faster

The first few times you play in a casino, the speed of the games might startle you. You may also think that the players are better than your home game cronies are. But after becoming familiar with the environment, you'll find that your skill level is right up there with your opponents' abilities. Most of them aren't students of the game. Recreational players want to have fun and that's it. Most of the regulars, who run the gamut of skill levels, don't bother to study the game. Though many of them have been playing in cardrooms for years, they simply repeat and reinforce the same errors they've been making for decades.

Don't worry too much about the skill level of your opponents when you first begin playing in a public cardroom. By studying and playing the game you should soon catch the field — begin to play as well, or better, than your opponents. Mind you, if you live in an area in which poker has only recently been legalized, you probably don't have any catching up to do at all. You can start ahead of the crowd and never look back. Think of yourself as a wire-to-wire winner. Your opponents may improve slowly, simply through osmosis. But through frequent play and study, you can improve at a much more rapid rate.

Chapter 2

Essential Strategic Considerations

● ●

In This Chapter

▶ Knowing what poker is and isn't

▶ Understanding the basics of the game

▶ Gaining a perspective on probability

▶ Looking at winning strategies

▶ Coping when all goes wrong

● ●

*B*asic strategic knowledge is critical for any poker player. If you have no basis for making decisions about whether to call, fold, raise, or reraise, then you might just as well play the lottery. Sure, you'll win occasionally because everyone gets lucky now and then. Without strategy and knowledge, you'll exercise no control over your destiny as a card player.

If you picked 100 poker players at random and asked them about the objective of poker, most would say something about winning the pot, but they couldn't be further from the truth.

The goal of poker — in addition to the enjoyment of playing the game — is winning *money*, not pots. If your goal was to win the most pots, that would be easy to do. Just play every hand and call every bet and raise until the bitter end. You'd win a lot of pots. In fact, you'd win every pot you possibly could. But you'd lose money. Plenty of it, and rapidly.

So the objective of poker is to win money. And that means tempering enthusiasm with realism by being selective about the hands you play. There's no need to play every hand. The very best players play relatively few hands, but when they do enter a pot they are usually aggressive and out to maximize the amount they win when the odds favor them.

This is the essence of poker: Anyone can win in the short run, but in the long haul — when the cards even out — the better players win more money with their good hands, and lose less with weak hands, than their adversaries.

Because of the short-term luck involved, poker is a game where even atrociously poor players can — and do — have winning nights. This is not true in most other competitive endeavors. Most of us would not have a prayer going one-on-one with an NBA basketball player, or attempting to hit a 95 mph big-league fastball. What's more, we realize it. Yet most of us think we are good poker players.

If you took a poll at any poker table, the majority of players would rate themselves significantly above average. But that's not the case. It can't be. In the long run, good players beat bad players — though the bad players will win just often enough to keep them coming back for more.

It's this subtle blend of skill and luck that balances the game. That balance also rewards good players who are realistic about how they assess their ability and that of their opponents. This chapter can help you develop those skills.

What Poker Is and Isn't

Poker is not one game but a variety of games that employ hand rankings, betting, and bluffing as strategic and tactical elements. In some forms of poker, like Seven-Card Stud, Texas Hold'em, Five-Card Draw poker, and Omaha, the best poker hand wins. What's the best hand? The rarer the hand, the higher it's ranked. Thus a straight flush, which is much less likely to occur than a full house, is ranked higher. That's why three-of-a-kind beats two pair, which in turn beats one pair.

In other games, like Lowball, Razz, or Deuce-to-Seven Kansas City Lowball, the lowest-ranked hand wins. In all but Kansas City Lowball, a hand composed of 5-4-3-2-A — called a *wheel* or a *bicycle* — is the best possible hand. In Kansas City, where straights and flushes count against you and an ace is always a high card, the best hand is 7-5-4-3-2. But don't worry about that game, it's not played very often. When it is, it's generally a high stakes, no-limit game — one you'd be better off avoiding for a long, long time.

If this isn't enough to confuse you, there are also *split* games, in which the highest and lowest hand split the pot. These games are usually played with an "8 qualifier." In order to split the pot, the low hand needs to be composed of five unpaired cards with the rank of 8 or lower. If there is no low hand, the high hand scoops the entire pot.

In casinos the two most popular "split" games are Omaha 8-or-Better, High/Low Split (usually abbreviated as Omaha/8) and Seven-Card Stud, 8-or-Better, High-Low Split (usually abbreviated Seven-Stud/8).

We Were All Beginners Once

In the beginning, we were all bad players — you, me, the guy winning all the money at your table tonight, as well as every player who has ever won the *World Series of Poker*. We were all bad. Once upon a time, Troy Aikman couldn't throw a football, Ken Griffey Jr. couldn't hit, and Michael Jordan was once cut from his high school basketball team. They were beginners too, and guess what: They were bad. Raw talent? Sure, they were blessed with an abundance of raw talent, but they all had to work long and hard to refine it.

So don't bemoan your current skill level as a poker player. You can improve, and you will if you're willing to pay the price. Every good poker player has been where you are now, and they've improved. To be sure, some progressed by leaps and bounds, while others have taken baby steps, one after the other, until they reached their goal.

Build a foundation first . . .

You can reach your poker-playing goals. You *do* have some innate potential as a poker player, and if playing winning poker is important, you need to build a foundation that will help you reach your potential as quickly as possible. Everyone who has progressed from neophyte to journeyman to expert to superstar shares one trait in common: They built a solid foundation, and that foundation allowed them to spread their wings and fly. And fly they can.

But in poker, as in life itself, you can't fly until you've built a rock-solid foundation and mastered the fundamentals. If you're still grappling with fundamentals, you're not yet ready to fly. But once those fundamentals are imprinted on your poker consciousness and you can execute them instinctively, then, and only then, can you think about digressing from these basics and improving.

. . . Then you can improvise

When you listen to great jazz musicians, you are hearing improvisation at its best. That improvisation, however, is based on a solid grounding of music theory. Charlie Parker, Miles Davis, the Modern Jazz Quartet, Sonny Rollins, Gerry Mulligan, Charles Mingus, Thelonius Monk: These jazz giants are masters of improvisation, but their innovation and creativity stood on a platform of musical theory, knowledge of time signatures, an understanding of harmony, skill in ensemble playing, and an ability to use rhythm to underpin melodic themes and harmony. Without possessing these basic skills, innovation would not have been possible. The price wasn't cheap, either. It took lots of playing, lots of years, and more clubs, sessions, and after-hours joints than those musicians would want to count. But the product was sweet, free-flowing music: riffs that seem to possess a life of their own, springing unbounded from horns, keyboards, and strings, and filling the night with magic.

Basic Poker Concepts

Your first efforts should center on learning basic poker concepts. Even when you understand them, this know-how must be continuously applied. The knowledge and abilities that compose basic poker skills are not a pill to be swallowed once. They need to be continuously refined.

Andres Segovia, the greatest classical guitarist of his generation, did not spend the majority of his practice time learning new pieces or practicing his concert repertoire. He spent four to six hours per day playing scales and études. Segovia spent 75 percent of his practice time on basics, and did this every day. You'll have to take our word for it, but this analogy holds true for poker, too.

Understand blinds and antes

Every poker game begins as a chase for the antes or blinds. An *ante* is a small portion of a bet contributed by each player to seed the pot at the beginning of each hand.

A *blind* is a forced bet by one or more players before any cards are dealt. In Stud games, players usually ante; in Texas Hold'em and Omaha Hold'em, blind bets are used. Regardless of whether a blind or an ante is employed, every game needs seed money to start the action. Without it, players could wait all day for unbeatable hands before entering the pot.

Playing for an empty pot would make for a slow and boring game. Blinds and antes serve the same purpose: to tempt and tantalize players, enticing them into the pot and creating action because there's a monetary target to shoot at.

Know your opponents

Suppose you're playing Texas Hold'em and have been dealt A♥K♥, and your opponents are Rick and Barbara, two players who are known for calling much too frequently.

"Fantastic," you say to yourself when you look at the flop and see J♥5♥9♣. "I have position, two overcards, and a nut-flush draw." You remember something about semi-bluffing and implied odds, and when your opponents check on the flop, you bet. They call. The turn brings 4♠, and it's checked to you. You bet, thinking that they might fold and you can win it right here.

WARNING!

Big-time pros can blunder

Even world-class professionals make mistakes. This situation occurred a few years ago at the final table of the main event at the Bicycle Club's Diamond Jim Brady tournament.

Three players remained: At that point, Player X had almost twice the number of chips as either players Y or Z (who were approximately equal in chip position). The payoffs were as follows: $230,000 to first place, $115,000 for second, and $55,200 for third. In a heads-up situation against Player X, Player Y went all in on the flop when two diamonds fell, giving him a flush draw.

It was all or nothing for Player Y the moment he chose to draw for his flush. If the flush came, Player Y would win the hand, double his stack, and be solidly ensconced in second place. If his flush didn't fall he would be out of the tournament. With two cards to come he had a 35 percent chance of making his hand and a 65 percent chance of busting out of the tournament.

Even if he did win that hand, however, there was no guarantee he would win the tournament or even capture second place. Thus he allowed himself to take a position as a 1.9-to-1 underdog in a situation where, even if he overcame those odds, he had no guarantee of a higher payoff in the tournament. As it happened, Player Y's flush never came, while Player Z made a remarkable comeback and went on to defeat Player X, who was the chip leader at the time.

The big winner in the confrontation between Players X and Y was Player Z. He went from a virtual tie for second/third place to a guarantee of second-place money — a difference of $59,800. Player Z, who had absolutely nothing at risk in that confrontation, would have been a winner regardless of the result. With Player Y knocked out of the tournament, Player Z guaranteed himself a payoff that was $59,800 more than he could count on before that hand was played. If Player Y won the hand, then Player Z would have still been in third place, but Player X would no longer have a big chip lead and would no longer be in a position to hammer away at the shorter stacks.

Why would a top tournament player make the strategic decision to contest that pot as an underdog, when the risk clearly outweighed the reward? It is very likely that Player Y was so focused on the situation at hand that he was, in that instant, unable to step back and grasp the issue in its broadest context. If that's the case, he was blind to the fact that Player Z also had a major stake in the outcome of that hand, even though he held no cards!

Just this momentary lack of awareness, entirely understandable when you consider the intense concentration required to survive as one of three finalists in a $10,000 buy-in, no-limit Hold'em tournament, could easily lead to an error in correctly bounding a problem. In so doing, the wrong strategy was selected.

Sometimes, one needs to look at poker problems from a variety of perspectives. Somewhere between the big picture and the nitty-gritty details, there's an appropriate perspective from which to examine most poker decisions.

Maybe you even have the best hand and would win in a showdown right now. Perhaps a heart — or even an ace or king — will come on the river (at the last common card). But you are up against players who sleep very well, thank you, each and every night of the week, secure in the knowledge that no one, but no one, ever steals a pot from them.

The river is no help; it's 4♣. Rick and Barbara check again. You still might have the best hand if you show it down. But you bet and you're called, and you lose to Rick, who holds a 6-5 of mixed suits.

"What went wrong?" you ask yourself. "I had the perfect opportunity to semi-bluff." Perfect, that is, only from the perspective of the cards on the table and those in your hand. But it was far from perfect if you stopped to consider your opponents. Your mistake involved considering only the cards while choosing a strategy. Semi-bluffing doesn't work with players who always call. You have to show them the best hand to take the money. While there was nothing you could have done to win that pot, you certainly could have saved a bet on the river.

Nothing was wrong with the strategy itself. It might have worked if the cards were the same but your opponents were different. Knowing your opponents is as important to winning at poker as understanding strategic concepts.

Strategy is situationally dependent. Skilled players realize they need to be aware of the big picture while simultaneously paying attention to small details. Understanding strategic concepts is only part of the battle. How, and under what circumstances to apply them, are equally important. If you can do this, you will find that you have become a better player and a more creative one, too.

Prepare to win

Success demands preparation. Knowledge, plus preparation and experience (and whatever innate talent one may have), equals know-how. That's what it takes to be a winning poker player. If you have that knowledge and you're losing, or you're just not winning as much and as often as you should, see Chapter 20, "(Almost) Ten Things to Consider Before Going Pro."

The primary step in making behavioral changes and eliminating bad habits is to be responsible for you. Adopt the irrevocable assumption that you are personally responsible for what happens to you at the poker table. If you put the blame on forces outside of yourself, you have not committed yourself to making changes; you're denying the problem.

A Little Probability

Consider a simple coin toss. With a very large number of tosses, do you believe that the number of heads and tails would be exactly the same? If you do, then you would also believe that these simulated players, each programmed to play identically from a strategic perspective, should have identical results after 3 million hands.

Understanding poker's fluctuations can provide some perspective when considering your short-term results. Not only can fluctuations persist for a long time before results can be attributed solely to skill, but there is no guarantee you will balance your books after the last hand is dealt. All that probability theory offers is the likelihood that your results will parallel your ability.

A short-term simulation

We used a computer to simulate 60,000 hands of $20–$40 Hold'em. That's about one year of play if you treated poker as a job and went at it eight hours a day. The objective was to determine how long it would take to get into "the long run," that elusive zone where luck is filtered out and only skill determines who wins and loses.

Because identical player profiles were loaded into the computer, the long-run expectation was zero. With identical profiles, each player should neither win nor lose. They should have broken even in the long run.

Nevertheless, there were four losers and five winners. Seat 9 lost $3.18 per hour while seat 6 won at the rate of $1.99. That's a difference of more than $5 per hour — and it was clear they never got into the long run, even after a year of simulated play.

A long-term simulation

If a year was insufficient to get into the long run, what about a lifetime? The computer was asked to play 3 million hands of $20–$40 Hold'em. At 30 hands per hour, 2,000 hours per year, that's 50 years of poker — about as long a run as we're likely to get.

After 50 simulated years, the big winner was ahead $60,214. The big loser was stuck $35,953. That's 60 cents per hour for the winner, while the big loser was in the red about 35 cents per hour. All the others at the table had results somewhere in between.

Did they get into the long run? Or does the 95 cents per hour difference between the big winner and big loser mean that even a lifetime isn't sufficient to get into the long run? Some probability theory will help us here.

Probability theory makes no promise to balance the books over the long haul. All it offers is this: The coin is as likely to come down heads as tails. Not that it will, only that it is *as likely to.* Because there is no reason why a coin should land on one side rather than the other, they are both equally likely to happen. Still, don't expect exactly half-and-half — even in a large sample. While you can expect results close to theoretical probability, remember this: The coin doesn't have a memory to give it heads this time and tails the next.

If you carry that logic over to the nine computerized Hold'em players, each had an equally likely chance to win. With identical playing profiles, each player's expectation was *break even.* The fact that they did not break even does not negate probability theory. After all, a break-even prediction was the best forecast you could have made, and there's no way anyone could logically predict seat three would win 60 cents per hour and seat one would lose 35 cents per hour. Maybe the best you can expect over a lifetime of poker is that only 1 to 1.5 percent of your results would be attributable to luck.

How many bad players does it take to make a good game?

In another simulation, two poorer players were introduced into the game. One played exceedingly tight. The other was much too loose. They also played for 50 years. The results: Mr. Too-Tight lost $3 million while Loose-Lee dropped nearly $4 million. Each of the seven other players was a lifelong winner in this game. The biggest winner was up $1.2 million. The smallest winner was ahead nearly $800,000.

These are pretty significant results, and they show the importance of game selection. Simply by substituting two poor players in this game (and they did not play that poorly, just somewhat worse than their competition), the big winner went from 60 cents to $12 per hour — a twentyfold increase.

Game selection, according to inferences that can be drawn from these simulations, is crucial to a winning player's long-term success. Why is it so important? Every subsequent decision made at the table relates only to the hand you are involved in. Game selection, however, has implications for every hand that you choose to play — or refrain from playing — when you are at the table.

Some Poker Perspective

The *information explosion* is everywhere, and poker is no different. More has been written about poker since 1985 than had previously been written in the entire history of the game.

Once you've made a commitment to reach for the stars, you have to decide where to begin. If you aspire to poker excellence, the first — and probably the most important step — is to develop a perspective that enables you to put each piece of information, each drop of data, each factoid, into a hierarchical structure. After all, some things are just a lot more important than others, and you might as well concentrate your efforts where they'll do the most good.

Why some tactics are important in poker and others aren't

Imagine that we could teach you a terrific tactical ploy that would require some real study and practice to perfect — but once learned, could be used to earn an extra bet from an opponent. What if we also guaranteed this ploy to be absolutely foolproof: It would work perfectly every time you used it. Have we piqued your interest?

But suppose that we also told you that this tactic works only in very special circumstances that occur about once a year. Do you still want to invest the time required to learn it? Probably not. While your ability to execute this particularly slick maneuver might brand you as a tough player in the eyes of your opponents, the fact that you might use it only once a year renders it meaningless. In the course of a year's worth of playing, one extra bet doesn't amount to a hill of beans. It doesn't even amount to a can of beans.

Frequent decisions

Tactical opportunities that occur all the time *are* important. Even when the amount of money attributed to a wrong decision is small, it will eventually add up to a tidy sum if that error is made frequently. Always defending your small blind in Hold'em, for example, is a good example. You have to decide whether to defend your small blind every round — and that's frequent. If you always defend it, you are investing part of a bet on those occasions when it is wrong to do so. At the end of a year, those mistakes add up.

Suppose that you're playing $10–$20 Texas Hold'em, with $5 and $10 blinds, and you decide to always defend your small blind, even when you're dealt hands like 7♥2♣. Just to keep this simple, we'll assume that your small blind is never raised. Based on the random distributions of cards, you're probably dealt a throwaway hand about one-third of the time. At the rate of 30 hands per hour, you'll be dealt the small blind three times every 60 minutes. If you always call, you'll wind up calling once each hour when you really shouldn't have. That's only $5 each hour, but after 1,000 hours of poker, you've essentially given away $5,000. It adds up fast, doesn't it?

Costly decisions

Playing correctly requires a great deal of judgment — the kind that comes from experience, not books. No matter how skilled a player you eventually become, you'll never reach the point where you always make these decisions correctly. Don't worry; that's not important. Just err on the side of protecting yourself from catastrophic mistakes, and you'll be on the right track.

Decisions that cost a significant amount of money when they occur, even if they don't happen too often, are also important. If you can't decide whether to call or fold once all the cards are out and your opponent bets into a fairly large pot, that's an important decision. If you make a mistake by calling when you should have folded and your opponent wins the pot — that's an error, but not a critical one. It cost only one bet. But if you fold the winning hand, that's a critical error, since the cost of that error was the entire pot.

Now we're certainly not advising you to call each and every time someone bets on the last card and you're unsure about whether you have the best hand, but deciding to call instead of fold doesn't have to be correct too often to render it the mistake of choice. If the cost of a mistaken fold is ten times the price of a mistaken call, you only have to be correct slightly more than 10 percent of the time to make calling worthwhile.

Decisions and subsequent actions

Choices can also be important because of their position on the decision tree. Those that are first in a long sequence of subsequent choices are always important, because subsequent choices are usually predicated on your initial selection. Make an incorrect move up front and you run the risk of rendering each subsequent decision incorrect, regardless of whatever else you might do. That's why the choice of which hands you start with in poker is generally a much more critical decision than how you play on future betting rounds. If you adopt an " . . . any cards can win" philosophy, you have set yourself up for a disaster that even the best players could not overcome on later rounds.

Poker's single most important decision

Choosing the right game is the most important decision you'll encounter as a poker player. Choose the wrong game and little else matters. Choose the right game and you might even make money even on nights when you're experiencing a below average run of cards.

Starting standards

After you choose the best game and select the best available seat (check out the sidebar "Getting the best seat in the house") at that table, what's important to winning play? Early decisions predicate subsequent choices, so deciding which hands to start with (your *starting standards*) is critically important.

It's only human nature to seek the best bang for the buck, and poker players are no different. There are hands where the return on your investment is positive, and others that will prove costly in the long run. In the heat of battle, you don't have the time to thoroughly assess your hand. You should have made these decisions long before you hit the table. That's why standards are critical. If you incorporate solid starting standards into your game, you are light years ahead of any opponent who has not done this — never mind how long he's been playing or how much experience he may have in other phases of the game.

Starting standards also provide a basis for deviation, but only under the right conditions. Those conditions are impossible to recognize — and capitalize on — unless you've developed standards and integrated them so completely into your game that they are second nature to you. Only when that's accomplished can you hope to find those very few exceptions that allow you to profitably deviate from them.

Hand selectivity

Hand selection is one of the most important keys to winning. Most of us play too many hands. I'm not referring only to beginners. Some players have been at it for years, and the single most important flaw in their game is that they still play too many hands.

After all, the majority of poker players are recreational players. They're not playing poker to make their living; they play to enjoy themselves — and much as they'd have you believe their goal in playing is to win money, that's really secondary to their main objective: having fun. The difference between a player who has come out to have fun and another who is playing to win money is that the recreational player will look for reasons to play marginal hands and to continue playing them even when subsequent betting rounds are fraught with danger. The money player will look for reasons to release hands, avoid unnecessary danger, and dump speculative hands whenever the potential reward is overshadowed by the risks.

Be aggressive, but be selective

Winning poker requires selectivity and aggression. Every top player knows that concept, and every credible poker book emphasizes it. If you have any doubts, consider the need to be selective. Picture someone who calls every hand down to the bitter end unless he sees that he is beaten on board. Her opponents would soon discover that it never pays to bluff her. Of course, every time they had the smallest edge, they'd bet, knowing that she will call with the worst of it. These *value bets* would soon relieve our heroine of her bankroll.

If selectivity is clearly correct, what about aggression? Consider the passive player. He seldom bets unless he has an unbeatable hand — and they don't come around all that often. More often than not you'll find yourself in pots where you believe, but aren't absolutely certain, that you have the best hand. Even when you are 100 percent certain that yours is the best hand at the moment, you might recognize it as one that can be beaten if there are more cards to come. This occurs more often than you might realize, and you can't win at poker by giving your opponent a free card. If they have to draw to beat you, make them pay the price.

TIP

Good games need bad players

Would you rather be the best poker player in the world at a table with the eight other players who are ranked second through ninth, or would you prefer being a good player at a table full of fish? Against a table full of weak players you'd win more money — much more, in fact, than the world's best player could ever win against tough competition!

Here's why. Most of the money you'll win at poker comes not from the brilliance of your own play, but from the ineptitude of your opponents. Never mind that you might be the world's best poker player. You're not all that much better than those immediately beneath you. And your opponents, all of whom are world-class players in their own right, will not present you with much of a target to shoot at. Bad players are another

story entirely. They offer huge targets. They call with weak hands. They stay in hopes of catching a miracle card. They believe that poker is like the lottery — all a matter of luck — and it's just a little while until everything evens out and they get theirs. And their bad play costs them money day after day.

The sad truth is that bad players simply don't realize the extent to which they bleed their money away. The gap between the good player and the fool is infinitely greater than the gap between the world's best player and any cluster of other world-beaters. It's not even close. That mythical journeyman professional poker player — the kind you aspire to be — may be a mile away from the world's best, but 10 miles ahead of the fools.

Patience

Patience is certainly related to the "be selective" portion of the "be aggressive, but be selective" mantra. Few players dispute the need to be selective. Nevertheless, most aren't very selective about the hands they play. After all, poker is fun, and most aficionados come to play, not fold.

When the cards aren't coming your way, it's very easy to talk yourself into taking a flyer on marginal hands. But there's usually a price to be paid for falling off the good-hands wagon.

Sometimes it all boils down to a simple choice. You can have a lot of fun, gamble it up, and pay the inevitable price for your pleasure, or you can apply the patience required to win consistently.

Position

In poker, position means power. It is almost always advantageous to act after you've had the benefit of seeing what your opponents do. Their actions provide clues about the real or implied values of their hands. This is true in every poker game, and is particularly important in fixed-position games, like Hold'em and Omaha. In these games position is fixed for the *entire hand*, unlike Stud, where it can vary from one betting round to another.

Getting the best seat in the house

Selecting the best available seat depends on the skills that your opponents have. Think about their playing style and level of experience.

Here are the types of players you want on your left:

- Timid players, who are likely to release their hands if you bet or raise
- Players who will call whenever you bet but will raise infrequently
- Predictable opponents

Here are the types of players you want on your right:

- Very aggressive players, especially those who raise too frequently
- Skilled, tough opponents
- Unpredictable players

Coping When All Goes Wrong

Unfortunately, no magic elixir eliminates the fluctuations everyone experiences at poker. But it's little consolation when you've been buffeted by the vicissitudes of fate to realize that you're not the only poor soul tossing about in the same boat. When all seems lost, you need to remember this: There *is* opportunity in adversity. In fact, losing provides the best opportunity to examine and refine your own game.

Let's face it. Most players don't spend much time in careful self-examination when they are winning. It's too much fun to stack the chips and revel in the money that's rolling in. But when they lose, they pore over each decision they made, wondering how they could have improved it. "What could I have done differently," they ask over and over. Losing turns them from expansive extroverts into brooding introverts whose inner-directed thoughts dredge them back over the same ground time and time again, in search of reasons and strategies that will prevent losses like these from ever happening again.

If you're on a losing streak

While no guarantees about future losses are available, we do recommend one course of action to any player mired in a losing streak: Just change gears. We all change gears during a poker game, sometimes consciously, as a planned strategy, and sometimes we just wind up playing differently than we did when we first sat down.

When you're losing, consider gearing down. Way down. This is a time for lots of traction and not much speed; a time for playing only the best starting hands. Not marginal hands, not good — or even very good — starting hands, but only the best hands. That means you'll be throwing away hand after hand, and it takes discipline to do this, particularly when some of these hands would have won.

When losing, most players want to minimize fluctuations in their bankrolls and grind out some wins. Gearing down accomplishes this, because you're not playing any of the "close call" hands you normally might. By playing hands that have a greater chance of winning, you're minimizing the fluctuations that occur with speculative hands. Of course, you're also cutting down your average hourly win rate, but it's a trade-off, because you are less apt to find yourself on a roller coaster ride. You can still win as much; it will just take more hours at the table.

Narrow the target

Gearing down also prevents your opponents from kicking you when you're down. When you're winning, your table image is quite different than when you're losing. Win, and you can sometimes bluff with impunity. It's a lot tougher when you're losing. After all, your opponents have watched you lose hand after hand. They believe you're going to keep losing. When you bet, they'll call — or even raise — with hands they might have thrown away if you had been winning steadily.

Chapter 3

Seven-Card Stud

. . . .

In This Chapter

▶ Getting to know antes, the deal, and betting structure

▶ Knowing when to hold or fold

▶ Recognizing winning hands

▶ Understanding the importance of live cards

▶ Looking at Seven-Card Stud in depth

▶ Starting hands

▶ Going beyond third street

. . . .

Seven-Card Stud is the most popular of all the stud games, and has been since it first appeared sometime around the Civil War. There are also six- and five-card variants, but they are not nearly as popular as the seven-card version. With three down cards and four exposed cards in each player's hand at the end of the hand, Seven-Card Stud combines some of the surprises of Draw poker, with a good deal of information that can be gleaned from four open cards.

Seven-Card Stud has five rounds of betting that can create some very large pots. Skilled Seven-Card Stud players need an alert mind and good powers of retention. A skillful player has the ability to relate each card in his hand, or visible in the hand of an opponent, to once-visible but now folded hands, in order to estimate the likelihood of making his hand, as well as to estimate the likelihood that an opponent has made his.

In Seven-Card Stud almost every hand is possible. This is very different than a game like Texas Hold'em, in which a full house or four-of-a-kind isn't possible unless the board contains paired cards, and a flush is impossible unless the board contains three cards of the same suit.

With nearly endless possibilities, Seven-Card Stud is a bit like a jigsaw puzzle. One must combine knowledge of exposed and folded cards with previous betting patterns in order to discern the likelihood of any one of a variety of hands that your opponent might be holding.

Because there are five betting rounds, contesting a pot can become quite expensive, particularly if yours is the second-best hand.

If You've Never Played Seven-Card Stud Poker

Seven-Card Stud requires patience. Since you're dealt three cards right off the bat — before the first round of betting — it's important that these cards are able to work together before you enter a pot. In fact, the most critically important decision you'll make in a Seven-Card Stud game is whether to enter the pot on *third street* — the first round of betting.

The next critical decision point is whether you should continue playing on the third round of betting, called *fifth street*. In fixed-limit betting games, such as $6–$12, fifth street is where the betting limits double. There's an old adage in Seven-Card Stud: If you call on fifth street, you've bought a through-ticket to the *river card* (the last card).

Getting personal — what you need to win

Being a winning Seven-Card Stud player requires more than technical poker skills. It also takes strength of character, determination, and grit.

✔ **Be patient:** In poker, money flows from the impatient to the patient. If you lack patience you will never become a good player, regardless of how much knowledge you acquire. Stud poker is a waiting game — one that requires the patience of a saint.

✔ **Be observant:** If you don't pay close attention to visible cards, you will have a hard time winning on a consistent basis. If you are not aware of the discards, it is too easy to lose money by drawing to hands you probably won't make.

✔ **Be determined — play only live hands:** This skill is closely related to the need to be observant. Don't throw money away on hands that are really much more of a long shot than they might appear.

✔ **Be studious:** Since you'll throw away most of your starting hands, there's plenty of down time that can be put to good use by observing your opponents. Learn the kinds of hands they play. Observe their mannerisms, too. See if you can pick up any telltale clues about what they might be holding.

✔ **Be aggressive:** Don't be afraid to raise or even reraise if you think you have the best hand. Don't be afraid to checkraise either. It can be a good way to trap opponents when you have a powerhouse hand.

✔ **Be judicious:** Don't feel like you must play every hand dealt to you — that's a sure-fire way to lose your hard-earned money. Remember the "F-word." We're not talking expletives here, either. In poker the "F-word" is *fold.* Don't ever be afraid to toss your hand away and wait for a better opportunity.

A sample hand

Figure 3-1 shows a typical hand of Seven-Card Stud after all the cards are dealt.

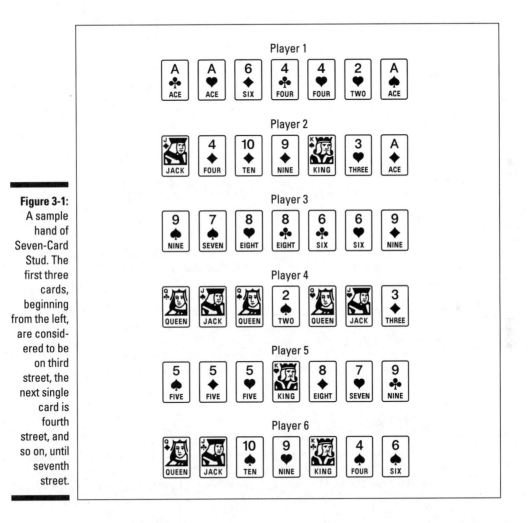

Figure 3-1: A sample hand of Seven-Card Stud. The first three cards, beginning from the left, are considered to be on third street, the next single card is fourth street, and so on, until seventh street.

At the conclusion of the hand, when all the cards have been dealt, the results are as follows:

Player 1 now has a full house, aces full of 4s. He is likely to raise.

Player 2 has an ace-high diamond flush.

Player 3, who began with a promising straight draw, has two pair — 9s and 8s.

Player 4 has a full house, queens full of jacks, but will lose to Player 1's bigger full house.

Player 5 has three 5s, the same hand she began with.

Player 6 has a king-high straight.

In Seven-Card Stud, each player make the best five-card hand from his seven cards. The highest hand out of all the players wins. (In Figure 3-1, Player 1 takes the pot.)

While most stud games do not result in this many big hands contesting a pot, you can see how the best hand changes from one betting round to another, and how a player can make the hand he is hoping for yet not have any chance of winning.

Antes, the Deal, and the Betting Structure

Before the cards are dealt each player posts an ante, which is a fraction of a bet. Each poker game begins as a chase for the antes, so this money seeds the pot.

Players are then dealt two cards face down, along with one face up. The lowest exposed card is required to make a small bet of a predetermined denomination. This bet (and the person who makes this bet) is called the *bring-in*. If two or more players have an exposed card of the same rank, the determining factor is the alphabetical order of suits: clubs, diamonds, hearts, and spades.

Betting

The player to the immediate left of the bring-in has three options. He may fold his hand, call the bring-in, or raise to a full bet. In a $20–$40 game, the antes are usually $3 and the bring-in is $5. The player to the bring-in's left can either fold, call the $5 bring-in bet, or raise to $20 — which constitutes a full bet.

If that player folds or calls the bring-in, the player to his immediate left has the same options. As soon as someone raises to a full bet, subsequent players must fold, call the full bet, or raise again.

Once betting has been equalized, a second card is dealt face-up and another round of betting ensues. This time, however, it is in increments of full bets. The player with the highest-ranking *board cards* (cards that are face up) acts first.

The first player to act may either *check* (a check, in actuality, is a bet of nothing) or bet. If a player has a pair showing (called an *open pair*), whether that pair resides in her hand or that of an opponent, she has the option to make a big bet in most cases. For example, in a $20–$40 game, the betting is still in increments of $20 on fourth street, except when there is an open pair. Then it is the discretion of any bettor to open for either $20 or $40, with all bets and raises continuing in increments that are consistent with the bet. (If the first two cards dealt face up to Brenda in a $20–$40 Stud game were a pair of jacks, then she or anyone else involved in that hand can bet $40 instead of $20.) This rule allows someone with an open pair to protect her hand by making a larger wager.

Raising

Most casinos allow three or four raises per betting round, except when only two players contest the pot. In that case, there is no limit to the number of raises permitted.

In Stud, the order in which players act (called *position*) is determined by the cards showing on the board and can vary from round to round. With the exception of the first round of betting on third street, where the lowest ranked card is required to *bring it in*, the highest hand on board acts first and has the option of checking or betting.

The highest hand could range anywhere from four-of-a-kind, to trips (three-of-a-kind), to two pair, to a single pair, or even the highest card, if no exposed pair is present.

Double bets

Betting usually doubles on fifth street, except if there's a player on fourth street who holds a pair. When there is, anyone involved in the hand has the option of making a double bet and those players still contesting the pot are dealt another exposed card. *Sixth street* is the same. The last card, called *seventh street* or *the river*, is dealt face down. At the river, active players have a hand made up of three closed and four exposed cards. The player who acted first on sixth street acts first on seventh street too.

Showdown

If more than one player is active after all the betting has been equalized, players turn their hands face up, making the best five-card hand from the seven cards they are holding, and the best hand wins in a showdown (see Figure 3-1).

Spread-limit games

Many low-stakes Seven-Card Stud games used spread limits rather than fixed limits. Many casinos will spread $1–$3 or $1–$4 Seven-Card Stud games. These games are usually played without an ante. The low card is required to bring it in for $1, and all bets and raises can be in increments from $1–$4 — with the provision that all raises be at least the amount of the previous bet. If someone bets $2 you can raise $2, $3, or $4 — but not $1. If the original bettor had wagered $4, you can fold, call his $4 bet, or raise to $8.

Know When to Hold 'em and Know When to Fold 'em

Seven-Card Stud requires a great deal of patience and alertness. Most of the time, you should discard your hand on third street because your cards either don't offer much of an opportunity to win, or they may look promising but really aren't because the cards you need are dead. (For details about dead cards, see the section titled "The Importance of Live Cards" in this chapter.)

What Kind of Hands Are Likely To Win?

Winning Seven-Card Stud generally takes a fairly big hand (usually two pair, with jacks or queens as the big pair). In fact, if all the players in a seven-player game stayed around for the showdown, the winning hand would be two pair or better more than 97 percent of the time. Even two pair is no guarantee of winning, however, since 69 percent of the time the winning hand would be three-of-a-kind or better, and 54 percent of the time the winning hand would be at least a straight.

A straight is the median winning hand: Half the time the winning hand is a straight or better, half the time a lesser hand will win the pot.

If you plan to call on third street, you need a hand that has the possibility of improving to a fairly big hand.

Since straights and flushes are generally not made until sixth or seventh street, you should raise if you have a big pair (10s or higher). In fact, if someone else has raised before it's your turn to act, go ahead and reraise — as long as your pair is bigger than his upcard. The goal of your raise is to cause drawing hands to fold so that your big pair can win the pot — particularly if it improves to three-of-a-kind or two pair.

Big pairs play better against a few opponents, while straights and flushes are hands that you'd like to play against four opponents (or more). It's important to realize that straights and flushes start out as straight- and flush-draws. *Draws* are hands with no immediate value and won't grow into full-fledged straights and flushes very often. But these draws have the potential of growing into very big hands, and those holding them want a lot of customers around to pay them off whenever they are fortunate enough to complete their draw.

The Importance of Live Cards

Stud poker is a game of live cards. If the cards you need to improve your hand are visible in the hands of your opponents or have been discarded by other players who have folded, then the cards you need are said to be *dead*. But if those cards are not visible, then your hand is *live*.

Many beginning Seven-Card Stud players are overjoyed to find a starting hand that contains three suited cards. But before you blithely call a bet on third street, look around and see how many cards of your suit are showing. If you don't see any at all, you're certainly entitled to jump for joy.

But if you see three or more of your suit cavorting in your opponents' hands, then folding your hand and patiently waiting for a better opportunity may be the only logical course of action.

Even when the next card you are dealt is the fourth of your suit and no other cards of your suit are exposed, the odds are still 1.12-to-1 against completing your flush. Of course if you complete your flush, the pot will certainly return more than 1.12-to-1, so it pays to continue on with your draw. But remember: Even when you begin with four suited cards, you'll make a flush only 47 percent of the time. (The sidebar "Consider the odds" offers more statistics.)

If you don't make your flush on fifth street, the odds against making it increase to 1.9-to-1 — which means you'll get lucky only 35 percent of the time. And if you miss your flush on sixth street, the odds against making your flush increase to 4.1-to-1. With only one more card to come you can count on getting lucky about only 20 percent of the time.

Consider the odds

Here are some odds that will help you put the game of Seven-Card Stud in perspective.

- ✔ 424-to-1: The odds against being dealt three-of-a-kind. (At an average of 30 hands per hour, you'll start with three-of-a-kind every 14 hours or so. That's why it hurts so much when you're dealt a hand like this and lose!)

- ✔ 5-to-1: The odds against being dealt *any* pair on your first three cards.

- ✔ 18-to-1: The odds against being dealt three suited cards.

- ✔ 3.5-to-1: The odds against making a full house if your first four cards make two pair.

- ✔ 6-to-1: The odds against making a straight if your first three cards are sequenced.

- ✔ 5-to-1: The odds against making a flush if your first three cards are suited.

- ✔ 1.2-to-1: The odds *in favor* of improving to at least two pair if you start with a straight flush draw like 10♦ J♦ Q♦.

- ✔ 1.4-to-1: The odds against making two pair if you start with a pair in your first three cards. The odds are 4.1-to-1 against making three-of-a-kind or better.

- ✔ 1.1-to-1: The odds against making a flush if you begin with three suited cards and catch a fourth card of your suit on the next round. But if you don't catch a fourth suited card on fourth street, the odds against making that flush jump all the way to 2-to-1!

- ✔ 4-to-1: The odds against making a full house if you hold three-of-a-kind and three other cards on sixth street.

This also holds true for straight draws. If your first four cards are 9-10-J-Q, there are four kings and an equal number of eights that will complete your straight. But if three kings and an eight have already been exposed, the odds against completing a straight are substantially higher and the deck is now stacked against you, and even the prettiest looking hands have to be released.

The first three cards are critical

Starting standards are important in Seven-Card Stud, just as they are in any form of poker. Those first three cards you've been dealt need to work together or contain a big pair to make it worthwhile for you to continue playing.

Position

Position (your place at the table and how it affects betting order) is important in every form of poker, and betting last is a big advantage. But unlike games like Texas Hold'em and Omaha, where position is fixed for all betting rounds during the play of a hand, it can vary in stud. The lowest exposed card always acts first on the initial betting round, but the highest exposed hand acts first thereafter.

Since there's no guarantee that the highest exposed hand on fourth street will be the highest hand on the subsequent round, the pecking order can very from one betting round to another.

Subsequent betting rounds

If you choose to continue beyond third street, your next key decision point occurs on fifth street — when the betting limits typically double. Most Seven-Card Stud experts can tell you that a call on fifth street often commits you to see the hand through to its conclusion. If you are still active on fifth street, the pot is generally big enough that it pays to continue to the sometimes bitter end. In fact, even if you can only beat a bluff on the river, you should generally call if your opponent bets.

By learning to make good decisions on third and fifth street, you should be able to win regularly at most low-limit games.

Seven-Card Stud in Depth

Seven-Card Stud is a game of contrasts. Start with a big pair, or a medium pair and a couple of high side cards, and you want to play against only a few opponents — which you can achieve by betting, raising, or reraising to chase out drawing hands.

If you begin with a flush or straight draw, you want plenty of opponents, and you'd like to make your hand as inexpensively as possibly. If you're fortunate enough to catch a scare card or two, your opponent will have to acknowledge the possibility that you've already made your hand or are likely to make it at the earliest opportunity. If that's the case, he may be wary of betting a big pair into what appears to be a powerhouse holding such as a straight or flush.

That's the nature of Seven-Card Stud. The pairs do their betting early, trying to make it expensive for speculative drawing hands, and those playing draws are betting and raising later — if they've gotten lucky enough to complete their hands.

Starting hands

Most of the time you will throw your hand away on third street. Regardless of how eager you are to mix it up and win a pot or two, Seven-Card Stud is a game of patience.

If you like to fish from the shoreline, daydream, meditate, or engage in other contemplative pastimes, Seven-Card Stud is right up your alley. But if you lack patience — or can't learn it — this game will frustrate you to no end.

Many players lose money because they think it's okay to play for another round or two and see what happens. Not only does this usually result in players bleeding their money away, the very fact that they entered a pot with less than a viable starting hand often causes them to become trapped and lose even more money.

Before making a commitment to play a hand, you need to be aware of the strength of your cards relative to those of your opponents, the exposed cards visible on the table, and the number of players to act after you do. After all, the more players who might act after you do, the more cautious you need to be.

Starting with three-of-a-kind

The best starting hand is *three-of-a-kind,* which is also called *trips.* But it's a rare bird, and you can expect to be dealt trips only once in 425 times. If you play fairly long sessions, statistics show that you'll be dealt trips every two days or so. While it's possible for you to be dealt a lower set of trips than your opponent, the odds against this are very long, and if you are dealt trips, you can assume that you are in the lead.

You might win even if you don't improve at all. While you probably won't make a flush or a straight if you start with three-of-a-kind, the odds against improving are only about 1.5-to-1. When you do improve, it's probably going to be a full house or four-of-a-kind, and at that point you will be heavily favored to win the pot.

With trips, you will undoubtedly see the hand through to the river, unless it becomes obvious that you are beaten. That, however, is a rarity.

Since you'll be dealt trips once in a blue moon, it's frustrating to raise, knock out all your opponents, and win only the antes. Since you are undoubtedly in the lead whenever you are dealt trips, you can afford to call and give your opponents a ray of hope on the next betting round.

The downside, of course, is that one of your opponents will catch precisely the card he needs to stay in the hunt and beat you with a straight or flush if you're not lucky enough to improve. When you have trips, you are hoping that one of your opponents will raise before it is your turn to act. Then you can reraise, which should knock out most of the drawing hands.

Most of the time the pot is raised on third street, the player doing the raising either has a big pair, or a more modest pair with a king or an ace for a side card. But your trips are far ahead of his hand. After all, he is raising to eliminate the drawing hands and hoping to make two pair in order to capture the pot. Little does he know that you are already ahead of him, never mind the fact that you also have ample opportunity to improve.

Your opponent will probably call your reraise, and call you all the way to the river especially if he makes two pair. Here's what usually happens. In the process of winning the pot, you earn three small bets on third street, another on fourth street, and double-sized bets on fifth, sixth, and seventh streets. If you are playing $10–$20, you will show a profit of $100 plus the bring-in and the antes. If you've trapped an additional caller or two who wind up folding their hand on fifth street, your profit will exceed $150.

Big pairs

A *big pair* (10s or higher) is usually playable and generally warrants raising. Your goal in raising is to thin the field and make it too expensive for drawing hands to continue playing. A single high pair is favored against one opponent who has a straight or a flush draw. Against two or more draws, however, you are an underdog.

It's always better to have a *buried pair* (both cards hidden) than to have one of the cards that comprise your pair hidden and the other exposed. There are a number of reasons for this. For one thing, it's deceptive. If your opponent cannot see your pair — or even see part of it — it will be difficult for him to assess the strength of your hand.

If fourth street were to pair your exposed card and you come out swinging, your opponent would be apprehensive about your having three-of-a-kind. This might constrain his aggressiveness and limit the amount you can win. But if your pair is buried, and fourth street gives you trips, no one has a clue about the strength of your hand, and they won't until you've trapped them for a raise or two.

Big pairs play best against one or two opponents and can sometimes win without improvement. But you're really hoping to make at least two pair. If you are up against one or two opponents, your two pair will probably be the winning hand.

Having said that, a word of caution is in order. It is critically important not to take your pair against a bigger pair, unless you have live side cards that are bigger than your opponent's probable pair. For example, if you were dealt J♦A♥/J♠, and your opponent's door card is Q♠, her most likely hand is a pair of queens if she continues on in the hand. (The slash mark indicates that the two cards to the left of the slash were dealt to the player face down. The card to the right of the slash was dealt face up.)

As long as your ace is live, you can play against the opponent. For one thing, she might not have a pair of queens. She might have a pair of buried 9s, in which case you are already in the lead. Even if she does have queens, you could catch an ace or another jack, or even a king. An ace gives you two pair that's presumably bigger than your opponent's hand, while trip jacks puts you firmly in the lead.

Even catching a live king on fourth street can help you. It offers another way to make two pair that is bigger than your opponent. You may be behind at this point, but you still have a number of ways to win.

Small or medium pairs

Whether you have a pair of deuces or a bigger pair is not nearly as important as whether your side cards are higher in rank than your opponent's pair. If you hold big, live side cards along with a small pair, your chances of winning are really a function of pairing one of those side cards — and aces up beats queens up, regardless of the rank of your second pair.

Small or medium pairs usually find themselves swimming upstream and need to pair one of those big side cards in order to win. While a single pair of aces or kings can win a hand of stud, particularly when it's heads-up, winning with a pair of deuces — or any other small pair, for that matter — is just this side of miraculous; it doesn't happen very often.

Playing a draw

If you have been dealt three cards of the same suit or three cards that are in sequence, the first order of business is to see if the cards you need are available. (Carefully check out your opponent's exposed cards to see if any of the cards you need are already out.) If the cards you need are not already taken, you can usually go ahead and take another card off the deck.

If you see that your opponents have more than two of your suit or three of the cards that can make a straight, you really shouldn't keep playing. If your cards are live and you can see another card inexpensively, however, go ahead and do so. You might get lucky and catch a fourth card of your suit, or you could pair one of your big cards and have a couple of ways to win. Your flush could get back on track if the fifth card is suited, or you could improve to three-of-a-kind or two big pair.

Drawing hands can be seductive because they offer the promise of improving to very large hands. Skilled players are not easily seduced, however, and are armed with the discipline required to know when to release a drawing hand and wait for a better opportunity to invest their money.

Beyond third street

Fourth street is fairly routine. You are hoping your hand improves and that your opponents don't catch the cards you need, or a card that appears to better their own hand.

When an opponent pairs his exposed third street card, he may well have made three-of-a-kind. When this happens, and you have not appreciably improved, it's usually a signal to release your hand.

Fifth street is the next major decision point. This is when betting limits typically double. If you pay for a card on fifth street, you'll generally see the hand through until the river, unless it becomes obvious that you are beaten on board. It's not uncommon for any number of players to call on third street and again on fourth. But when fifth street rolls around, there are usually only two or three players in the hand.

Often it's the classic confrontation of a big pair — or two pair — against a straight or flush draw. Regardless of what kind of confrontation seems to be brewing, unless you have a big hand or big draw, you will probably throw away many of your once-promising hands on fifth street.

In fact, if you throw away too many hands on sixth street, you can be sure that you are making a mistake on both fifth and sixth street.

If you are fortunate enough to make what you consider to be the best hand on sixth street, go ahead and bet — or raise if someone else has bet first. Remember, most players will see the hand through to the river once they call on fifth street. When you have a big hand, these later betting rounds are the time to bet or raise. After all, good hands don't come around all that often. When you have one, you want to make as much money as you can.

When all the cards have been dealt

If you've seen the hand through to the river, you should consider calling any bet as long as you have a hand that can beat a bluff (assuming you are *heads up* — playing against just one other player). Pots can get quite large in Seven-Card Stud. If your opponent was on a draw and missed, the only way for her to win the pot is to bluff and hope you throw away your hand. Your opponent doesn't need to succeed at this too often to make the strategy correct. After all, she is risking only one bet to try to capture an entire pot full of bets.

Most of the time you'll make a *crying call* (a call made by a person who is sure he will lose) and your opponent will show you a better hand. But every now and then you'll catch her *speeding* (bluffing), and win the pot. And you don't have to snap off a bluff all that often for it to be the play of choice.

Seven-Card Stud is a complex game with a number of strategic elements. Take a look at the sidebar "Master a winning strategy."

Master a winning strategy

Become a winning Seven-Card Stud player by mastering these strategic elements:

✔ **If you have a big card showing** and no one has entered the pot on third street when it's your turn to act, you should raise and try to steal the antes.

✔ **This game requires immense patience,** especially on third street. If you don't have a big pair, big cards, or a draw with live cards, save your money.

✔ **Drawing hands offer great promise.** But to play them, your cards must be live. Draws are also more playable if your starting cards are higher in rank than any of your opponents' visible cards. This can enable you to win even if your draw fails but you are fortunate enough to pair your big cards.

✔ **After all cards have all been dealt** and you have a single opponent who comes out betting, you should call with any hand strong enough to beat a bluff.

✔ **Seven-Card Stud requires strong powers of observation.** Not only must you be aware of whether the cards you need are live or not, you must also be aware of the cards most likely to improve your opponent's hand.

✔ **Fifth street, when the betting limits double,** is a major decision point. If you buy a card on fifth street, you've probably committed yourself to see the hand through to its conclusion.

Chapter 4

Texas Hold'em

• •

In This Chapter

▶ Understanding the basics

▶ Taking a deeper look

▶ Starting hands

▶ Getting to know the ins and outs of raising

▶ Playing the flop

▶ Playing the turn

▶ Playing the river

▶ Knowing what to do if you make your draw

▶ Making smart moves when the pot gets big

• •

Texas Hold'em is the most popular game played in casino poker rooms. Although playing expertly requires a great deal of skill, Hold'em is easily learned and deceptively simple. It is a subtle and complex game, typically played with nine or ten players to a table and is a faster, more action-filled game than Stud or most other games. Texas Hold'em is also the fastest growing poker game in the world, and it is the game used to determine the world champion at the World Series of Poker.

Basic Rules

In Hold'em, two cards are dealt face down to each player, and a round of betting takes place. On the first round, players may either call or raise the blind bet, or they must fold their hand. Most casinos allow a bet and three or four raises per betting round, with one exception: When only two players contest the pot there is no limit on the number of raises permitted.

When the first round of betting is complete, three communal cards, called the *flop*, are turned face up in the center of the table. That's followed by another round of betting. On this and each succeeding round, players may check if no one has bet when it is their turn to act. If there is no bet, a player may check or bet. If there is a bet, players may fold, call, raise, or reraise.

A fourth communal card — called the *turn* — is then exposed. Another round of betting takes place. Then the fifth and final community card — known as the *river* — is placed in the center of the table followed by the last round of betting. The best five-card poker hand using any combination of a player's two private cards and the five communal cards is the winner.

That's all there is to the play of the game. Yet within this simplicity lies an elegance and sophistication that makes Texas Hold'em the most popular form of poker in the world.

Blind Bets

Before cards are dealt, the first two players to the left of the dealer position are required to post blind bets, which are used instead of antes to stimulate action. (Those two players post their bets before they see any cards and, thus, are "blind.")

In a $10–$20 Hold'em game, blinds are usually $5 and $10. Each blind is considered *live*. Because blinds represent a forced, first bet, the blind bettors can raise (but only on the first round) once the betting has gone around the table and it is their turn to act again.

Unlike Stud, where position is determined by each player's exposed cards, referred to as his *board*, the player with the dealer button (see the section "Position, position, and position," later in this chapter) acts last in every round of betting — with the exception of the first one.

Hold'em in General

While Hold'em is exciting, exhilarating, and enjoyable, you should know *something* before diving in and plunking your money down — even if you are playing the lowest-limit game in the house. This section offers a few of those *somethings* we wish we had known when first making the transition from Seven-Card Stud to Texas Hold'em.

Hold'em only looks like Stud; it plays differently

With a total of seven cards, some of which are turned face up and others down, Hold'em bears a resemblance to Seven-Card Stud. But this furtive similarity is only a "tastes like chicken" analogy.

One major difference is that 71 percent of your hand is defined on the flop. As a result, your best values in Hold'em are found up front; you get to see 71 percent of your hand for a single round of betting.

Staying for the turn and river demands that you either have a strong hand, a draw to a potentially winning hand, or good reason to believe that betting on a future round may cause your opponents to fold. Because there are only two additional cards dealt after the flop, along with the fact that the five communal cards play in everyone's hand, there are fewer *draw-outs* in Hold'em than Stud. (A draw-out happens when you draw cards that make your hand better than your opponent's.)

Also, because Hold'em uses exposed communal cards in the center of the table that combine with two hidden cards in each player's hand to form the best poker hand, it is more difficult for an opponent to draw-out on you than in Stud poker. For example, if you were dealt a pair of jacks and your opponent held a pair of 9s, the presence of a pair of 5s among the communal cards gives each of you two pair. But you still have the best hand. Unless one of those 5s helped an opponent complete a straight, the only player helped by that pair of 5s would be an opponent fortunate enough to have another 5 in his hand.

The first two cards are critical

You'll frequently hear players say that any two cards can win. While that's true as far as it goes, it doesn't go far enough. The whole truth is this: While any two cards can win, they won't win enough to warrant playing them. Like all forms of poker, you need *starting standards*. Players who lack starting standards take the worst of it far too often. See Chapter 2 for more detail about starting standards.

Position, position, and position

There's an old real estate bromide that says the three most important features of any property are location, location, and location. In Hold'em, the important features are position, position, and position. Where your place is at the table (your *position*) is so important that some two-card holdings, which can't be played profitably from early position, are cards you might raise with when you're last to act.

In a typical nine-handed game, *early position* includes both blinds and the two players to their left. The fifth, sixth, and seventh players to act are in *middle position*, and the eighth and ninth players are in *late position*.

Because casino games are dealt by house dealers, a small disk — called a *puck*, a *buck*, or, most commonly, a *button* — is used as a marker to indicate the player in the dealer position. That player is always last to act. The button rotates clockwise around the table with each hand that's dealt. The expression "passing the buck" does not refer to dollar bills, but to poker. And President Harry S. Truman, an avid poker player himself, had a sign on his desk in the White House that read, "The buck stops here."

The flop should fit your hand

No matter how sweet your first two cards may appear, an unfavorable flop can render them nearly worthless. A key concept is that the flop must fit your hand. We call this concept "fit or fold." If the flop doesn't strengthen your hand or offer a draw to a very strong hand, you should usually release it.

Suppose you called on the first round of betting with A♦J♦, and the flop is Q♦5♦3♠. You don't have a strong hand at this point. What you do have, however, is a hand with extremely strong potential. If another diamond falls on the turn or the river, you'll make a flush. Not any flush, mind you, but the best possible flush, since your ace precludes any of your opponents from making a higher one.

Even if you don't make a flush but were to catch a jack or an ace instead, that may be enough to win the pot.

Beyond the flop

As a general rule, you shouldn't continue beyond the flop without a strong pair and a decent side-card (or *kicker*), or a straight or flush draw with at least two opponents to ensure that the pot is big enough to make it worthwhile.

Because of the communal cards, players frequently have the same hand, with the exception of their unpaired side card, or kicker. When that happens, it's the rank of each player's kicker that determines who wins the pot in question. That's why most Hold'em players love to be dealt A-K (or "Big Slick," as players call it). If the flop contains either an ace or a king, the player holding Big Slick will have the top pair with the best possible kicker.

Game texture — the relative aggressiveness or passivity exhibited by the players — is also important in determining whether to call that bet or raise. But a feeling for the game's texture and how it should influence your play can be obtained only from live game experience. In the absence of that experience, err on the side of caution. It costs less.

Success at Hold'em demands that you be patient, pay close attention to position, and take comfort in the knowledge that good hands are run down less often than the best Seven-Card Stud hands.

Hold'em in Depth

Combinations of poker hands number literally in the millions; in Hold'em, however, there are only 169 different two-card starting combinations. That number, of course, assumes that a hand like K♦Q♦ is the equivalent of K♣Q♣. If three diamonds were to appear on the flop, the K♦Q♦ would be significantly more valuable than K♣Q♣. But the future can neither be predicted nor controlled, and these two hands have identical value before the flop.

Each one of these 169 unique starting combinations fits into one of only five categories:

- ✔ Pairs
- ✔ Connecting cards
- ✔ Gapped cards
- ✔ Suited connectors
- ✔ Suited gapped cards

That's it. Five categories. That's all you have to worry about.

If you are not dealt a pair, your cards will be either *suited* (of the same suit) or unsuited. They also can be *connected* (consecutive) or *gapped* (unconnected). Examples of connectors are K-Q, 8-7, and 4-3. Unconnected cards might be one-, two-, three-gapped, or more, and would include hands like K-J (one gap, with Q missing), 9-6 (two gap, missing 7-8), or 9-3 (five gap, missing 4-5-6-7-8).

Small gaps make more straights

Generally, the smaller the gap, the easier it is to make a straight. Suppose that you hold 10-6. Your only straight possibility is 9-8-7. But if you hold 10-9, you can make a straight with K-Q-J, Q-J-8, J-8-7, and 8-7-6.

Every rule has exceptions. A hand like A-K can make only one straight. It needs to marry a Q-J-T. An A-2 is in the same boat and needs to cozy up to a 5-4-3. Although connected, each of these holdings can make only one straight because they reside at the end of the spectrum.

Other exceptions include a K-Q, which can make a straight only two ways, by connecting with A-J-10 or J-10-9; and 3-2 is in a similar fix. The only other limited connectors are — yes, you guessed it — Q-J and 4-3. These two holdings can each make three straights. The Q-J needs A-K-10, K-10-9, or 10-9-8. It can't make that fourth straight because there is no room above an ace. The 4-3 is similarly constrained because there is no room below the ace. But any other connectors can make straights four ways, and that's a big advantage over one-, two-, or three-gapped cards.

Unless you are fortunate enough to wrap four cards around one of your four-gappers, there's no way these cards can make a straight. But don't worry about that. If you take our advice, you will seldom, if ever, play hands that are four-gapped or worse unless they are suited — and then only under very favorable circumstances.

Gapped cards

Gapped cards, in general, are not as valuable as connectors because of their difficulty in completing straights. But if you were to make a flush there's no need to be concerned about the gap. After all, a flush made with A♥6♥ is just as good as an A♥K♥ flush. But A-K is more valuable for other reasons. Suppose that flush never comes. You can make a straight with A-K; you can't with A-6 (unless four cards come on the board to help your straight).

You might also win if you catch either an ace or a king. If an ace flops, you'll have made a pair of aces with a 6 side-card, or kicker, and could easily lose to an opponent holding an ace with a bigger companion. But any pair you'd make with the A-K would be the top pair with the best possible kicker.

Acting last is a big advantage

Acting later in a hand is a big advantage, so you can afford to see the flop with weaker hands when you're in late position. If you're last to act, you've had the advantage of knowing how many opponents are still in the pot and seeing how each of them acted on the current round of betting. That's a big edge, because some starting hands play better against a large number of opponents, while others play better against a smaller field.

In late position you'll also know which of your adversaries are representing strength by betting or raising. The later you act, the more information at your disposal. And poker is a game of information — incomplete information, to be sure, but it's a game of information nevertheless.

Starting Hands

Some starting hands are so strong they can be played in any position. You don't get these hands very often, but when you do, you are generally a favorite from the get-go to win that pot.

The following table shows that we recommend playing any pair of 7s or higher in early position, as well as the twelve suited and six unsuited card combinations.

Playable hands in early position

Pairs	7s through aces
Suited	Aces with a king, queen, jack, or 10
	King with a queen, jack, or 10
	Queen with a jack or 10
	Jack with a 10 or 9
	10 with a 9
Unsuited	Aces with a king, queen, jack, or 10
	King with a queen or jack

When you are the fifth, sixth, or seventh player to act, then you are in middle position and can safely play smaller pairs like 6s and 5s. You can also add ten additional suited hands and four more unsuited combinations to your playable repertoire if the pot has not been raised.

Playable hands in middle position

Pairs	5s and 6s
Suited	Aces with a 9, 8, 7, or 6
	King with a 9
	Queen with a 9 or 8
	Jack with an 8
	10 with an 8
	9 with an 8
Unsuited	King with a 10
	Queen with a jack or 10
	Jack with a 10

In late position you have the advantage of acting last or next-to-last. As a result, you can add a variety of hands to your arsenal. Most are bargain basement specials, however, that should be played only if the pot has not been raised. Moreover, you should be disciplined enough to release them if the flop brings anything less than an abundant harvest of friendly cards.

Playable hands in late position

Pairs	4s, 3s, and 2s
Suited	Aces with a 5, 4, 3, or 2
	King with an 8, 7, 6, 5, 4, 3, or 2
	Jack with a 7
	10 with a 7
	9 with a 7 or 6
	8 with a 7 or 6
	7 with a 6 or 5
	6 with a 5
	5 with a 4
Unsuited:	King with a 9
	Queen with a 9
	Jack with a 9 or 8
	10 with a 9 or 8
	9 with an 8 or 7
	8 with a 7

If you are new to the game, have been playing indiscriminately, or have an any-two-cards-can-win philosophy, you may believe these recommendations are too tight. They're not. In fact, they are somewhat loose.

A hand like K♥2♥, while playable in late position, is a pretty sorry excuse for a Hold'em hand. If you flop a king and there's any appreciable action, it's fairly apparent that someone else has a king with a bigger kicker than yours. If you flop a 2, you've guaranteed yourself the lowest pair on board. Even if you are incredibly lucky and flop a flush, there's no assurance that it is the best flush. Probably the very best flop you could hope for is something like A♥2♣2♦, which gives you three deuces with a strong kicker. You also have three cards to a flush, and while the odds against catching two more hearts are long indeed, it is an additional way to win. Players call this a *backdoor* draw. More importantly, an ace on the board guarantees a call or two from any opponents holding an ace in their hand.

Still, K♥2♥ and a lot of the other playable hands in late position are vulnerable from any number of directions, and it takes some degree of skill to navigate your way through the murky waters of a Hold'em pot in a rickety canoe like this one.

Getting lucky

Sometimes you'll get lucky. Lou Krieger, one of this book's authors, recalls being dealt K♦4♦. The pot wasn't raised, and six players called before it was his turn to act, so he called too. The flop was A♦ J♦ 5♦. Not only did he flop the nut (best possible) flush, but two of his opponents held aces and were in a mood to raise.

The two opponents were attempting to knock out any opponents who may have held a large, lone diamond card. Neither one realized the other had an ace. They were never able to chase the fellow who held J♣5♥ and flopped two pair in the blind, nor did they dissuade a woman who called from middle position with 9♦8♦, and was drawing nearly dead to Krieger's larger flush.

Krieger was lucky. He won a big pot against some opponents who should have known better. This kind of pot doesn't come around every day, but it does occasionally, and its largess is still underwriting his periodic calls from late position in unraised pots with hands like K♦4♦.

The Art of Raising

Raising adds spice to the game of poker and money to the pot. Raising is an act of aggression and causes everyone to sit up and take notice. When there's a raise or reraise, the level of excitement escalates. Sometimes you'll be raised, and sometimes you'll do the raising. Regardless of whether you're the raiser or raisee, it's time to sit up and take notice whenever a raise is made.

You've been raised

If the pot has been raised before it is your turn to act, you must tighten up significantly on the hands you play. Savvy players might raise with almost anything in late position if no one except the blinds are in the pot, but if a player raises from early position, give him credit for a good hand, and throw away all but the very strongest of hands.

 Remember that you need a stronger hand to call a raise than to initiate one. After all, if you raise, your opponents might fold, allowing you to win the blinds by default. If you call a raise, you have to give your opponent credit for a strong hand, and you should generally only call if you believe your hand to be even stronger.

When someone's raised after you've called

When an opponent raises after you've called, you are essentially committed to calling his raise, seeing the flop, and then deciding on the best course of action.

But when you call only to find yourself raised and raised again by a third opponent you should seriously consider throwing your hand away unless it is extremely strong.

Suppose that you called with a hand like 10♥9♥. Just because this hand may be playable in a tame game doesn't mean you must play it. In a game with frequent raising it may not a playable hand because it is speculative and best played inexpensively from late position. The ideal way to play this hand is from late position, with a large number of opponents, in a pot that has not been raised. Now this hand is worth a shot. You can always throw it away whenever the flop is unfavorable.

When should you raise?

Hold'em is a game that requires aggressive play as well as selectivity. You can't win in the long run by passively calling. You have to initiate your share of raises too; and here are some raising hands:

- ✔ You can always raise with a pair of aces, kings, queens, jacks and 10s. In fact, if someone has raised before it's your turn to act and you have a pair of aces, kings, and queens in your hand, go ahead and reraise. You probably have the best hand anyway. Reraising protects your hand by thinning the field, thus minimizing the chances of anyone getting lucky on the flop.

- ✔ You can also raise if you're holding a suited ace with a king, queen, or jack, or a suited king with a queen. If your cards are unsuited, you can raise if you're holding an ace with a king or queen, or a king with a queen.

- ✔ If you are in late position and no one has called the blinds, you can usually safely raise with any pair, an ace with any kicker, and a king with a queen, jack, 10, or 9. When you raise in this situation, you're really hoping that the blinds — which are, after all, random hands — will fold. But even if they play, your ace or king is likely to be the best hand if no one improves.

Playing the Flop

Defining moments are crystallized instances in time, forever frozen in memory, imprinted into consciousness, never to be forgotten. Like Neil Armstrong walking on the moon, and the first home run you hit in Little League, these magical moments shape the way you perceive and value the world around you.

Hold'em also has its defining moment, and it's the flop. (See the section "Basic Rules" for details about the flop.) Unlike Seven-Card Stud, where cards that follow your initial holding are parceled out one by one with rounds of betting interspersed, when you see the flop in Hold'em, you're looking at five-sevenths of your hand. That's 71 percent of your hand, and the cost is only a single round of betting.

The implications of this situation should be abundantly clear: If the flop does not fit your hand, be done with it. Playing long-shot holdings after the flop is a sure way to lose money. After the flop, the relationship between the betting and cards-to-come is reversed. Now you're looking at spending 83 percent of the potential cost of a hand for the remaining 29 percent of the cards!

Fit or fold

Fit or fold. That's what you have to decide on when playing the flop. *Fit* can take one of three forms. The flop fits because

- ✔ It improves your hand.
- ✔ It offers a draw that figures to pay off handsomely if you hit it.
- ✔ You hold a big pair before the flop.

If you don't improve to a big hand or a draw with a nice potential payoff, then get out (fold) — and do it now.

Flops you're going to love, flops to fold on

While you're not going to like the flop most of the time, there are those rare instances when it fits like a custom-made suit. When you're lucky enough to flop a straight flush, four-of-a-kind, a full house, or the nut flush, your major worry is not whether you'll win, but how much money you can extract from your opponents.

Your first order of business is to examine the texture of the flop. Based on the betting pattern prior to the flop, try to determine if one or more of your opponents has made a hand or has a draw to a hand that would be second-best to yours.

Take a look at how you can handle different types of flops:

Lovable flops

- **Straight flush:** Bet the house, the farm, and mortgage your soul. You shouldn't lose.

- **Four-of-a-kind:** If there are two pair on board, and you have the smaller of the two pair, it is possible — though very unlikely — that you can lose this hand. But if there's only one pair on board and you have the matching pair in your hand, you have the practical *nuts*. You can lose only to a straight flush or royal flush, unless a bigger communal comes along and someone else has a bigger four-of-a-kind. But don't worry; you'll seldom, if ever, lose with hands like these.

- **Full house:** A terrific hand, but you have to examine the board to make sure that yours is the best possible full house before you bet the farm. But don't be afraid to raise with a full house; it's probably a winner.

- **Nut flush:** If you have an ace-high flush when all the cards have been dealt, and no pair is on the board — which means that a full house or four-of-a-kind is not possible — you've got the best possible hand. Just keep betting or raising and don't stop.

- **Nut straight:** If you have the highest possible straight, and there's no possibility of a flush or full house, you've got the best hand, period. Bet and raise for all you're worth.

Likable flops

- **Set with safe board:** If you're lucky enough to hold 8♣8♦ and the flop is 8♥K♠2♦ you've flopped a *set* (three of a kind), and there's not much to be wary of. There's no flush or straight draw, and anyone holding a king in his hand is going to pay you off.

- **Trips:** If you have A♥8♠ and the flop is 8♣8♦7♠ you've got trips. It's not quite as good as it would be if the pair were in your hand, because anyone holding 8-7 will have flopped a full house. But that won't happen very frequently, so go ahead and bet and raise as long as the board is not threatening.

Good flops

- **Two pair:** If you flop two pair but they are not the top two pair, you have a good hand but one that is still vulnerable. Stay with it, however, unless it appears obvious that you are beaten.

- **Top pair:** A lot of Hold'em pots are won with one pair, and that one pair is usually the top pair on board. Your primary concern with top pair and an apparently safe board is determining whether your kicker is bigger than your opponent's.

- **Overpair:** If the board is 8♥7♠2♣, and you hold 10♦10♠ you have a pocket pair that is higher than the highest card on the board. In poker parlance, that's called an *overpair*. It's better than top pair, and usually a hand to consider raising with.

Dangerous flops

- ✔ **Kicker trouble:** Even if you flop top pair, your hand is only as strong as your kicker. It's a lot nicer to make top pair with an ace kicker than a weaker one.

- ✔ **Suited board:** Flops where all the cards are of the same suit or are sequenced, like 10-9-8 are dangerous. Someone may already have made a straight or a flush, and even if you've been lucky enough to flop a set, you are heading uphill and may have to see the board pair — giving you a full house — in order to win. With top pair, or even two pair, discretion is usually the better part of valor with suited or sequenced flops.

Overcards

An *overcard* is a card higher than the highest card on the board. Should you play overcards or not? Many of your opponents will routinely call with over-cards. Suppose you call before the flop with K-J, you're up against three opponents, and the flop is 8-6-3 of mixed suits. What should you do if someone bets? Do you call, hoping the next card off the deck is a king or jack — one of the six remaining cards in the deck that presumably gives you a winning hand? Or are you better off folding, and waiting for a flop that fits your hand?

Making a good decision involves knowing your opponents and the hands they are likely to play. Then examine the flop. Is it the kind of flop that will tend to hit one or more players? Or is it so ragged that it's unlikely any of your opponents are holding cards the flop would have paired? You should also be aware of how many opponents you're facing. The more opponents, the more likely the flop will hit at least one of them.

If you're unsure what to do, err on the side of caution until you gain enough playing experience to feel comfortable in these situations.

Flopping a draw

When you flop a four-flush or a four-straight, you'll have to decide whether to continue with your draw. Here's how to make that decision:

You'll need enough opponents so that the size of the pot offsets the mathe-matical odds against completing your hand. How many opponents do you need? If you're facing three or more, it's typically worthwhile to draw. If you're holding two large cards, like A-Q, you're probably favored against any lone opponent regardless of whether you make your hand. You might also win by pairing either of your cards on the turn or river. Sometimes just two big cards will be sufficient to win in a showdown.

Six tips for winning play on the flop

Here are six tips that will help you play successfully on the flop:

- If the flop doesn't fit your hand, most of the time you'll have to release it. The flop defines your hand.

- When you flop a big hand, give your opponents an opportunity to make the second-best hand, but avoid giving them a free card later that could beat you.

- If you're new to Hold'em, err on the side of caution. It costs less.

- When you have a hand with multiple possibilities, play it fast. It has value exceeding any of its component possibilities.

- Be selective about the hands you plan to play both before and after the flop, but be aggressive when you have a hand that warrants it.

- If you flop a draw, stick with it as long as the pot promises a greater payoff than the odds against making your hand.

Multiway possibilities

You'll occasionally flop hands that offer a plethora of possibilities. Assume you hold 8♥7♥, and the flop is 7♣6♠5♥. You've flopped top pair, as well as a straight draw, and you have backdoor flush potential (see the "Starting Hands" section for more about backdoor draws).

When you flop a hand with more than one way to win, your hand is stronger than any of its individual components. Your pair may win by itself. Your hand could improve to trips or two pair. You might make a straight on the turn or river, or make a flush if the next two cards are both hearts.

Here's another example: You hold A♣J♣ and the flop is A♥9♣4♣. Chances are you hold the best hand and are favored to win even if your hand does not improve. You may also get lucky and turn your good hand into a great one. A jack gives you two pair, and ace gives you three aces, and any club makes the nut flush.

With a hand this promising you want action. Get more money into the pot by betting or raising. And if you think one of your opponents is going to bet, you can try for a checkraise.

Playing the Turn

The *turn card* is the fourth card dealt face up and is common to everyone's hand. Some poker pundits have suggested that the turn plays itself. While you can't play the turn on autopilot, you shouldn't get yourself into too much trouble unless you've already made the mistake of seeing the turn when you shouldn't have. If that's the case, you've already thrown good money after bad.

Much of the time you won't even see the turn. You'll have thrown away most of your hands before the flop and released others once you saw that the flop didn't fit. If there's no logical reason to be in the pot by the turn, you should have folded. It's very easy to squander your bankroll one bet at a time. Poor players do just that, calling one more bet and then another. While calling any one bet may be insignificant by itself, collectively it can break you.

If you've made it to the turn you should be holding a good hand, a promising draw, or believe your bluff can pick up the pot.

TIP

Seven slick tips to improve your play on the turn

While the turn is not as difficult to play as the flop, here are some tips for the critical choices you'll face here:

✔ Raise when you have the top two pair on the turn, unless the board is three-suited or otherwise threatening.

✔ If you have an open-ended straight draw or flush draw with two or more opponents, call a bet on the turn. However, if the board is paired, and there's a bet and raise in front of you, be wary. You could be up against a full house.

✔ Bet, or check (planning to raise), when you're sure you have the best hand. Make it expensive for opponents who are on the come to draw out.

✔ If you hold a draw, try to make your hand as inexpensively as possible.

✔ If you have a hand you would call with, betting — rather than calling — is a superior strategy if you think there's any chance your bet will cause your opponent to fold.

✔ Be alert to picking up a draw on the turn. It could allow you to continue playing a hand you otherwise would throw away.

✔ "Should I checkraise or should I bet?" comes up frequently. Unless you think your opponent will bet *and* call your raise, you should come out betting.

What to do when you improve on the turn

Your hand can improve on the turn in one of two ways. The first, and best, happens whenever the turn card improves your hand. But you'll also benefit if you had a good hand going in, and the turn — while not helping your hand — did nothing to improve your opponent's either.

If you have top two pair on the turn and an opponent bets, you should usually raise. If you are in late position and none of your opponents have acted, go ahead and bet. If you're in early position, check with the intention of raising if you are fairly certain one of your opponents will bet. If you think your opponents might also check, forget about trying to checkraise and come out betting.

If you have the best hand, betting gets more money into the pot and makes it expensive for anyone to draw-out on you. But it's not a totally risk-free strategy. If your opponent has made a set or turned a straight, you can count on being raised or reraised.

What to do when you don't improve on the turn

It's unfortunate, but true: Most of the time the turn card will not help you. What's a player to do?

If you have an open-ended straight or flush draw and you're up against two or more opponents, you should usually call a bet on the turn. However, if the board is paired and there's a bet and raise in front of you, be wary. You may be facing a full house. If you are, you're drawing dead. (See the section about slang in Chapter 15 for more about drawing dead.)

You may be facing a set or two pair. Once again, knowing your opponents will help you determine what they might be holding. If you're up against someone who never raises a three-suited board unless he can beat that probable flush, release your hand.

If the turn didn't help and there is a bet in front of you, not only has the cost gone up, but the number of future betting rounds has decreased. You have less opportunity to punish your opponents if you make your hand. Moreover, many of them will probably fold on the turn too, leaving you with fewer opponents to punish, if indeed you were to get lucky on the river.

Should you continue with a draw?

Flopping four-flush or an open-ended straight draw is a common situation. If it's relatively inexpensive, you'll invariably stay for the turn card — particularly when you're certain yours will be the best hand if you make it. But most of the time the turn card will not help you. Players call that a *stiff*. After all, if you've flopped a four-flush there are only nine remaining cards of your suit in the deck.

Even if you don't complete your straight or flush on the turn, it usually pays to see the river card in hopes that deliverance is at hand, and you can reap the rewards.

Should you checkraise or come out betting?

Suppose you were dealt Q-J, flopped an open ended straight draw when 10-9-5 showed up on board and made your hand when an 8 appeared on the turn. If you're really lucky, one of your opponents holds 7-6, or J-7 and made a smaller straight. You'd love to see that, since they'd be drawing dead, absent flush possibilities.

If you try for a checkraise and your opponents all check behind you, you've cost yourself some money. Should you bet, hoping to get some more money into the pot? Or are you better off checkraising and trying for a bigger payday, bearing in mind you may not get any money into the pot at all if your opponents also check.

It's time to put on your Sherlock Holmes hat and do some detective work by reconstructing the play of the hand. Was there a lot of action before the flop, suggesting that your opponents held big hands or big pairs? Did they raise on the flop, suggesting they might have been trying to force any straight draws to fold? Or did they just check and call, suggesting that they were also on the come, and have now made their hand — albeit a lesser one than yours.

But an opponent holding a single big pair might also check, since the turn showed straight possibilities. If you think this is the case, you're better off leading with a bet, since she may call, but would throw her hand away if she were the bettor and you raised.

If your opponent was also drawing, you might want to check, hoping she will try to steal the pot by bluffing. Another possibility is that she made a smaller straight than yours, and will bet from late position. If that's the case, you can raise with the assurance she will not lay her hand down — even if she suspects you have the nut straight.

This is a case where recalling the play of the hand is more important than knowing the tendencies of your opponents. If you can deduce what kind of hand — or hands — your opponents are likely to hold, you can decide whether to come out betting or try for a checkraise. Remember, unless you think your opponent will bet *and* call your raise, betting is the preferred course of action.

Bluffing on the turn

Suppose that you raised with A-K before the flop and then bet into two opponents when the flop was J-7-3. You don't suspect any strength, and know your opponents are solid enough players to release a hand when they think they're beaten.

Because your opponents have to consider the possibility that you're holding an overpair or a jack with a good kicker, it will be difficult for them to call with anything less than a hand like J-8. Of course, if your opponents are calling stations, they'll call with almost anything, and you'll have to become adept enough at knowing their proclivities, so you don't try to bluff someone who never releases a hand.

A good player also understands that you might be betting a hand like A-K. But he may not call even if he holds a hand like 8-7, since he can't be certain about what you have, and could be beaten if his inclination about your bluff is wrong.

Should you bluff on the turn?

Knowing whether to attempt a bluff on the turn is a tough call. These five tips can help you decide.

✔ Don't bluff bad players. To beat a bad player, you're simply going to have to show down the best hand.

✔ Know your opponent. Will she release a hand, or will she call ". . . to keep you honest?"

✔ Do you think your opponent is *on the come* (see the section on slang in Chapter 15), and will release his hand if he does not improve on the turn?

✔ How much money is in the pot? The larger the pot, the more likely someone will call simply for the size of the pot. Most players will abandon a small pot more readily than a big one.

✔ Mentally review the hand's play. Would your betting or raising pattern cause a good player to assume you have a big hand? If she doesn't believe you hold a much better hand, don't bluff.

Your bet may cause an opponent to lay down the best hand. Even if he calls, the river could bring an ace or king and win the pot for you. But if you bet and are raised, throw your hand away. Sure, someone may be making a move on you. But it doesn't happen frequently enough to worry about, particularly in low-limit games. Most of the time you'll be beaten when you're raised in this situation.

Playing the River

If you're still contesting the pot while awaiting that last card on the board (the *river* card), you should have a strong hand, or a draw to what you believe will be the best hand if you make it. If you're playing with reasonably prudent opponents, what may have begun as a confrontation between five or six will probably be reduced to two — or perhaps three of you — once all the board cards have been exposed.

Realized versus potential value

Prior to the last card, many strategic considerations are predicated on your chances for subsequent improvement. You could, for example, bet a hand composed of a pair and four flush. Taken together, that pair, coupled with its potential for a flush as well as the possibilities of improving to two pair or trips, made it worth playing. And its worth was made up of both realized and potential value.

Once the river card is exposed, your hand no longer has any potential value. Its value is fully realized — for better or worse. If that flush draw never materialized, you're left with one pair, and it may not be enough to win the pot. More importantly, your strategic thinking has to change too. You have no remaining potential upon which to base decisions.

What do I do when I make my draw?

Many Hold'em newbies automatically check a good flush from early position, hoping to checkraise, thereby trapping their opponents for an additional bet. Others will always bet. These are two very different strategies. Which is correct?

Here's part one of the general rule on checkraising: Do it when you believe you will have the best hand most of the time *you are called.*

Part two of the general rule on checkraising states that you need to be certain your opponent will bet if you check. It's no fun to check a big hand only to have your opponents check behind you, especially when you know they would have called if you had bet.

If you are not certain you'll hold the best hand if you are called, or you aren't sure one of your opponents will bet if you check, do not checkraise.

Top pair on the river

An enduring dilemma is what to do when you're holding top pair against one or two opponents and all the cards are out. Now you have to decide whether to check or bet, or if your opponent acts first, whether to call, fold, or raise.

If you're observant, you will have noticed that some opponents will almost always bet top pair on the river, unless there is a strong threat of a flush or straight. Others seldom bet one pair, even when the board is not threatening. Most, however, fall somewhere in between. This is a judgment call. There is no formula to help you determine the best course of action, but there are some things you can do to clarify your decision.

Suppose you are first to act and raise before the flop with A-K. Two opponents call. You bet the flop and the turn. Now the board shows A-Q-4-7-9 of mixed suits. All the cards are out, no one has folded, and it's your turn to act. Should you bet or check?

You'll beat any pair, but lose to any two pair. Unless one of your callers held a pocket pair of 9s and made a set on the river, you can probably dismiss the notion that there is a set out against you. If one of your opponents either flopped or turned a set, he would have raised on the turn — when the betting limits doubled.

Your real concern, of course, is whether one of your opponents holds two pair. If an opponent held A-Q she probably would have raised before the flop, called on the flop and raised your bet on the turn. An opponent holding A-7, A-4, Q-4 or Q-7 would probably have raised on the turn.

If your opponents would raise with any two pair and call with lesser hands, like A-8 or Q-J, you'll want to bet. If they had made two pair on the turn, that's when they would have likely raised. Except for the chance that they are holding A-9, Q-9, 9-7, or 9-4, your bet on the river will elicit a call, and you'll win.

Now imagine the same scenario, but this time your opponent is first to act. If she bets, should you fold, call, or raise, and if she checks, should you bet?

TIP

Five tips for navigating the river

Navigating the river can be tricky. Follow this map and you'll avoid many of the sandbars along the way.

✔ Once the river card is exposed, your hand no longer has any *potential* value. Its value has been *realized*.

✔ Your decision to check or bet if no one has acted — or to fold, call, raise, or reraise if there has been action — can be based only on your hand's realized value.

✔ When you make two pair it will usually be the best hand. But if the turn or river brings a third suited card, be careful — your opponent could have made a flush.

✔ When it's heads up, and the pot is large, it's better to err by calling with the worst hand than by folding the winner.

✔ Overcalling requires a hand strong enough to beat legitimate calling hands.

If your opponent is very aggressive and tends to overplay weak hands, you can raise if you suspect she is betting a weaker hand than yours. If she is a tight player, just call her bet. If she is a real rock who seldom, if ever, bluffs, then throw away anything less than top pair with a very big kicker whenever she bets on the river.

The key, of course, is to know your opponents and their tendencies. Top pair on the river is a very common situation, and it is critically important that you learn to play it well.

When the Pot Gets Big

Pots sometimes grow quite large, particularly when there has been a raise before the flop. This can tie a lot of players to the pot, and if the flop provides a flush- or straight-draw to your opponents, you can be certain they'll be there to the end.

If the straight or flush cards fail to come, a bet will usually drop any opponents who were drawing. Often there are only two or three opponents contesting a very large pot on the river.

You might be in there with second pair, or perhaps top pair with a marginal kicker, and your opponent comes out betting. You're holding a hand you'd throw away if the pot were small, but with all that money in it, what should you do? Suppose you're playing in a $3–$6 Hold'em game and the pot is $90 by the time you reach the river. If your opponent bets, the pot now contains $96, and is offering you 16-to-1 on your money. If you call and are beaten, the cost is only an additional $6.

If you throw your hand away and your opponent was bluffing, you made a $96 mistake.

The answer should be obvious. If you believe this to be a situation in which your opponent would bluff more than one time in 16, go ahead and call. Only if you are sure your opponent would never bluff, you can comfortably throw your hand away.

You're always better off committing the small error of calling with a losing hand, than the catastrophic error of folding a winner. In the situation cited above, even if your opponent would only bluff one time in ten, you are far better off calling than folding.

If you were to call ten times, you'd lose $6 on nine occasions, for a loss of $54. On the tenth occasion, you'd win a $96 pot, for a net profit of $42. If you divide that $42 profit by each of the ten times you called, your decision to call is worth $4.20 each time you make it — regardless of whether you win that particular pot.

If you are second to act and think there's some chance you have the best hand, even if you don't consider yourself the favorite, you may want to raise if your opponent comes out betting. By doing this, you may get the third opponent to lay down his hand. If your first opponent was betting a fairly weak hand in hopes that you might fold, he, in turn, may now fold if he suspects you're holding a powerhouse. A play like this also adds some deception to your game. But like all deceptive plays, you have to use it sparingly.

Five tips for winning Hold'em play

If you play Hold'em correctly, you'll have incorporated all these tips into your game.

- Play few hands from early position. You'll throw lots of hands away, but you'll be saving money.

- Position is critical in Hold'em. Certain hands that you would fold in early position can be raising hands in late position.

- Fit or fold: If the flop does not help your hand, you must consider folding, regardless of how sweet it may have looked before the flop.

- Many of your opponents will play A-K as strongly as a pair of aces or kings, but it is not. A-K is a powerful drawing hand, but it usually needs help on the flop to win the pot.

- Hold'em only looks like Seven-Card Stud. In reality, it's a very different game due to the use of community cards, the positional aspect of the game, and the fact that on the flop you will see 71 percent of your hand for a single round of betting.

Chapter 5

Seven-Card Stud Eight-or-Better, High-Low Split (Seven-Stud/8)

In This Chapter

▶ Diving into basics if you've never played before

▶ Getting acquainted with the antes, the deal, and betting structure

▶ Knowing when to hold or fold

▶ Recognizing winning hands

▶ Understanding the importance of live cards

▶ Exploring the starting standards

▶ Looking at Seven-Stud/8 in depth

▶ Digging into the differences between Seven-Stud/8 and Seven-Card Stud

▶ Driving and braking

▶ Knowing what to do after all the cards are dealt

Seven-Card Stud 8-or-Better, High-Low Split — we'll call it Seven-Stud/8 for convenience sake — is a game that continues to grow in popularity. Games where the high and low hands divvy up the money often have very large pots. Since the pot is divided in half much of the time, many players who wouldn't ordinarily be in the hand if it was plain, old, garden-variety Seven-Card Stud (where there's one winner only: the best high hand) are in there slugging it out.

If You've Never Played Seven-Stud/8 Before

In Seven-Stud/8, the best high hand and the best low hand split the pot, assuming, of course, that there is a low hand. There's always a high hand, but in order to have a low hand, a player must have five unpaired cards in his hand with the rank of 8 or lower. That's called an *8-qualifier*.

One could probably play with a 9-qualifier, or any other qualifier for that matter, but the game is well balanced with an 8-qualifier. Each player receives seven cards that can be used in any combination to make hands. In other words, you can make a low hand and a high one, and perhaps win the high and low portions of the pot. Winning both portions of the pot is called *scooping* — you use different combinations of the seven cards in your hands (or even the same five cards) to form two distinctly different five-card holdings.

For example, if your seven cards were A♦J♦9♦7♦5♦4♠2♣, you're high hand would be an ace-high flush, composed of A♦J♦9♦7♦5♦. Your low hand would be called a *7-low,* and would be made up of 7♦5♦4♠2♣A♦.

Now you've already discovered something very important about Seven-Stud/8: You can use aces as both the highest and lowest card in the deck. When you're dealt an ace, it's like receiving two cards for the price of one, and that's an important concept to remember.

Seven-Stud/8 has five rounds of betting, just like it's high-hand-only cousin. This creates large pots on occasion because some players are trying to make a high hand, while others are hoping to make the best low hand. Skilled players need to be alert and be aware of the cards that are *live,* as well as those that have been folded. (For more on live cards, see the section "The importance of live cards" in this chapter.)

Personal skills required to win at Seven-Stud/8

Becoming a winning Seven-Stud/8 player requires more than technical poker skills. It also takes strength of character, determination, and grit.

✔ **Be patient:** If you lack patience you will never become a good Seven-Stud/8 player, regardless of how much knowledge you acquire.

✔ **Be observant:** If you don't pay close attention to visible cards, you will have a hard time winning on a consistent basis. If you are not aware of the discards, it is too easy to lose money by drawing to hands you probably won't make.

✔ **Be determined:** Play live hands, and play low hands. Don't throw money away on hands that are really much more of a long shot than they might appear.

✔ **Be studious:** Since you'll throw away most of your starting hands, there's plenty of down time that can be put to good use by observing your opponents. Learn the kinds of hands they play. Observe their mannerisms too. See if you can pick up any telltale clues about what they might be holding.

✔ **Be aggressive:** Don't be afraid to raise, or even reraise if you think you have the best hand, or the only hand in your direction.

✔ **Be judicious:** Don't feel like you must play every hand dealt to you. You won't start with three low cards very often, but even some of those holdings are not playable, particularly when an ace raises on third street. Discretion — in poker, as it is in war — is usually the better part of valor. Don't be afraid to wait for better opportunities.

The goal of every high-low split game is to try to scoop the pot and win all the money. In the absence of that, you should always try to be the only player heading in your direction, regardless of whether that is high or low.

Antes, the Deal, and the Betting Structure

Before the cards are dealt each player posts an ante, which is a fraction of a bet — just like in traditional Seven-Card Stud. Antes seed the pot and stimulate action.

Players are then dealt two cards face down, along with one face up. The lowest exposed card is required to make a small bet of a predetermined denomination. This bet (and the person making that bet) is called the *bring-in*. If two or more players have an exposed card of the same rank, then the alphabetical order of suits (clubs, diamonds, hearts, and spades) determines the bring-in.

If Ron has the 2♦ and Amber the 2♣, Amber would be required to *bring it in* based on the order of suits. While an ace can be used as both a high card and a low card in this game, for purposes of establishing the bring-in, an ace is considered to be high, and Amber's 2♣ is the lowest card in the deck.

Betting

The player to the immediate left of the bring-in has three options. He may fold his hand, call the bring-in, or raise to a full bet. In a $20–$40 game, the antes are usually $3 and the bring-in is $5. The player to the left of the bring-in can either fold, call the $5 bring-in bet, or raise to $20 — which constitutes a full bet.

If he folds or calls the bring-in, the player to his immediate left has the same options. Once someone raises to a full bet, subsequent players must do one of the following: fold, call the full bet, or raise again.

Once betting has been equalized, a second card is dealt face up, and another round of betting ensues. This time, however, it is in increments of full bets. The player with the highest-ranking board cards acts first.

If there are two high cards of the same rank, the order of the suit determines who acts first. The highest suit is spades, followed by hearts, then diamonds, and finally, clubs.

The first player to act may either check or bet. But unlike traditional Seven-Card Stud, an open pair on board does not afford a player the option of making a big bet.

Betting order

Just like Seven-Card Stud play for high, the lowest exposed card always acts first on the initial betting round, but the highest exposed hand acts first thereafter.

Since there's no guarantee that the highest exposed hand on fourth street will be the highest hand on the subsequent round, the pecking order can very from one betting round to another. For more on betting order, see "Position" in this section.

Raising

Most casinos allow three or four raises per betting round, except when only two players are contesting the pot. Then there is no limit to the number of raises permitted because either player can end the raising bar by calling her opponent's last bet.

Position

Betting order (who bets when) depends on the person's place, or position, at a table. Position is determined by the cards showing on the board and can vary from round to round. With the exception of the first round of betting on third street, where the lowest ranked card is required to *bring it in*, the highest hand on board acts first, and has the option of checking or betting.

The highest hand could range anywhere from four-of-a-kind, to trips, to two pair, to a single pair, or even the highest card, if no exposed pair is present.

Double bets

Betting usually doubles on *fifth street* (the fifth card dealt), and those players still contesting the pot are dealt another exposed card, followed by a round of betting. Sixth street is the same. The last card, called *seventh street* or the *river*, is dealt face down. At the river, active players have a hand made up of three closed and four exposed cards. The player who acted first on sixth street acts first on seventh street, too.

Showdown

If more than one player is active after all the betting has been equalized, players turn their hands face up, making the best five-card hand — or hands — from the seven cards they are holding. The best high hand wins half the pot, and the best low hand, assuming there is a qualifying low hand, wins the other half. The players don't have to disclose which way they are going (although some home games are played with such a *declare*).

In most home games where players have to declare whether they are going high, low, or both ways, the usual rule is that if you declare in both directions but lose in one of them, then you are ineligible to win the other half of the pot. (In other words, you either win the whole pot or lose the whole pot.) Declaration is usually done with coins. Players put one, two, or three coins (for low, high, or both, respectively) in their hands and open their fists for a simultaneous declaration. Declaring adds another element of strategy to the home game. In casino games, however, there is no declaration. "Cards speak" is the rule in public card games. (See Chapter 1 for details on cards speak.)

Having the best high hand and the best low hand in the same hand is possible. If you held 6-5-4-3-2 in your hand, you'd have a 6-high straight as your high hand and a 6-low as your low one. That's a very strong hand, one that's sometimes good enough to scoop the entire pot — much to your opponents' consternation.

Know When to Hold 'em and Know When to Fold 'em

Seven-Stud/8 requires patience. Many people love playing high-low split games because with two ways to win, they think they will have an opportunity to play more hands. The best Seven-Stud/8 players play few hands and generally look for those with two-way possibilities. They want hands that have the potential of becoming low as well as high hands. After all, the objective of this game is to scoop pots, not split them.

What Kind of Hands Are Likely To Win?

Certain high hands, which are playable in Seven-Card Stud, are quite vulnerable hands in Seven-Stud/8. Starting with a pair of kings or queens in Seven-Card Stud is usually a good hand. In Seven-Stud/8, however, most players are looking for low hands that have the potential to become high hands, too.

Consequently, an ace with two other low cards is very playable. With an ace, a player can skewer a pair of kings or queens by catching a companion ace — even if he was initially trying to make a low hand.

Because most players look for low hands with the potential to become high hands too, winning high hands tend to be smaller than the high hands typically made in Seven-Card Stud.

What's a good low? It all depends on what your opponents' hands look like. An 8-7 low can be a terrific hand, as long as all your opponents have face cards showing and appear to be heading off along the high road. But an 8 low is a terrible starting hand if you look around the table and see lower cards staring back at you.

The importance of live cards

Live cards (cards that help your hand and that are still available) are just as important in this game as they are in Seven-Card Stud played for high. If you are trying to complete a low hand, you should be aware of the number of exposed low cards so that you can estimate your chances of completing your hand.

Although conventional wisdom suggests starting with low hands that can become high ones, when most of the low cards are all out, there's not much point in continuing with a drawing hand — and all lows are drawing hands until fifth street, at least.

Starting standards: The first three cards are critical

Starting standards (starting hands that you should play) are important in Seven-Stud/8, just as they are in any form of poker. Some experts say they are even more important in a split-pot game. Because there are generally a multitude of opponents at the start, it's a good rule to have the best draw if you are trying for a low hand. If you don't have a draw to the best low hand, you'll have to rely on getting lucky twice: first, by catching a good card and again, by hoping that your opponent catches a bad one.

Your first three cards need to work together to make it worthwhile for you to continue playing. If they work together in both directions, so much the better.

For example, beginning with a hand like A♥4♥3♥ is an incredibly good hand. Not only do you have a draw to a low hand, you also have the possibility of making a flush for high. If another ace comes your way, you will have a big pair and may even improve to two pair or three-of-a-kind. It's also possible to wind up with a straight; two pair with a low; or a *flushy-low,* if you get lucky enough to make both a flush and a low hand.

One can't do much better than 3-4-5 as a starting hand. Not only do you have three low cards, but you have straight potential on both sides, and any ace, 2, 6, or 7 on the next card significantly improves your hand. If you're fortunate enough to start with 3♥4♥5♥, you have a hand that can improve to a flush as well as a straight or a low.

Even if you catch a card like J♥, you've improved. Now you have four to a flush, and although the jack does nothing for your possibilities of making a low hand, you're not dead either. That fourth heart keeps you in the hunt, and if the next card is, for example, the 7♣, you have a draw to a low along with your flush draw — with two chances to complete your hand in one or two directions.

Suppose you catch the A♥ on sixth street. What can be better? You've made an ace high heart flush and a 7-5 for low. Now you can typically raise with impunity. If you have two or three opponents who look like they're going low, you will probably take the high side and may scoop it all.

If your opponents are all going high, you will certainly win the low end and still stand a good chance of scooping, too. With two or more opponents, your half of the pot should be quite healthy, particularly if you've been able to continue raising your opponents — all of whom are contesting the other end of the pot.

If you can scoop, you'll be stacking chips for the next two hands. When you have a lock on one end of the pot and are freerolling toward the other, you can reel in some big pots when you're lucky enough to scoop. (For more details on freerolling, see the section titled, "Beyond third street" in this chapter.)

Playable hands

Generally, a desirable starting hand has a two-way possibility that enables you to scoop a big pot when you get lucky. For example, A♦2♦3♦ is a perfect starting hand. It begins with three cards to a wheel — the very best possible low — yet it can easily become a high hand too, by making either a straight or a flush. If you get extremely lucky, you might even make a straight flush. Most starting hands are not in its league — not by a long shot. Still, there are many others that are very playable:

Ace hands

An ace showing on third street is guaranteed to give pause to your opponents. Aces are like two cards in one, since they're simultaneously the highest and the lowest card in the deck. When you're showing an ace your opponent has no idea whether you are going high or low. If your hole cards are 6-5, you're working on a very good low. On the other hand, if you have another ace in the hole, you have the highest hand at that point unless one of your opponents was dealt three of a kind — and that's very unlikely.

Continue to catch low cards and your opponent will assume you are drawing to a low hand. If you catch a high card and continue to contest the pot, your opponent won't know what you have. You could be holding a pair of aces. You might have paired one of your hole cards and now have two pair, or simply caught a bad card and are foolishly chasing the field for the low side.

Suppose you start with 6♣5♦ hidden and an A♥ as your exposed card, catch a 3 on fourth street, then pair your ace on fifth street. Now your opponent must take a very hard look at his own hand. He'll see that you've paired aces and has to consider the possibility that you're holding three of them.

Your opponent also has to consider that you're holding 4 to a good low along with a pair of aces as a valid possibility. If you're holding this kind of hand against a lone opponent, you stand an excellent chance of scooping the pot. Aces are not only the most potent card in this game, they are also the most powerful *scare card* you can hold. Any card or series of cards that appear to give you a powerful hand will often "scare" your opponents and cause them to play cautiously. This can often be a good motivation for you to bluff.

Most of your opponents will play an ace with any two low cards, even if they are very rough. How playable is a hand like 8-7-A? That depends on your opponents' hands. If your opponents are all showing high cards, you have the only low draw. If you make your hand half the pot will be yours. But if other low cards are showing you are faced with having to make the best low.

One-way low hands

A *one-way low hand* is one that has little or no possibility of becoming a high hand too. One of the problems with one-way low hands that are unlikely to make a straight — like 7-3-2, for example — is that they will not make a high hand unless the holder is fortunate enough to make two pair with a low, or gets very lucky and makes a flushy-low (a hand that is both a flush and a low). Since you aren't likely to make a straight, your chances to scoop are reduced substantially. It doesn't necessarily render your hand unplayable, but it does tend to limit you to playing for one end of the pot only. When you set off down that road, you should make sure you are the only one headed in that direction.

Whenever your opponent shows an ace on third street in a heads-up confrontation, it spells trouble if all you hold is a one-way low. Not only does your opponent's hand look to be a better low than yours, it's also a better high. That ace has surrounded you, and regardless of the direction you are heading, it's probably uphill. Your opponent often either scoops or splits the pot. As for your one-way low, you split the pot or you get scooped. You're better off folding one-way hands most of the time that you're heads-up against an opponent showing an ace.

An ace is like two cards in one

The ace is both a low and a high card, so holding one is like having an extra card. It's almost like playing eight cards against your opponent's seven. But as strong as an ace is, not every hand containing an ace is playable. A hand like 9-8-A probably won't win regardless of whether you're trying to build a high hand or a low one. You'll find more than enough hands to play in Seven-Stud/8, so do yourself a favor: Even when your ace is smiling out at the world, toss it away if your hole cards are dogs.

Two-way hands

Two-way hands are the most desirable of all. With a little bit of luck, low hands can become high hands, but high hands don't become low hands very often.

If you begin with a hand like 6-5-3 you're on your way to a good low, but with a bit of luck you might also make a straight and scoop the pot. Three low-suited cards are even better because they can make a flush or a straight to go along with a low hand.

On the other hand, try starting with three high cards and see how difficult it is to go low. After all, if you were dealt Q-J-10, you have a straight working, but how are you ever going to make a low hand and scoop? You can't. It's that simple. That doesn't mean you can't ever play high cards; but it does mean you have to consider the situation very carefully.

Disguised hands

While high hands can sometimes masquerade as low ones, it's tough for a high hand to cloak itself in disguise. After all, if you call with a jack showing, you'll have a tough time convincing anyone that you are working on a low hand. You might have a pair, a straight draw, or a flush draw. Your opponents won't know that, but they will know where you're headed, and that's more important.

High hands

If all of your opponents are building low hands, and you have a good high hand working, you should usually go ahead and play it. Unless one of your opponents makes a low straight or a flush, chances are your high hand can hold up. If you both make two pair, yours will likely take the high side.

Whenever you are the only player going high and you are up against two or more opponents trying to make a low, you're in good shape unless someone begins catching aces.

High against low: one-on-one

You can also play a high hand profitably when you are up against one opponent who looks like he is working on a low hand. If you have even so much as a high pair on third street, your odds of winning are good. Here's why: You already have a hand. Your opponent, particularly if she starts off with a one way low — where making a straight is just about impossible — is still drawing, and has no guarantee of succeeding.

Your opponent might start off with four low cards and catch three high cards in succession and never take the low side. You will usually take the whole pot or split it; while your opponent — unless she is fortunate enough to make a two-way hand or back into a better high hand than yours — will either split the pot or lose it. This is almost a "heads I win, tails you lose" encounter, and you can't hope for much more than that.

If you are going to draw for a low hand, you'd ideally like to be up against a gaggle of high hands — a guarantee that you'll take half the pot if you make a low. You seldom want to compete with a bunch of low hands for half the pot against a lone high hand.

Powerhouse hands

Another time it pays to go high, regardless of how many opponents you are up against, is when you start with a powerhouse hand. If you were dealt three jacks, for example, you shouldn't mind any number of opponents who also appear to be going high. You already have three-of-a-kind, along with a good chance of improving to a full house or better. You are heavily favored, and you should exploit the opportunity for all it's worth by betting and raising at every opportunity.

Seven-Stud/8 in Depth

When playing Seven-Stud/8, conventional wisdom suggests that you begin with a low hand and try to scoop the pot by making a high hand, too. That's a lot easier than starting with high cards and hoping to make a low one. The objective of this game is to scoop pots — not split them — so it's important to play hands that have two-way potential. Most of the time, that means starting with low cards.

Beyond third street

Choosing to continue beyond third street means that your next key decision point occurs on the very next betting round. If you hope to make a low hand but catch a high card on fourth street, it severely diminishes your chances of completing your hand. If you catch a fourth low card, however, you stand a good chance of succeeding.

If you catch a good card on fourth street and an opponent (who also has what looks like a low draw) catches a high card, then you can raise if someone bets. That tactic makes it very difficult for any opponent to call once he sees two low cards on your board. If you can chase other low draws out of the pot, it no longer matters how good your low is, as long as it is the only low hand in the battle.

If you make the only low hand, you can raise whenever someone bets — and you can do so with the complete assurance that half of all the money going into that pot will soon be yours. This nifty but rare situation is called *freerolling* — where you hold the best possible low hand and there is no cost or risk to drawing for the high hand.

Calling on fifth street in Seven-Stud/8 does not necessarily represent the same commitment to the hand that it does in Seven-Card Stud. If you have a low draw and catch a bad card on sixth street while an opponent catches a very good one, it can be correct to release your hand in the face of a bet.

But if you have a high hand and are still active on fifth street, the pot is generally big enough to continue to the end.

When everyone has low cards showing

If you find yourself up against a few opponents on third street with 2s, 3s, 4s, 5s, or 6s showing, you can usually be certain they are also going low. When one of your opponents has an ace as his *door card* (the first card dealt face up), he could be going high or low, or have a two-way hand like A-2/A. (The two cards to the left of the slash were dealt face down. The card to the right was dealt face up.) With a low door card other than an ace, you can safely assume that most of your opponents also will have two other low cards.

The following scenario can be a real dilemma: If you start with three low cards and three opponents also call with low board cards, you can assume that there are probably 12 cards between and ace and an 8 already out. If that's the case, it means that 12 out of the 32 low cards, or 38 percent of all the low cards in the deck, have already been dealt.

To illustrate some important concepts, imagine the following:

- ✔ No aces are showing.
- ✔ You hold three good low cards.
- ✔ Three of your opponents also appear to be going low.
- ✔ A player showing a king also calls.

It's obvious why the king is in the pot — he's going high. Four of you are trying for the low side, and one or two may have two-way hands. Approximately 20 low cards remain in the deck — more, if some of your opponents are poor players who will play weak hands like 3-J/2, and fewer, if others folded hands like 3-7/10. You'll never know for sure, but you are in the ballpark.

Suppose you started with 3-4/5. Catching another 3, 4, or 5 is not what you are hoping for. An 8 gives you four cards to a low — but against three other opponents heading in the same direction yours is probably the worst four-card low of the lot.

Either a 2 or a 6 is a perfect catch. With either of those cards you have a good low draw along with an open-ended straight draw for high. An ace is a terrific low card — in addition, it provides an inside draw to a wheel. Catching a 7 keeps you in the hunt by providing a good-but-not-great four-card low, along with an inside straight draw for high.

Your opponent with the high hand is in a good situation at this point. Not only does the distribution of high versus low cards help her, she is not really hurt if she holds a big pair and catches a low card. In fact, that's one low card her opponents can't catch. Moreover, if she catches high cards she may make two pair or trips, assuming she started with a big pair and a big, live side card.

Frustrations can mount in Seven-Stud/8, particularly when you start with three good low cards and catch a face card or a bad low card and have to abandon your hand. That's the nature of the game. The frustration factor in Seven-Stud/8 causes many players to play almost any starting hand, and that's when they lose money. Even experienced players occasionally lose patience after waiting for good starting hands that they have to release once they've caught a bad card or two on subsequent betting rounds.

Do big hands equal big profits? Not always

Big hands are not always big money makers, and that's often frustrating. You might be dealt three kings and catch the fourth king on the next card against one opponent who is obviously drawing for low. You can bet and raise to the hilt, but if he makes a low hand, you'll only split the antes and the bring-in when all the shouting is done. That's not much of a return on four-of-a-kind, endlessly raised, is it?

Jamming the pot

When you make a two-way hand that has a lock on at least one side, you can — and should — *jam* (raise as much as possible) the pot at every opportunity. You get to scoop the pot if you're lucky, and whenever there are multiple opponents, each dollar you bet generates a profit even when you split it.

Tread lightly on the other side of this two-edged sword, however, and avoid situations where you are the one being sliced and diced. You can't avoid this entirely. You might find yourself against two or three high hands, while you have the only low draw. There's no guarantee that you'll complete your hand, and if you do not catch the cards you need, you may wind up calling all the way to the river only to fold your hand.

Nevertheless, you *can* avoid drawing for one side of the pot whenever your hand figures to be second best if your opponent also completes his draw. There are some players who will always draw to an 8-low against opponents who are drawing to a low that's obviously better. When both players make their hand, the second-best hand suffers for his indiscretion.

Seven-Stud/8 is filled with twists and turns, and that's what makes it such an exciting game: It's the made hand versus the big draw. It's going to the river with a two-way draw. It's starting out low and finishing high. It's freerolling to a scoop, and it's the frustration of making a very big hand that only chops the antes when your opponent takes the other half of the pot.

When you hold the only low hand

When you make the only low hand, you're guaranteed half the pot. You also have more good drawing cards available to you. If you're the only one going low, catching an 8 is as good as any other low card. Make your hand early and you can enjoy jamming the high hands with impunity. When you're competing with others for low, however, there's no guarantee that yours will be the best one. It doesn't pay to jam the high hands if you might not capture your share of the pot. There's nothing more vexing — or costly — than making a low and losing to a better one, particularly if the signals were there all along.

Take these concepts to heart

Here's the lowdown on low cards:

Just because you have three low cards doesn't mean you have a playable hand:

- ✔ **You do,** even with an inherently weak hand, like 2-7/8, if it's the only low hand against more than one opponent who is going high.

- ✔ **You don't** if your opponents have better low draws, and you don't have a two-way hand.

When two or three players begin with low draws, don't be surprised to catch high cards. The deck is probably full of high cards at that point.

Players who start with any three low cards, particularly those with neither straight nor flush potential, are doomed to usually draw for only half the pot with no guarantee they'll complete their low. Face it, there is *always* a high hand; there doesn't necessarily have to be a low one. This is a money-losing proposition in the long run.

How Seven-Stud/8 Differs From Seven-Card Stud

How well you play your first three cards in Seven-Card Stud poker is one of the keys to success. Successful play demands an awareness of whether the cards that can improve your hand are still alive. Seven-Card Stud players also need to anticipate what players acting after them might do, based on their door cards.

These considerations also hold true for Seven-Stud/8. But that's where the road forks. In Seven-Card Stud once you decide to play the hand you've been dealt, the next major decision point is fifth street — buy a card there and you've bought a through-ticket to the river. Seven-Card Stud pundits do not usually offer much salient advice about play on fourth street. It's almost as though you're expected to play it on autopilot.

How you play that fourth card is critical, however, when you play Seven-Stud/8. Misunderstanding its importance can be a major blunder.

If you play Seven-Stud/8 correctly, most of the time you'll be starting with three low cards — and it is these three low cards that make fourth street so very critical. If you start with three low cards, you'll still need to catch two cards lower than a 9 — that do not pair your hand — out of the next four cards dealt to you, in order to make a low hand. In other words, half of your next four cards must be small for you to succeed.

Suppose you catch a high card on fourth street, or a card that pairs one of the three cards already in your hand. If you catch a face card on fourth street you'll usually find four dragons raising their fire-breathing heads.

First, you have substantially reduced your chances of making a low hand. Now two of the next three cards must be low for you to even have a chance at half the pot.

Second, you can't possibly make your hand until sixth street. Even when you do make it, you'll have one less round of betting to jam the pot if you are lucky enough to be competing against two or more opponents who are slugging it out for the high side.

Third, if you catch a high card and someone else going low catches a smaller one, she is now far ahead in the race. She needs only one more low card out of the final three that she will be dealt in order to complete her hand. Meanwhile, you need to catch two low cards out of the next three to even compete in the race — and there's no guarantee yours will be the best low hand. If your opponent makes a low hand before you do, you can expect her to raise anytime there is a bet. A skillful opponent will make it expensive for you to stick around and draw out on her.

Fourth, you might catch a low card that pairs one of your hole cards. Yes, it's true: You do have a start at a high hand, but it's a marginal one. There is one saving grace, however. An opponent who is also going low will not know you paired. If she catches a face card, she'll probably fold if you bet or raise before it's her turn to act. Even if you can eliminate her, however, you'll still need to make a low hand to escape with half the pot.

Suppose you started with a terrific low hand, like 5-4/3 and catch an 8 on fourth street. This is not nearly as bad as catching a face card, since you have a four-card low, but how will you feel about your hand if you look over and see that one of your opponents is showing a 6-5 and another a 4-3? The only way you have the best low draw on fourth street is if both your opponents have at least one bad card in the pocket.

Hidden Hands

Hidden hands (like a pair of aces in the hole with a low door card or finding that you've been dealt three 4s) are terrific in Seven-Stud/8 because they are rather rare. When you think someone is trying to make a low hand, they usually are. If you have a high hand that looks like a low one, however, you stand a very good chance of winning a big pot. You can keep betting and raising, because the opponent who mistakenly thinks he has the only high hand will be betting and raising too. He'll think you and the other low hand are slugging it out for half of the pot, while he's guaranteed his share. He won't suspect that he's the one who's going to be sliced and diced at the showdown.

Sometimes you can scoop the pot by making a two-way hand — any low straight stands a terrific chance of scooping, as does the relatively rare and wonderfully nicknamed flushy-low (a flush and low hand). Even two pair with a low will frequently scoop a fairly big pot. Most of the time, however, you'll be playing a one-way hand, and when you are, the only way to scoop is to eliminate opponents who are heading in the other direction.

Driving and Braking

If you're dealt a big pair early, you have a hand that already has some intrinsic value. If you start with three low cards, however, all you have is a draw — as yet unrealized — and as good as those three low cards look, there's always a chance that a low hand will never be completed. If three of your next four cards are 9s or higher you will have missed your low and unless you miraculously back into a high hand, you'll lose the pot too.

Nevertheless, if you make the only low hand by fifth or sixth street, along with a chance to improve to a high hand too, you have half the pot won against opponents who hold *high-only* hands, and you can bet or raise with complete safety. If you make a straight, or any other good high hand to complement your low, you might scoop the pot. What's more, you're in a good freeroll position.

Some interesting strategic concepts include knowing when to drive a hand by betting or raising, and understanding when to put on the brakes by trying to complete your hand inexpensively. If you have a high hand, you need to bet and raise early and often to make it as expensive as possible for anyone drawing to a low hand to play against you. After all, you want to avoid splitting the pot. You'd also like to avoid the indignity of an opponent's low draw backing into a high hand and scooping the entire pot right out from under your nose.

The only way to ensure that you'll win the entire pot when you have a high hand is for the low draw to release his hand. Your opponent is not going to do that of his own accord; you must induce him to do so. The best way to accomplish this is to bet at him, or raise when he bets. Remember, before fifth street, it's impossible for your opponent to have a completed low hand. He may have a terrific draw, but it's still a draw, not a made hand — and even a single high pair is temporarily the better hand at that juncture.

From a practical standpoint, you'll find it nearly impossible to force an opponent to release a low draw unless he catches a face card on fourth or fifth street. If he does, and you come out betting, he'll realize that the odds against his completing a low hand have just escalated, and *drawing* for half a pot might start looking like the losing proposition it often is.

Driving and braking in Seven-Stud/8

Keep the following rules of the road firmly in mind:

✔ **When you have a high hand, drive it (by betting or raising) until fifth street,** or until it appears your opponent has made a low hand. Then apply the brakes.

✔ **If you have a low hand, draw inexpensively most of the time.** After all, there's no guarantee that you will complete your hand, so why make it any more expensive than necessary?

✔ **If you have the only low draw against two or three high hands, go ahead and bet — or raise.** Take this step (an exception to the preceding bullet) if you start with three low cards and catch another on fourth street.

✔ **If you are the only hand drawing for low against two or more high hands, some players contesting the high side will probably fold later in the hand.** When you have the only low draw against two or more high hands, bet or raise to get their money into the pot.

✔ **Seven-Stud/8 is a game that requires a certain amount of *gambling,*** and situations like these — where the size of the pot looks like it will exceed the odds against making your hand — are prime gambling opportunities.

You won't always be so lucky. If your opponent keeps catching low cards (also known as *babies*), he's probably going to complete his low hand. If you bet and he raises on fifth or sixth street with a low board showing, you can be certain he's made a low hand and is now freerolling for a high hand, or worse yet, already has a better high hand than yours, as well as a low one.

If you suspect your opponent has made a low hand, it's time to stop driving and apply the brakes. (See the sidebar "Driving and braking in Seven-Stud/8.) Once your opponent has made a low hand, the strategic elements have now completely reversed themselves — as long as your high hand has no low possibilities. At best, you are now the player taking aim at half the pot. At worst, you will get scooped. Since that's the case, what earthly reason could you have for betting into this pot?

The best you can do is break even — which will happen a lot of the time — although you'll lose the entire pot occasionally. If your opponent has made a low hand and you are foolish enough to bet your high hand, he's going to raise at every opportunity. He has nothing to lose. Half the pot is already his, and he has an opportunity to win it all.

When All the Cards Have Been Dealt

If you've seen the hand through to the river, you usually should call any bet if you think you can escape with half the pot. If your opponent appears to have a low hand, sometimes even a paltry pair can capture the high side of the pot.

If it's heads-up and you have a high hand while your opponent appears to have made a low hand, there's no point in betting. At best, you'll just split the pot. At worst, he'll have a high hand to complement his low and might scoop the entire pot.

TIP

Seven-Stud/8: Winning strategies

Become a winning Seven-Stud/8 player by mastering these strategic elements:

- **If the shoe fits, steal it:** If you have the only ace showing, no one has entered the pot on third street when it's your turn to act, and you have the only low card showing, you should raise and try to steal the antes.

- **Be patient, especially on third street:** If you don't have three low cards, the best high hand, a draw to a straight or a flush, save your money.

- **Maneuver well on fourth street — a major decision point:** If you begin with a low draw and catch a complementary low card on fourth street, you have an outstanding chance to make a low hand.

- **Call if you have a viable hand:** Once the cards have all been dealt and your opponent comes out betting, you should usually call with any hand that stands a good chance of taking your half of the pot.

- **Stay alert:** Like its cousin, Seven-Card Stud, this game demands strong powers of observation to know whether the cards you need are live. You also must be able to determine whether you have the best hand in your direction, and whether you have a chance to scoop.

- **Play good drawing hands (just don't play all of them):** Drawing hands can offer great promise. But to play them, your cards must be live. Low draws are more playable than high draws, because they offer the chance for you to make both a high and low hand and scoop the pot.

Chapter 6

Omaha

· ·

In This Chapter

▶ Getting acquainted with Omaha/8

▶ Knowing when to hold 'em and when to fold 'em

▶ Covering Omaha/8 in depth

▶ Playing the turn

▶ Playing the river

▶ Playing Omaha High-Only

· ·

*O*maha Hold'em, 8-or-Better High-Low Split Poker is quite a mouthful — so you can just call it Omaha/8 for short. "The game of the future," as many poker pundits predict, is a variation of Texas Hold'em in which each player receives four cards dealt face down. Like its cousin, Texas Hold'em (see Chapter 4), five community cards — which every player can use — are dealt face up in the center of the table. The best high hand and the best low hand split the pot.

As in most split-pot games, lots of chips may be on the table because some players are trying to make the best low hand, some the best high one, while others are trying to scoop the entire pot.

Omaha/8 also creates action because each player is dealt four cards rather than the two that Texas Hold'em players receive. Naturally, with four cards to choose from, many players don't have any trouble finding a hand they think is worth playing.

Although you may get confused at times trying to ferret out the best five-card poker hand from among the five community cards on the center of the table and the four private cards in each player's hand, don't worry — if you can play Texas Hold'em, you can play Omaha/8. We also cover Omaha High (a high-only variation of Omaha/8 that is played less frequently) later in this chapter.

Playing Omaha/8 for the First Time

Omaha/8 looks almost like Texas Hold'em, which you've undoubtedly mastered after reading Chapter 4, but you can expect four major differences:

- ✔ Omaha/8 is a high-low split game, which means more players in each pot, more chips in the center of the table, and more action.

- ✔ Each player must make his best five-card poker hand by using exactly two cards from his hand and three communal cards. In Texas Hold'em, you can form the best hand using two, one, or even none of your private cards. If you are playing Texas Hold'em and you hold the ace of spades when the board contained four additional spades, you have a flush. But in Omaha, you have nothing at all. That's because you must play two cards — no more, no less — to make a valid Omaha hand.

- ✔ Because you have four cards to work with, you can form six different starting combinations. In other words, by receiving four private cards, you have six times as many potential starting hands as you do as you do in Texas Hold'em. As a result, the winning hands tend to be quite a bit bigger than they do in Texas Hold'em.

- ✔ Straights and flushes are common; and two pair, which is often a winning hand in Texas Hold'em, seldom wins in this game. Regardless of how powerful a high hand you make, whenever three unpaired communal cards with a rank of 8 or lower are on the board, someone probably made a low hand and that big pot you were hoping to win has effectively been chopped in half.

Blind bets

Before any cards are dealt, the first two players to the left of the dealer position are required to post blind bets, which are used instead of antes to stimulate action. (For a more thorough discussion of blind bets, see Chapters 2 and 4.)

In a $6–$12 Omaha/8 game, blinds are usually $3 and $6. Each blind is considered *live*. Because blinds represent a forced, first bet, the players forced to post those bets can raise (but only on the first round) after the betting has gone around the table and it is their turn to act again.

Unlike Stud poker, where position is determined by the cards showing on the board, the player with the dealer button acts last in every round of betting — with the exception of the first one.

The deal and betting structure

Four cards are dealt face down to each player, and a round of betting takes place. On the first round, players may either call or raise the blind bet, or fold their hands. Most casinos allow a bet and three or four raises per betting round, with one exception. When only two players contest the pot, the number of possible raises is unlimited.

When the first round of betting is complete, three communal cards, called the *flop*, are simultaneously turned face up in the center of the table. Another round of betting follows. On this and each succeeding round, players may check if no one has bet when it is that player's turn to act. If there is no bet, a player may check or bet. If there is a bet, players must either fold, call, raise, or reraise.

A fourth communal card — called the *turn* — is then exposed. Another round of betting takes place. Then the fifth and final community card — known as the *river* — is placed in the center of the table, followed by the final betting round.

The best five-card high poker hand and the best five-card low poker hand split the pot — with these provisos:

- A player must use exactly two cards — no more, no less (from among his four private cards) to construct a poker hand.

- To have a low hand, a player must combine any two unpaired cards with a rank of 8 or lower with three unpaired communal cards with a rank of 8 or lower.

A player can make a high and a low hand by using different cards from his hand to construct the two hands. For example, if your private cards are A♣2♦3♥K♥ and the five communal cards are Q♥9♠7♥6♥4♠, you have a flush. The flush is made by mating your K♥3♥ with the communal Q♥7♥6♥. You'd have a low hand too, which would be created by combining your A♣2♦ with the board's 7♥6♥4♠.

You'd have a terrific two-way hand. Although it's possible for an opponent to have made a bigger flush if she held the A♥ and any other heart in her hand, no one could have a better low hand than you do. You could be tied for low by anyone who also has an ace and a 2. In that case, you'd simply split the low side of the pot. But take our word for it, this is a terrific holding, and one that doesn't come around all that often.

Beginning players often have difficulty in determining the best Omaha hand. Before you plunk your money down and get in a game, we recommend dealing out some hands and trying to identify the best high and best low hands.

A sample hand

Figure 6-1 shows a sample hand of Omaha, with all cards dealt.

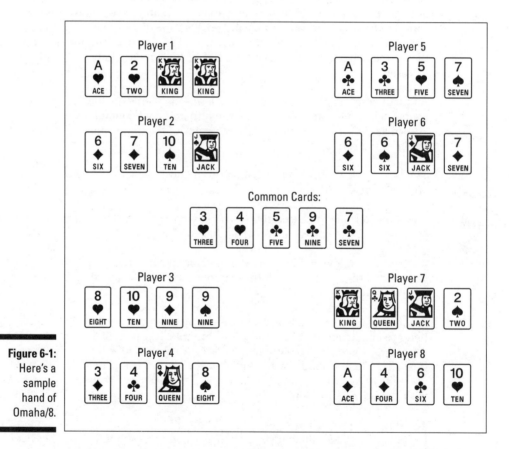

Figure 6-1:
Here's a sample hand of Omaha/8.

So, at the end, when all the common cards are dealt out, the hands are as follows in Table 6-1:

Table 6-1	Possible Hands in Figure 6-1	
Player	*Best High Hand*	*Best Low Hand*
1	5 high straight	5 low wheel (the best possible hand)
2	7 high straight	7-6 low
3	Three 9s	No low hand
4	Two pair — 3s and 4s	8-7 low
5	Ace-high flush	7-5 low
6	7 high straight	7-6 low
7	No pair	No low hand
8	Pair of 4s	6-5 low

You can see that Player 1 will win the low and Player 5 will win the high. Player 8 has a good low, but may lose a lot of money.

Knowing When to Hold 'em and When to Fold 'em

Although Omaha looks confusing, you can take solace in the fact that even professional casino dealers sometimes have trouble determining the best hand. Having to look for high as well as low hands with so many card combinations probably leads to brain-lock on occasion. Don't worry. When you get used to the game, you will be able to quickly spot potential draws and winning combinations.

With four cards in their hands, many players can always find something worth playing. These players are, of course, playing far too many weak hands that really don't warrant an investment and should be discarded rather than played. Even beginning Omaha/8 players can be considered a favorite in lower-limit games simply by playing better starting cards than their opponents play.

Even experienced players often fail to realize that split-pot games are illusory in the sense that it appears as though one can play many more hands than they can in a game where only the high hand wins. But winning players are more selective than their opponents, and they enter pots only with hands that are superior to those that their opponents play most of the time.

Omaha/8 seems even more confusing when you have a two-way hand and must determine whether you have the best low hand as well as the best high one.

Although determining the best high and low hands (see Figure 6-1) requires concentration, Omaha/8's underlying precept is simple: The ideal hands are those that can capture the entire pot. That usually means beginning with low hands that also offer an opportunity to grow into a straight or flush. You can also start with big, high cards and hope for a flop containing nothing but high cards. When this happens, the pot will tend to be a bit smaller. But it won't be split either. Whenever the flop contains three big cards, all the one-way low draws have to fold. Their investment is *dead money* in the pot, and the pot will go to the winning high hand.

Position, position, and position

Position is fixed for the entire hand in Omaha/8, just as in Texas Hold'em. This means that if you are in late position and the pot has not been raised, you can see the flop with hands that are a bit weaker than you normally would consider playing, because you have less chance of being raised. Position can give you an opportunity to get lucky with certain hands that can't profitably be played in a raised pot.

In a typical nine-handed game, early position includes both blinds and the two players to their left. The fifth, sixth, and seventh players to act are in middle position, and the eighth and ninth players are in late position.

The flop should fit your hand

Poker writer Shane Smith coined the phrase, "fit or fold." It's particularly true in Omaha/8. The flop must fit your hand, by providing you with a good, strong hand or a draw to the best possible hand. If the flop doesn't meet those criteria, you likely should release your hand.

Omaha/8 in Depth

Nearly endless combinations are possible with four-card starting hands, but you need not be concerned with too many of them — most are easily recognizable as hands you will release with neither remorse nor regret.

The best Omaha/8 starting combinations are coordinated, and they work together in some way. Many of your opponents will play hands in which only three of the four cards are coordinated, and others will play any four cards that look good.

Starting hands

The following sections offer examples of Omaha/8 starting hands; of course, these are not the only possibilities. In the first example, a hand like A-2-3-5 is just about as good as A-2-3-4.

The very best

- ✔ **A♣2♣3♦4♥:** A suited ace with three low cards can make the nut low, as well as a straight, and the nut flush. By having sequenced low cards, you have protection against being counterfeited if one, or even two, of your low cards hit the board. You are said to be *counterfeited* if one of your low cards is duplicated on the board, thus weakening your hand considerably. For example, you hold A-2-7-9, and the board is 3-4-8. At this point, you have the best possible low hand (8-4-3-2-A). Suppose the turn card is a deuce. Now your low hand is 7-4-3-2-A, but it is no longer the nut low, and if an opponent holds A-5 in his hand, he will have an unbeatable low hand, as well as a 5-high straight (called a *wheel* or *bicycle* for a high hand, too).

- ✔ **A♣K♦3♦4♣:** A-K double-suited offers two flush combinations, two straight combinations, a draw to a very good low hand, and protection against making a low and having it counterfeited.

- ✔ **A♣A♦2♦3♣:** A pair of aces, two nut flush draws, a low hand with counterfeit protection, and a draw to the nut low are the features of this hand.

- ✔ **A♣A♥K♣K♥:** No low possibilities here, but a double-suited A-K is a very powerful hand, because you can make a straight, two flushes, and sets of aces or kings that can become a full house if the board pairs.

- ✔ **A♣2♣3♦9♥:** Only three of the cards are coordinated, but with a large number of players in the pot, you have a draw to the nut low with counterfeit protection.

Very good hands

- ✔ **A♣2♣5♦5♥:** Flush draw, nut low draw, straight draw are some of the possibilities. You might also flop a set to your pair of 5s. A-2 suited with any pair can be counterfeited for low and is not as strong as the very best hands, but it is a good hand nevertheless.

- ✔ **A♣Q♣J♦10♥:** You'd like to see either all picture cards on the flop in hopes of making the best possible straight, or three clubs. If you flop a flush and two small cards are present, you must bet or raise at every opportunity to make it as costly as possible for low hands to draw against you. If a low hand is made, you've lost half your equity in this pot.

✔ **2♣3♦4♥5♠:** You're hoping an ace falls along with two other low cards. If it does, you've made the nut low and you probably have a straight draw, too.

✔ **A♥3♦5♠7♥:** Although this is good low draw along with nut flush possibilities, you won't make the best possible low hand unless the community cards include a 2. But you can easily make the second best low hand, which often spells trouble. Suppose that David holds A-3-x-x, Karen has 3-4-x-x, and Abby has A-2-x-x. Suppose that, at the end of the hand, the board is K-K-8-7-5. All three players made low hands, but Abby made the best possible low hand. David's hand is the second-best possible low hand, and if he were to bet and Abby were to raise, David would lose the low half of the pot.

Other playable hands that aren't ready for prime time

✔ **K♣2♣3♦4♥:** This hand offers a draw to a flush, though it's not the nut flush, and a draw to a low hand that won't be the best low unless an ace hits the board. Nevertheless, it is playable in late position, although this kind of hand often must be released if the flop doesn't fit it precisely.

✔ **K♣K♦10♦10♠:** Here's a hand that can make a straight, albeit with great difficulty, and can make a flush, although it is not the best flush. The hand can improve to a set or a full house, too. It's playable, but it's the kind of hand that looks a lot stronger than it really is.

✔ **8♠9♥10♦J♣:** This is a straight draw with no flush possibilities. If you make a 5-6-7-8-9 straight, any low hand will take half of this pot. If you make a big straight, you run the risk of losing the entire pot to a higher one. Mid-range cards are dicey holdings in Omaha/8, and this is another of those hands that looks a lot better than it is.

✔ **K♣Q♦2♦3♣:** This is a good-looking hand that can also lead to trouble. On the plus side, it's double-suited, providing two flush draws. And two straight draws are also possible, as well as a low hand. But the down side is that neither flush draw contains an ace, and you can't make the best possible low unless an ace appears among the communal cards. This hand and many others like it are what poker players call *trouble hands*. They're seductive, and even when you catch what appears to be a good hand, it might be more trouble than it's worth. Hands like this are always treacherous and often can be disastrous.

✔ **5♣6♦7♦8♣:** Mid-range cards spell trouble — even double-suited, as in this example. With mid-range cards, you stand very little chance of scooping a pot. On the other hand, you can be scooped, particularly when you make a straight and your opponent makes a higher card straight.

Getting good at hand selection

Every form of poker requires a blend of skills. But in Omaha/8, hand selection far outweighs other skills. Because any hand that is *possible* is also *probable* in Omaha/8, you need not be an expert at reading your opponents. Just reading the community cards to ascertain the best possible hand is usually enough. Bluffing, too, is not nearly as important in Omaha/8 as in other forms of poker.

For example, if you are playing Texas Hold'em and all the cards are out, you may be successful if you try to bluff against one or two opponents. But not in Omaha/8. With four starting cards in their hands, each player has six starting combinations. Trying to bluff two players is like trying to run a bluff against a dozen starting hand combinations. The tactic's not going to work most of the time.

In fact, if you never bluffed at all in Omaha/8, you'd probably be better off.

Because one does not need to bluff, or even possess the ability to read his opponents, the critical skill required to win at this game is hand selection.

Some players start with almost any four cards, and if you can exert the discipline to wait for good starting cards — hands that are coordinated, with cards that support each other in some discernable way — you can have an edge over most of your opponents.

Acting last is a big advantage

You can afford to see the flop with weaker hands when you're in a late position. The later you act, the more information you can expect at your disposal, and poker is a game of information — incomplete information, to be sure, but a game of information nevertheless.

Looking for a flop

Before you decide to call with the four cards you've been dealt, ask yourself what kind of flop would be ideal for your hand. And when you see the flop, determine which hand would be perfect for it. This kind of analysis will help you ascertain how well the flop fits your hand.

Here are eight convenient ways to characterize Omaha/8 flops:

- ✔ **Paired:** When a pair flops, the best possible high hand is four-of-a-kind (which players refer to as *quads*), unless a straight flush possibly exists. Although flopping quads is a rarity, a full house is a distinct possibility.

- ✔ **Flush or flush draw:** Three or two cards of the same suit.

- ✔ **Straight or straight draw:** Three or two cards in sequence, or gapped closely enough so that a straight is possible.

- ✔ **High:** Three or two cards above an 8. If three cards higher in rank than an 8 flop, no low hand is possible.

- ✔ **Low or low draw:** Three or two cards with the rank of 8 or lower.

These groupings are not mutually exclusive. Some of these attributes can appear in combination. For example, if the flop were A♣2♣2♦ it would be both *paired* as well as *low*, and contain a *flush draw* as well as a *straight draw*.

It's important to recognize when a flop has multiple possibilities and to understand how your hand stacks up in the pecking order of possibilities.

Suppose you called on the first round of betting with A♦2♦3♣K♠, and the flop is Q♦5♦4♠. You don't have a completed hand at this point. But do have a draw to the best flush and the best low hand. In poker parlance, you have a draw to the nut flush and the nut low. Any diamond gives you the best possible flush. Of course, if that card happens to be the 4♦ someone else could make a full house if that player holds a pair of queens or a pair of 5s in his hand, or he would make four-of-a-kind if he is holding a pair of 4s.

If any card with the rank of 8 or lower falls, and it does not pair one of the low cards on the board, you have the best possible low hand. You also have a straight draw, and if a third diamond shows its face and doesn't pair the board, you also hold the nut flush.

If a 2 falls, then the 2 in your hand is said to be counterfeited, because that 2 on the board belongs to everyone. Nevertheless, you still have the best possible low hand. That third low card in your hand provides insurance against being counterfeited.

The unpleasant experience of being quartered

When you win only one-fourth of a pot because you've split the low half of that pot with another opponent, both of you are said to have been *quartered*.

If only three players contest a hand, and two of them tie for low, each of the low hands loses money even though each wins one-fourth of the pot. Here's how to figure it: Suppose each of you put $40 dollars in the pot. If you are quartered for low, the high hand takes half of the $120 in the pot for his share. The remaining $60 is then divided in half. Each of the low hands receives $30. Because each of you contributed $40, the return on your investment is only 75 cents on the dollar — if you keep winning pots like that, you'll go broke.

With four players in the pot, you can be quartered and break even. With five or more players, you come out a bit ahead if you're quartered. Nevertheless, being quartered is anything but a journey down the primrose path.

Worse than being quartered is playing hands that do not have much of a chance to make the best hand in one or both directions. If you play mid-range cards, like 9-8-7-6, you may make a straight but wind up splitting the pot with a low hand. If you make the bottom end of a straight with Q-J-10, you don't have to worry about a low hand taking half the pot, but you do have to worry about losing the entire pot to a bigger straight.

Playing low draws that do not contain an ace and a 2 is an invitation to make the second-best low hand, which is how many Omaha/8 players lose money. They play hands that look good, but are not good enough to become the best hand in their direction.

Beyond the flop

As a general rule, you shouldn't continue beyond the flop without the best possible hand or a draw to the best possible high hand, low hand or both.

With six conceivable two-card combinations in each player's hand, a lot of hands are possible, so make certain that you'll have the best hand if you catch the card you need.

Here's an example: Suppose the flop is K-8-7 of mixed suits, and you hold 2-3 among your four cards. If 4, 5, or a 6 hits the board, you'll make a low hand but so will your opponent who was drawing to an A-2. Once you see the flop, here are some things to think about before deciding whether to keep playing:

   ✔ **Draw quality:** If you make your hand, will it be the nuts? Suppose you have Q♠J♠ among your starting cards and the flop contains two other spades. Although you have a flush draw, two higher flushes are possible. This is a dangerous hand. Drawing to the second or third best straight, drawing to the second or third best low hand, or thinking you have this pot won because you flopped the third best or second best set are common variations on this theme. Omaha/8 is a game of drawing to the nuts.

- **Pot percentage:** How much of the pot are you hoping to win? Do you have a hand that might scoop the pot if you make it? Are you drawing for the top half of the pot or drawing for low only? More than one player can have a draw to the best low hand, and unless you have at least four opponents, you can expect to lose money whenever you are quartered.

- **Opponents:** Some hands play better against large fields; others play well short-handed. With a flush draw or a straight draw, you need five or six opponents to make the draw worthwhile if you figure to split the pot.

- **Pot size:** Determine how much money will you win if you scoop the pot, if you take half of it, or if you are quartered.

- **Raised or not:** When the pot is raised before the flop in Omaha/8, the raiser usually has a superb low hand, such as A-2-3-4, or A-2-3-K, with the ace suited to another of his cards. If the flop contains all big cards, you probably have nothing more to fear from the raiser.

What to Do When You've Been Raised

If the pot has been raised before you act, tighten up on the hands you play. When you are raised before the flop, the raiser invariably has an outstanding low hand. If you have any low draw other than A-2 along with protection against being counterfeited, throw your hand away.

Since bluffing is infrequent in Omaha/8, if you are raised after the flop, the raiser usually has one of the following:

- The best possible high hand
- The nut low with a draw to a high hand
- A big hand with a draw to a good low

As in all forms of poker, you need a stronger hand to call a raise than to initiate one. Before you call a raise in Omaha/8, give your opponent credit for a strong hand — and quite possibly a strong hand in one direction and a draw to an equally strong hand in another. Call only if you believe your hand is stronger.

Flopping a draw

Here's how to decide whether to continue with your draw if you flop a 4-flush or a 4-straight.

When you're facing three or more opponents, a draw is worthwhile if you think you'll win the entire pot by making your hand. If you have a draw to a high straight or flush and you are certain one of your opponents already has a low hand, half the pot will go to your opponent, so you'll need five or six opponents to make the draw profitable.

But if you have a draw and only two low cards are on the board, don't be afraid to bet, or even raise to make it expensive for opponents to draw for their half of the pot. If that low hand never materializes, their investment is dead money and you'll claim it if you make your hand.

Table 6-2 shows how likely you are to make a low hand.

Table 6-2	Likelihood of Making a Low Hand		
Number of Different Low Cards Dealt to You	*Chances Before the Flop of Making a Low Hand*	*Chances of Making a Low Hand if Two New Low Cards Flop*	*Chances of Making a Low Hand if One New Low Card Flops*
4	49%	70%	24%
3	40%	72%	26%
2	24%	59%	16%

Playing the Turn

If you survived the flop, keep playing if you have done any of the following:

- ✔ Flopped the best high hand.
- ✔ A draw to the best high hand.
- ✔ Flopped the best low hand.
- ✔ A draw to the best low hand.
- ✔ Flopped a two-way hand. You may not have the best possible hand in each direction, but if you believe you can win in one direction and have a shot at the other, keep playing.

By answering the questions in the next four sections, you should be able to gauge whether it's a good idea to continue playing.

How do my opponents play?

If your opponents are loose players, you can draw to the second best high hand; but if your opponents are tight players, you probably don't want to continue unless you have a draw to the best hand or have already made it.

What in the world could my opponent be holding?

If the pot has been raised, you have to think about what kinds of hands your opponent would raise with, as well as the hands other players in the pot need to justify calling a raise.

Where do I sit in relation to the other bettors?

If you think you might be raised if you call, you need a much stronger hand than you would if you have no reason to fear a raise.

Playing the turn at Omaha/8

If you survive the flop, here are some tips for playing the turn successfully:

✔ Bet or raise aggressively if you've made the best possible hand on the turn.

✔ If you have the nut low along with another low card to protect your hand from being counterfeited, bet and call all bets, but be wary of raising. You do not want to drive out other hands that would otherwise pay you off, and you want to avoid being drawn and quartered.

✔ If you have the nut low hand along with a draw to a high hand, feel free to raise from late position. In this situation you want to get more money into the pot. You'll probably win the low end, and you want that additional money in the pot in case you win it all.

✔ Call with a draw if the pot odds exceed the odds against making your hand and you know you'll have the best hand if you catch the card you need.

How much will it cost to see the hand through to its conclusion?

This is poker's essential risk/reward issue. The amount of money you're likely to win if you make your hand should be higher than the odds against making your hand. In other words, if you think you'll win $30 on a $5 investment, it pays to stick around as long as the odds against making your hand are less than 6-to-1.

If you can win $30 for an investment of $5, the relationship between the cost of your investment and the size of the pot is 30-to-5, which reduces to 6-to-1.

If the odds against making your hand are only 3-to-1, then this represents a good bet. But if you were a 9-to-1 underdog, you're better off folding your hand.

Playing the River

Because of all the straight, flush, and full house possibilities generated when each player's four-card private hands combine with five board cards, an Omaha/8 game is frequently decided on the last (or *river*) card. Omaha/8 is very different than Texas Hold'em in this regard. Texas Hold'em is a flop game, and the best hand on the flop is frequently the best hand on the river.

But that's not the case with Omaha. If there are five active players going into the river, you can be sure that at least three of them have one or more drawing combinations in their hands. Even the two players currently holding the best high and low hands also might have draws to better hands. With so many possibilities, you might imagine that almost any card will help someone.

Although the suspense can be frustrating, just imagine your joy when your draw comes in and you scoop a big pot. But the river can be treacherous, and here are some tips for navigating it safely.

When you make the best high hand

If you have the best high hand after all the cards have been dealt, you can bet or raise without fear. You are assured of capturing at least half the pot, and may scoop it if there is no low.

This is the time to be aggressive. Get as much of your opponent's money in the pot as you can; at least half of it will come back to you.

When you have the best low hand

Having the best low hand is not as simple as holding the best high hand. If you are absolutely sure you have the only nut low, you can bet or raise just as if you have the best high hand. But if one of your opponents has the same hand — and this is very common in Omaha/8 — you will be quartered. Making money when this happens is difficult. You need at least five players in the pot to show a profit, and it won't be much of a profit at that.

Suppose that five of you each have $20 in the pot. If you are quartered for low, you and the other low hand will each receive $25 — a scant $5 profit on your investment. The high hand will take $50, for a profit of $30.

If you have a two-way hand, you can be aggressive with it, particularly if you know you have the best hand in one direction. In the $20 per-player example, you would have won $100, for a net profit of $80, if you were able to scoop the pot.

That's why Omaha/8 and other split games are somewhat slippery slopes. Scooping the pot is not merely twice as good as winning one side of the confrontation — the win is usually much better than that.

Eight secrets for winning at Omaha/8

Here are a few thing to keep in mind when you set off to learn Omaha/8:

- Each player has four private cards, which yields six times as many starting combinations as Texas Hold'em hands.

- With all these combinations, hands tend to be bigger in Omaha than in Hold'em, and a hand that is *possible* is usually *probable*. For example, a full house is only possible with a paired board in Texas Hold'em and Omaha/8. But a full house is much more common in Omaha because players have six times the number of starting hand combinations than they do in Texas Hold'em.

- Exactly two — no more, no less — of your hole cards must be used to form five-card hands.

- Omaha/8 is a split-pot game. Anytime you have a high hand and see three low cards on the board, your high hand has just lost some value. Chances are you'll be splitting the pot.

- Play few hands from early position. You'll throw lots of hands away, but you'll be saving money.

- Play coordinated hands. If your first four cards do not work together, throw away your hand and wait for a better opportunity.

- Fit or fold: If the flop doesn't help your hand, or offer a very strong draw in one or both directions, fold your hand.

- The best strategy is to play low cards that have the potential of making high hands, too.

Exploring Omaha High-Only

Omaha is not necessarily a high-low split game; you can play it as a high-only game, too. You'll find Omaha played as a high-only game in some casinos, although it is not nearly as popular as its 8-or-Better cousin.

Omaha High-Only is often played pot-limit in card casinos. Betting can escalate extremely quickly in these games, and the last thing we'd ever advise a beginning player is to play pot-limit or no-limit poker.

Much of the time, Omaha High-Only makes an appearance during a major poker tournament — the kind that takes place over a week or longer — and the game is usually played as pot-limit.

Omaha High-Only is very popular in European card casinos, but in England, Ireland, and much of continental Europe, pot-limit games are the rule rather than the exception.

The mechanics of Omaha High are identical to those of Omaha/8. Each player receives four cards in his starting hand. After a round of betting, three communal cards are flopped. A betting round, a fourth communal card, and another round of betting follows. Then a fifth community card is placed on the board. A final betting round follows and the best five-card hand wins the pot. As in Omaha/8, a player must use precisely two cards from her hand and combine them with three of the community cards to form her best poker hand.

So far, so good. Everything looks the same. But if you play Omaha High-Only, you can expect some major differences in strategy.

✔ **Ditch low hands:** Because low hands won't win a thing in this game, why play low cards? A hand like A-2-3-4 is a powerhouse in Omaha/8, because it can easily make the best low hand and capture half the pot. But this low hand is a real dog in Omaha when it's a high-only game.

✔ **Mid-range is okay:** In Omaha/8, you rarely play a hand like 9-8-7-6. If you make the best possible straight, you probably have to give up half the pot to a better low hand, and if you make the lower end of a straight, such as 8-9-10-J-Q, you face a very good chance that someone has a bigger straight. But if you're playing for high only, you never have to worry about a lower hand snatching half the pot out from under your nose.

✔ **Wrap it:** When played for high, Omaha is often a game of straights and flushes. Because each player is dealt four private cards that can combine to form six distinctly different two-card combinations. Making a straight or a flush is not quite the rarity it is in Texas Hold'em, where each player has only one two-card combination to work with. Wherever there is a possible straight due to the array of communal cards, an Omaha hand is much more likely to have the right two-card combination than a Hold'em hand.

Of course, whenever the board is paired, someone may have a full house or four-of-a-kind. But beyond those possibilities, straights and flushes are the name of the game. No one can possibly make a flush without three community cards of the same suit. That's where *wraps* come into play. If you have four sequenced cards, or four cards with a small gap, you can make a straight in any number of ways. Here's an example of a hand that requires "wrappped" attention.

In Omaha, you can have as many as 20 opportunities to make a straight. If you began with J-10-7-6 and the flop was 9-8-3, you'd make a straight with a queen, jack, 10, 7, 6, or 5. Four of those cards are in your hand, but with two more board cards to be dealt, you can expect to complete a straight more than 70 percent of the time. By comparison, in Texas Hold'em the maximum number of cards you can have that will complete your straight is eight.

✔ **Big flushes:** If you're going to make a flush, you may as well think big. There's nothing more frustrating than making a flush and losing to a bigger one. For obvious reasons, you'd much rather make a straight with a hand like 9-8-7-6 than a flush.

You may want to introduce Omaha High-Only as well as Omaha/8 into your home games to see which version you prefer. But if you're in a poker club or casino, you won't have the luxury of becoming acquainted with a game before you enter serious play. The best way to learn Omaha High-Only under these circumstances is to find an inexpensive tournament. Even if the tournament event is pot limit, you can afford to play and learn as long as the cost to enter the tourney is within your poker budget.

Chapter 7

Home Poker Games

Home poker games have been around forever. A good home poker game gives you something to look forward to with friends and colleagues.

This chapter gives you advice on home games and how to set one up successfully.

Setting Up a Home Game

A successful ongoing home poker game requires good planning and well-thought-out rules. The key to a good game, of course, is a friendly, fair game that people will want to keep coming back to on a regular basis.

This section shows you some key considerations for establishing a fair and fun game.

Rules

A good home game has rules established well before the game begins to avoid any controversy. Try to follow the rules that normally apply in card clubs and casinos so as to not confuse people who play in both.

Your rules should encompass answers to at least the following questions:

✔ Is checkraising allowed?

✔ How will antes be put up? By each player or only by the dealer?

✔ What is the best low hand? (The great majority of card clubs say that A-2-3-4-5 is the best low, even though it's a straight.)

✔ If you play a high-low game, how will the parties declare their hand? (Chips in the hand is the most common method.)

✔ In a high-low game, if one person goes both ways, what happens if he ties one way?

✔ Who splits the pot if a player going both ways wins only one way?

✔ What constitutes a misdeal?

✔ What happens if there is a misdeal?

✔ If the pot is split up between two players, who gets any odd chip?

Think about putting your rules on paper. Memories fade as to what was agreed upon, so it's helpful to bring out the rules in the event of any controversy.

Dealer's choice

Many home games involve a variety of poker games, but *dealer's choice* is usually the deciding factor on the actual game to be played. That is, the dealer can choose the game she wishes to play for that hand or for a round.

The dealer may also designate any special rules such as:

✔ Whether there will be a high-low split.

✔ Whether the betting will increase in certain instances.

✔ Whether there is a wild card.

✔ Whether there is a bet or not after there is a "declare" of low or high in split games.

Of course, the dealer's decisions should be reasonable. You can't have a situation where the rules unduly favor the dealer.

Harry Truman on poker

President Harry Truman was a poker player. Here was his advice on the stakes of a home game:

"Poker among friends and colleagues should not drive anyone to the poorhouse, but should be expensive enough to test skill and make it interesting."

Betting stakes

The betting stakes for a home game need to be agreed on clearly in advance. On the one hand, you want the stakes to be meaningful — enough to keep up people's interest and to allow bluffing and other strategies to potentially be effective. But on the other hand, you don't want the stakes to be so high that players can lose a very large sum in one night. Huge swings can ultimately kill a game, as people will drop off for fear that they can't continue sustaining significant losses.

Some games allow an increase in the stakes in certain poker games or in the last hour of the game.

But remember, a home game is also often about camaraderie and friendship, so if you are going to err on betting stakes, err on the low side.

Wild cards

Most poker purists play without wild cards, but some games do incorporate wild cards. A wild card is specified by the dealer and can be used to greatly improve a hand. So, if you are playing with a wild card or cards, you have to expect the hands to be better than those in regular poker. Gauge your betting accordingly.

The typical choices for wild cards are:

- ✔ **Joker:** The joker can be used as any card or, alternatively, for only aces, straights and flushes.
- ✔ **Deuces:** Each 2 card is wild. So a hand consisting of 4-4-2-2-J is 4-4-4-4-J.
- ✔ **One-eyed jacks:** The jack of spades and jack of hearts have only one eye each, and these jacks when played as wild cards can be any card you wish.

Our preference is to play without wild cards. Wild cards introduce a high element of luck. So if you are a great poker player, you don't want to introduce a greater luck component in your game that your opponents can benefit from.

A trick to mitigate losses

Some home poker players try to ease the pain of losing big by using the following strategy: Set aside a few dollars from each pot. At the end of the night, the big loser (or the two big losers)

receive the set-aside amount. This is effectively a wealth transfer from the winners to the losers, but it lessens the loss.

Time limit

Before the game starts, set a time when the game will end and stick to it. By setting the time limit, everyone is on notice and whining can be avoided by people who are losing and want to continue playing past a reasonable hour.

Near the end, it's often appropriate for the host of the game to announce that the time is drawing near and that three more hands or one more round will end the game. That warning enables players to plan their end strategy accordingly.

Food and drinks

The host for the game should arrange for appropriate food and drinks in advance. Here is our favorite poker food:

- Chips and dip
- Pizza
- Pigs in a blanket
- Licorice
- Cashews
- Beer and soda

Don't get any of that frou-frou stuff like salads and broccoli. If you do, you should suffer humiliating comments from your friends.

Reimbursing the host for all of the expenses in getting the food and drinks is also appropriate. This is best accomplished by taking a few dollars from each pot until the right amount is set aside.

Paying up

The rules should clearly set forth in advance as to how the losers will pay and the winners compensated. The key issues to address are:

- Will payment be in cash or check?
- Will payment be at the end of the night or at the next game?

Game Options

Home games typically have more game options than card clubs or casinos. The type of games is limited only by the imagination of the players. This section describes a number of the most common home games.

Seven-Card Stud

Seven-Card Stud is very popular and can be played high-only or high-low. Two down cards and one up card is first dealt to each player. Four more cards are dealt, three up, and the last one down, with betting intervals following each card. From the seven cards played, the best five cards win. Head over to Chapter 3 for a detailed description of the game.

Texas Hold'em

In Hold'em, each player receives two cards face down, and then a bet ensues. Then three common cards are dealt face up, followed by a common fourth and a common fifth card, with betting intervals. The best five cards out of the two in your hand and the five on the board constitutes the hand. See Chapter 4 for details and great tips.

Omaha High

In Omaha High, each player gets four cards face down, and then a bet occurs. Then three cards are dealt face up all at once on the board as common cards, with a betting round. Then a fourth common card is dealt face up with a bet, with a betting round, and a fifth common card is dealt face up with a common card and with a betting round. A player must use two (and only two cards) from his hand, together with three of the common cards. Hands in Omaha tend to be higher than those in Seven Stud or Hold'em because of the greater number of cards dealt out and the greater number of possibilities. Check out Chapter 6 for some terrific tips on Omaha.

Omaha High-Low, 8-or-Better

Omaha High-Low, 8-or-Better (Omaha/8) is played in the same way as Omaha (four cards in your hand, five common cards ultimately on the board), but there is a high hand and a low hand that splits the pot. A qualifying hand of 8 or better is needed for a hand to be in contention to win half of the pot. Check out Chapter 6 for advice on playing this game.

Pineapple

Pineapple starts with three cards dealt face down to each player, and then a betting round ensues. Then three common cards are dealt face up followed by a betting round. Then each player must discard one of the cards in his hand. Then a fourth common card is dealt face up followed by betting, followed by a fifth common card face up and then betting. The best five cards from the two in your hand and five on the board are played. Pineapple can also be played high-low.

Five-Card Draw

In Five-Card Draw poker, each player is dealt five cards face down. After the deal, a betting round occurs. After the betting round, beginning with the player on the dealer's left, a player may discard one or more cards, and the dealer then deals her from the deck as many cards as she has discarded (the *draw*). A player does not have to draw and can stay *pat*. (For example, if you already have a straight, flush, or full house, you should stay pat and not draw any cards.)

After the draw, there is another betting round, followed by the show of hands. Some games limit the number of cards that can be drawn, some not.

In one variation of Five-Card Draw, a person is allowed to bet only if she has a pair of jacks or better.

Lowball

Lowball is like Five-Card Draw, but the lowest hand wins the pot. Ace always counts as a low card and A-2-3-4-5 is the best possible low. Straights and flushes don't count, although some players play that 6-4-3-2-A is the lowest hand.

Like Five-Card Draw, five cards are dealt face down, followed by a betting round. Then a player may discard cards to improve his hand, followed by a final betting round.

The best hand is referred to by the highest card in your hand. If two players have the same card that is the highest card, then the next lowest card counts. For example,

> 7-6-5-4-2 beats 8-6-4-3-2
>
> 7-5-4-2-A beats 7-6-4-3-A
>
> 6-5-3-2-A beats 6-5-4-2-A

No pair beats any pair. So even K-10-9-8-7 Beats 2-2-3-4-5.

Lowball is typically a game that should be played conservatively, waiting for pat hands or hands with one-card draws.

Five-Card Stud

In Five-Card Stud, each player gets one card down and one card up initially, followed by a bet. Then each player gets a second up card, followed by a bet. A third and fourth card face up is given to each player, each followed by a bet.

The best high hand at the end wins. There are variations of the game where players are allowed to buy one or two replacement cards after all five cards are dealt. The game can also be played high-low, although in this variation, no minimum 8-low-or better is typically required.

A high pair in regular Five-Card Stud can often win the hand.

Baseball

Baseball is typically a version of Seven-Card Stud, where each player gets two cards down, four cards dealt face up, and a final card face down. But in Baseball, all 9s and 3s are wild. If a 4 is dealt face up, it entitles the player to an extra down card.

Baseball is a game where big, big hands often come up. With eight wild cards, you can see four of a kind easily, with straight flushes and five of a kind happening not infrequently.

Black Mariah

Black Mariah (sometimes referred to as Chicago) is a Seven-Card Stud game, except that the high spade in the hole splits half the pot. Sometimes Q♠ counts as the highest spade.

If you have the highest spade in the hole in the first two cards you get, you can keep betting and raising at will.

Indian Poker

Indian Poker is a one-card game dealt face down to each player. Each player, without looking at his card, simultaneously places it on his forehead so that other player can see all cards but his own. Then there is a single round of betting, and then a showdown.

Razz

Razz is Seven-Card Stud, played low. Each player starts with two cards down and one card up. Each player must ante initially, and the high card on the board is typically required to make a small bet. Subsequent players may then call or raise.

As long as he stays in, a player gets ultimately a total of three hole cards and four exposed up cards. The best hand is A-2-3-4-5. The key to this game is starting with three low cards and being able to read your opponents' hands and remember what cards have been already played and folded.

Crisscross (or Iron Cross)

Five cards are dealt to each player face down. Then five cards are placed face down on the board as common cards, in two intersecting rows forming a crisscross arrangement. The common cards are revealed clockwise, with the center card last, and with betting after each exposed card.

Two cards from a player's hand and one row from the crisscross are used. The game can be played high-only or high-low.

Poker Etiquette in Home Games

Basic etiquette plays a vital role in society, and it even applies to poker. Players who are rude and inconsiderate may soon find themselves excluded from games or the object of silent derision. We're not saying you need to stick a doily under your beer or soda bottle, but keep the following do's and don'ts in mind.

Do . . .

- ✔ **Be honest:** Don't try to short-change the pot or otherwise cheat.

- ✔ **Play quickly:** No one likes a slow player.

- ✔ **Be courteous and friendly:** No one likes a whiner.

- ✔ **Be a good winner:** Gloating and making fun of other players is a definite no-no.

- ✔ **Be a good loser:** We all lose. It happens. But show some class and don't show your temper, swear or throw cards. Definitely don't insult the other players.

- ✔ **Let the other players know if you plan to leave early:** It's courteous to let the other players know in advance if you plan to quit early.

- ✔ **Bet in sequence:** Bet, call, or fold when it's your turn. Acting out of turn can adversely affect another player's hand.

Don't . . .

- ✔ **Give a player advice in the middle of a hand even if he asks for it:** This is a no-win proposition: Either the player who asked will be upset at you if the advice is wrong or the person who loses against the player will be mad at you.

- ✔ **Look at another player's hand, unless you have permission:** Some players strongly object to your looking at their hand.

- ✔ **Play poker with a guy named "Doyle," "Amarillo Slim" or "Harpo":** These guys are too good for your normal home game.

More Information On Home Games

A variety of books can help you to win at your home game. Head to your local bookstore or log onto amazon.com or barnesandnoble.com. Here is a short list of some of the books:

- ✔ *Poker: Over 25 Games and Variations, Plus Tips, Strategy, and More,* by Seth Godin

- ✔ *The Rules of Neighborhood Poker According to Hoyle,* by Stewart Wolpin

- ✔ *Thursday-Night Poker: How to Understand, Enjoy — and Win,* by Peter O. Steiner

- ✔ *How to Win at Strip Poker,* by Herbert I. Kavet (Yes, there really is a book with this title.)

- ✔ *Hold 'Em Poker,* by David Sklansky

- ✔ *Getting the Best of It!,* by David Sklansky

- ✔ *Caro's Fundamental Secrets of Winning Poker,* by Mike Caro.

Part II

Advanced Strategy

The 5th Wave   By Rich Tennant

"You know, I'm not great at reading poker faces, but I think I'd bet against his hand."

In this part . . .

*P*laying and winning poker involves much more than the luck of the draw, and this part covers two pretty important aspects of the game: bluffing and money management. Chapter 8 offers some guidelines on both performing bluffs and reading bluffs from other players. In Chapter 9, we actually use math to help you decide how to proceed when you're winning, losing, and breaking even.

Chapter 8

Bluffing

*B*luffing is poker's magic elixir. It's the sleight of hand where high art and drama reside. It's the place where myths are made. After all, what's a western movie without a poker scene with one player trying to bluff another out of a big pot?

To those who do not play poker or who have only a nodding acquaintance with it, bluffing is where those folks focus most of their attention when they think about the game.

What Is Bluffing, Anyway?

Ask most poker players to define bluffing and they'll tell you about betting a weak hand with the hope of driving other players out of the pot. After all, without bluffing, poker would be a boring game. Bets would be made and the best hand would win. Always.

The cards figure to break even in the long run; without the possibility that someone is bluffing, then each player would have the same expectation — and when all was said and done, no one would win any money.

Does this conversation ring a bell?

Non-Player: "You're a professional poker player? Wow — you must have a real poker face."

Professional Player: "Why do you say that?"

Non-Player: "Don't you need a poker face because you have to bluff all the time?"

Professional Player: "Actually, bluffing is only a small part of the game, and good players don't really bluff that often."

Non-Player: "Hmmm. It's not like that in the movies."

Professional Player: [shrugging his shoulders with the resigned weariness of one who's had similar conversations far too many times] "Well, few things really are . . . "

But some players win most of the time and some players lose most of the time. And it's often bluffing — or more precisely the possibility that one's adversary might be bluffing — that goes a long way toward separating the winners from the losers. Bluffing, after all, is merely a form of deception — and deception is an essential component in winning poker.

After all, if your opponents always knew what cards you had they'd be tough to beat. Deception is the art of keeping others off balance. Like a misdirection play in football, or a baseball player hitting behind the runner into an area vacated by the infielder on a hit-and-run play, deception is a required skill for any poker player.

Different Kinds Of Bluffs

Bluffing comes in several forms — the reason for bluffing frequently depends on the cards you hold, what you think your opponents have in their hands, and what you think they believe you have.

- ✔ **Betting — or raising — with a helpless hand.** With this technique, you have a weak hand but act as if it's a strong one. The maneuver is reversible, too: You can act weak when holding an extremely powerful hand in order to lure opponents into a trap.

- ✔ **Betting or raising on the inexpensive betting rounds.** You use this bluff in order to get a free card later on in the hand — when the cost of bets double.

- ✔ **Betting with a *semi-bluff*.** Noted poker theorist David Sklansky, who coined the term, defines the semi-bluff as " . . . a bet with a hand which, if called, does not figure to be the best hand at the moment but has a reasonable chance of outdrawing those hands that initially called it."

With a semi-bluff, as opposed to a bluff with a helpless hand, a player has two ways to win:

- His opponent might think the bluffer has the hand he's representing and release his own hand.
- If the opponent calls, the bluffer might catch the card he needs and beat his opponent that way.

The Importance of Bluffing

Some players — and it's only a few of them, to be sure — never bluff. After you figure out who they are, playing against them is easy. If they bet once all the cards are out, you can safely throw your hand away unless you believe that your hand is superior to theirs. If it is, you should raise.

Famous bluffs: Baldwin versus Addington

During the 1978 World Series of Poker No-Limit Hold'em championship Bobby Baldwin, then a professional poker player and now president of the Bellagio Hotel in Las Vegas, was matched up against San Antonio real estate investor Crandall Addington for all the marbles.

Addington was heavily favored at the time, having about $275,000 in chips to Baldwin's $145,000. Baldwin bet before the flop and Addington called. The flop was Q♦4♦3♣. Baldwin bet $30,000. What could he have? A flush draw or straight draw was a possibility. So was a pair of queens.

Addington called without a moment's hesitation, a sure sign he also had a good hand. The A♦ fell on the turn, making a straight and a flush distinct possibilities. Baldwin made a $95,000 bet, adding it to the $92,000 already in the pot, and leaving himself with only a few remaining chips if he lost the hand.

Addington went into deep thought. If Addington called and won, Baldwin would be nearly broke, and he would almost surely be the winner. If he called Baldwin's bet and lost, the tables would be turned and Baldwin would then be favored to win the event. If he folded, he would still have a substantial chip lead on Baldwin and still be favored to grind him down as the tournament wore on.

Addington folded. As Baldwin gathered in the pot, he tossed his cards toward the center of the table. They were the 10♥9♥. Baldwin had successfully bluffed with a completely hopeless hand that could have never won in a showdown. Players call that a *naked* bluff, and Baldwin used it to win a $92,000 pot with absolutely nothing — not even a draw.

That move turned the tide, and Bobby Baldwin became the 1978 World Series of Poker champion — although whether he *won* it or *stole* it right out from under Addington's nose is subject to interpretation.

Other people are habitual bluffers. When they bet, you have to call as long as you are holding any reasonable hand. Although habitual bluffers will also make real hands every now and then, the fact that they bluff far too often makes your decision easy. By calling, you'll win far more money in the long run than you would save by folding.

Keep 'em guessing

We have no easy answer about players who bluff some, but not all of the time. Opponents who bluff some of the time are better poker players than those found at either end of the bluffing spectrum. Better players, of course, can keep you guessing about whether or not they are bluffing. And when you're forced to guess, you will be wrong some of the time. That's just the way it is.

Of course, you might be able to pick up a tell (a revealing gesture) and know when your opponent is bluffing, but that's not too likely in most cases. The sad truth is that players who keep you guessing are going to give you much more trouble than predictable opponents.

In most low-limit games, players bluff much too often. After all, when you play fixed-limit poker, all it costs is one additional bet to see someone's hand. And the pots are usually big enough, relative to the size of a bet, to make calling the right decision.

Here's an example: Suppose the pot contains $90, and your opponent makes a $10 bet. That pot now contains $100, and the cost of your call is only $10. Even if you figure your opponent to be bluffing only one time in ten, you should call. By calling, the laws of probability suggest that you'd lose a $10 bet nine times, for a loss of $90. Although you'd win only once, that pot would be worth $100. After ten such occurrences, you'd show a net profit of $10. As a result, you could say that regardless of the outcome of any particular hand, each call was worth one dollar to you.

The threat of bluffing

The threat of a bluff is just as important as a bluff itself. A good player — one who bluffs neither too often nor too infrequently, and seems to do so under the right conditions — has something else going for her too. It's the *threat* of a bluff. Does she have the goods or is she bluffing? How can you tell? If you can't, how do you know what to do when she bets?

These answers don't come easily, and even top-notch players are not going to have a terrific batting average in most cases. As a result, the threat of a bluff combined with the bluff itself, is designed to help a player win some pots that she would otherwise lose and to win more money in pots where she actually has the best hand.

After all, if you have the best hand and come out betting, your opponent won't always know whether you're bluffing or not. If there's a lot of money in the pot, she'll probably call. That's the less costly error. After all, if she were to throw the winning hand away and relinquish a big pot, that's a much more costly *faux pas* than calling one additional bet.

Bluffing and the threat of bluffing go hand in hand. A bluff can enable a player to win a pot she figured to lose if the hands were shown down. The threat of a bluff enables a player with a good hand to win more money than she would if her opponent knew she never bluffed.

The Bluffing Paradox

A successful poker player has to adopt a middle-ground strategy. This means that sometimes you'll be called when you bluffed and lose that bet. Other times you will release the best hand because an opponent successfully bluffed you out of the pot.

Neither scenario is enjoyable. Just remember that making errors is inevitable when you deal with incomplete information. One can call too often or not enough. One can bluff too often or not at all. And the only way to eliminate errors at one extreme is to commit them at the other.

Very cautious players, who never call unless certain of winning, avoid calling with a lesser hand, but often relinquish a pot they would have won. Players who call all the time win just about every pot they can possibly win, but find themselves holding the short straw far too often when the hands are shown down.

The paradox is that good players make both kinds of errors some of the time to avoid being a predictable player at either end of the bluffing-calling spectrum. After all, there's a relationship between risk and reward. If you are never caught bluffing, you are either the best bluffer in the history of poker or you are not bluffing often enough. If you are caught almost every time you bluff, you're bluffing much too frequently.

If you call all the time, you will never lose a pot you could have won, and if you seldom call, your opponents will learn that they can win by betting and driving you off the pot unless you have a very strong hand.

Bluffing, after all, is much like mom's advice: "All things in moderation."

Famous bluffs: Jack Straus and the 7-2

The late Jack Straus, who won the 1982 World Series of Poker, was a man known for his creativity, flair, and imagination at the poker table, as well as his willingness to risk all he had if he liked the odds. Once, in a No-Limit Hold'em game, Straus was dealt a 7 and a 2 of different suits.

That starting hand is one of the worst in the deck — one the overwhelming majority of players would throw away without a moment's hesitation. But not Straus; not this time. "I was on a rush," he said, "so I raised."

One player called. The flop was 7-3-3, giving Straus two pair, albeit with a kicker that couldn't even beat the board. As Straus bet again, he realized he had made a mistake. His opponent, who didn't hesitate as he reached for his chips, raised Straus $5,000. Straus realized his opponent had a big pair in the hole, and the logical move would have been to give up the bluff and release his hand.

But Straus called, which must have caused his opponent to question whether he, indeed, had the best hand. The fourth card was a 2. It paired Straus' other hole card, but it was worthless since there was already a communal pair of 3s on the board.

Straus fired out a bet: $18,000. As his opponent paused to consider whether Straus had a hand or was bluffing, Straus leaned forward, saying: "I'll tell you what, just gimme one of those $25 chips of yours and you can see either one of my cards — whichever one you choose."

After another long pause, Straus' opponent tossed over a single green chip and pointed to one of the two cards that were face down in front of Straus. Straus flipped over the 2. Now there was another long pause.

Finally Straus's opponent concluded that both cards were the same, and that Straus made a full house — 2s full of 3s — and threw the winning hand away.

"It was just a matter of psychology," Straus was reputed to have said later. But to most observers it wasn't psychology at all. It was magic, pure and simple.

Not All Bluffs Are Created Equal

Not all bluffs are the same. Some work better in one situation that others, so let's look at the various kinds of bluffs and distinguish between them.

Bluffing on the end with a hopeless hand

This is the classic bluff of movie lore. You're up against an opponent or possibly two of them. You have a hopeless hand. Perhaps it's a straight draw that didn't materialize. Maybe it's a busted flush draw.

The hidden benefits of being caught

Bluffing won't succeed all the time. Observant opponents notice when you are caught bluffing. Once others realize that you don't have a legitimate hand every time you bet, your good hands will attract more calls than they would if you left your opponents with the impression that you never bluffed at all.

That's one of the benefits of bluffing. Not only will you be able to steal a pot every now and then, but a failed bluff or two can serve as potent advertising. As a result, a player who bluffs every now and then can expect to make more money on his good hands, too.

If the hands were to be shown down, you know you couldn't possibly win. So you bet. "Nothing ventured," you think to yourself, "nothing gained." If someone calls your bluff, you lose a bet you would have saved had you checked. But checking, of course, is tantamount to relinquishing your opportunity to win the pot.

If you bet, there's always the chance that both your opponents will fold. If someone doesn't call you, then you win the entire pot. Suppose that pot contains $100 and the cost to bet is $10. Your bluff doesn't have to succeed all of the time — or even most of the time — for it to be a good decision.

If bluffing fails nine times and succeeds only once, you will still be a winner in the long run. You'll have lost an extra $10 nine times, or $90, but you will win $100 on one occasion, for a net win of $10. That net figure may not be a spectacular profit, perhaps, but enough to prove that bluffs have to succeed only every now and then to be worthwhile.

Bluffing with more cards to come

When you bluff with more cards to come, you usually have two ways to win. The bluff might succeed on its own merits, causing an opponent to lay down the best hand. In addition, you might catch the card you need on a succeeding round and actually make the winning hand.

Imagine that you're playing Hold'em and you raised before the flop with K♥Q♥, and two other players call. Suppose the flop is J♣6♥4♥. If you come out betting on the flop, you have any number of ways to win this pot. Your opponents could fold, and you'd win right there. But even if one or both call, you certainly shouldn't mind. After all, any of the nine hearts in the deck can complete your flush. Moreover, any of the three kings or three queens will

Famous bluffs: Stu Ungar versus Ron Stanley

In the 1997 World Series of Poker, Stu Ungar had been dominating the final table. He was chip leader from the start, and rather than nursing his lead while his opponents eliminated themselves, Ungar attacked early and often.

Once, Ungar raised on seven successive hands in a row. Bluffing? Of course he was. But none of his opponents wanted to risk early elimination to find out for sure. Each subsequent rung on the pay ladder was a significant increase in winnings, so each of Ungar's adversaries was apparently content to cautiously inch his way upward.

After Las Vegas professional Ron Stanley stole the blinds a few times, he moved within $200,000 of Ungar. For a moment, it looked like he might overtake Ungar.

But a few hands later, the two chip leaders began a heads-up duel. With Ungar in the big blind, Stanley quietly called. The flop was A♠9♥6♠.

Stanley, a seasoned professional, had noticed that each time Ungar flopped top pair with an ace, he checked the flop and bet on the turn. Once again he checked behind Stanley, suggesting that he might be holding an ace once again.

An 8 fell on the turn. Stanley, who had a 9 in his hand and second pair, bet $25,000. Ungar raised $60,000 and Stanley called.

The last card was a king. Stanley checked and folded when Ungar bet $225,000. Ungar brashly turned up his cards, showing Q-10. It was a total bluff. He had no hand whatsoever, and Ron Stanley had released the best hand.

Seemingly unnerved by Ungar's bold action, Stanley was eliminated shortly thereafter, while Ungar proceeded to run over the rest of his opponents — who by this time all seemed to realize that they were only playing for second place, not the championship.

give you a pair that is probably superior to whatever your opponents are holding. In addition, there are three tens in the deck (exclusive of the 10♥, which completes your flush) that will give you a straight draw.

A lot of good cards are in that deck, and you are rife with potential. When you couple the chances of making the best hand on the turn or the river with the possibility that your adversaries will fold if you bet, you are probably an odds-on favorite to win the pot one way or another.

Bluffing and Position

In most instances, acting last — after you've had a chance to see what your opponents do — is a big advantage. But when you're bluffing it's often advantageous to act first.

If your opponent checks and you bet, he's likely to realize that you are trying to take advantage of the fact that he's shown weakness. As a result, he is more likely to call — or even raise, if he's a very aggressive player — with marginal hands.

But betting from first position conveys the image that you really do have a strong hand. After all, you are betting into someone who could have a really powerful hand. Your opponent, of course, will realize that and be more prone to release a marginal hand than he would be if he checked and then you bet. (For more details about position, see Chapter 3.)

Bluffing More Than One Opponent

The odds against a bluff succeeding increase significantly as you add additional opponents to the equation. The more opponents, the more someone is likely to call to keep you from winning a sizeable pot by bluffing. "I had to call to keep you honest" is a frequently heard expression at any poker table.

Suppose you were facing a single opponent and thought that your bluff would succeed one-third of the time. Those aren't bad odds, particularly when the money in the pot exceeds the odds against a successful bluff. Suppose the pot contains $90 and the price of a bet is $30. If this situation were to repeat itself and your estimate of successfully bluffing was accurate, you would bet $30 twice and lose, but you'd win $90 the third time. In the long run, this is an opportunity with a positive expected value.

But what happens if you add a third player to the mix? Once again, you figure that your chances of successfully bluffing the additional player are one chance in three. The presence of a third player will, of course, increase the size of the pot. Let's assume that the pot now contains $135.

Looking for "tells"

Perhaps a poker player's most important skill is the ability to get into the minds of his opponents. Poker legend, Doyle Brunson, once proclaimed he could beat anyone at the poker table — even if he didn't look at his own cards.

Brunson insisted, as long as his opponents were unaware of the fact he wasn't looking at his cards, he could pick up enough visual cues from his opponent's mannerisms and tendencies to beat them at the game and win money.

Brunson's unique outlook on the game reaffirms one of his most celebrated quote: *Poker is not a game of cards. It's a game of people.*

Although the size of the pot has increased arithmetically, the chances against your bluff succeeding can be argued to have grown geometrically.

While the size of the pot increased, it usually does not increase to a point where it offsets the very long odds against successfully bluffing through two opponents.

Bluffs work best against a small number of opponents. The fewer the better. Three is almost always too many, and even running a bluff through two players is both daunting and difficult. There is one exception, however. Assume that there are no more cards to come. If you are first to act and are facing two opponents, you can bluff if you think that the last player to act was on a draw and missed her hand.

Suppose you are playing Hold'em and there are two suited cards on the flop. If Phyllis, the third opponent, simply calls on the flop and the turn, chances are she may have had a flush draw that never materialized. If that's the case, she is very likely to release her hand against a bet on the river, even if she suspects that you're bluffing. When all is said and done, she might not even be able to beat a bluff.

Famous bluffs: Texas Dolly versus the masked duo

On the quiet evening of April 29th, 1998, Doyle "Texas Dolly" Brunson returned home after winning a major poker tournament. Doyle is a two time winner of the World Championship of Poker. He had $85,000 in uncashed casino chips in his pocket.

Brunson was startled by two robbers who were waiting for him at his doorstep. The masked men forced Brunson and his wife, both in their late 60s, into their Las Vegas home and demanded all the cash and jewels in the house.

The Brunsons were tied up together and forced to lie on the living room floor while the two robbers made repeated threats to kill both of them if they refused to cooperate and hand over the money and jewels.

But Brunson had other ideas.

Drawing upon his vast poker experience, Brunson outfoxed the bandits. He feigned a heart attack, clutching his chest. As the two robbers watched in horror, Brunson gasped for air.

Fearful of a possible murder rap, the robbers panicked. They ran out the door and were never seen again.

Doyle Brunson may have bluffed many poker players in high-stakes poker games. But he most certainly would agree — this was his greatest bluff of all.

But Stan, the player in the middle, has a lot to worry about. If you bet, not only does he have to worry about whether you have a real hand, he also needs to concern himself with the player to his left. Even if the player in the middle has a marginal hand — the kind he'd call you with if the two of you were heads-up — he might release it. After all, Stan has two concerns: Your hand might be stronger than his, and the third player might also have a better hand.

When your opponent in the middle is a good player — good enough to release a marginal hand rather than stubbornly call " . . . to keep you honest" — you might use the implied threat of the third adversary to force the man in the middle to shed his holding.

Bluffing Strategies

Bluffing is tricky business. You never know for sure if you'll be called or if you'll be able to steal a pot out from under your opponent's nose. The next time you're inclined to perform larceny at the poker table, keep these tips in mind:

- ✔ **Be aware of how many players you'll have to bluff your way through.** While one or even two players can be bluffed, don't think about trying to bluff more than two opponents unless you really have strong reasons to believe you'll succeed.

- ✔ **Understand that a bluff doesn't have to work to make it the correct decision.** After all, you're usually just risking one bet to win an entire pot full of bets. Bluffing has to work only some of the time to be the right choice. And even when you're caught, a bluff can be successful if it causes opponents to call when you are betting a strong hand.

- ✔ **Avoid bluffing players who are either experts or brain dead.** Instead, aim your bluffs at good opponents. Poor players will usually call " . . . to keep you honest," while experts are more likely to see through your chicanery.

- ✔ **Don't bluff for the sake of bluffing.** Some players will bluff just to "advertise." There's no need to do that. Bluff if you believe you have a reasonable chance to succeed. You'll get plenty of advertising value because some of your bluffs will be picked off regardless of how well you assess your chances for success.

- ✔ **Never bluff a hopeless hand when there are more cards to come.** Instead, think about semi-bluffing, which allows you to win the pot two ways: Your opponents may fold, or you might hit your draw. (See the section "Bluffing with more cards to come" in this chapter.)

- ✔ **Take the opportunity to bluff if all of your opponents check on the previous betting round.** It's even better if they've all checked on an expensive betting round. But your chances are diminished if any newly exposed cards appear to have helped one of your opponents.

> ✔ **Imply specific hands.** Bluffs that seem to represent specific hands, such as a flush or a straight, have a much better chance to succeed than bets that appear to come out of the blue.

> ✔ **Zero in on weak players.** It's much easier to bluff players who have shown weakness by checking, than to bluff those who have shown strength by betting on the preceding round.

> ✔ **Strive for a tight, aggressive image** by playing the kinds of starting hands recommended in this book. This kind of image has a much better chance of running a successful bluff than a player with a loose image. If you are seen as selective, tight, and aggressive, your opponents will not suspect a bluff when you bet. When you have a license to steal, use it.

> ✔ **Attempt a bluff occasionally when all the cards are out and you have nothing, but don't overdo it.** But if you have enough to beat a draw, save that additional bet and try to win in a showdown.

Famous bluffs: Johnny Chan versus Erik Seidel

In this "reverse" bluff, Johnny Chan bluffed Erik Seidel into thinking he held the best hand, lured him into betting, and won a $1.6 million pot during the final stages of the 1988 World Series of Poker.

Chan had won the World Series the previous year and had been on a roll ever since. Here he was, 12 months later, with a chance to win back-to-back titles. But he'd need some magic to accomplish it. Seidel, a former commodities broker from New York, left Wall Street for the life of a professional poker player; and now he had a big chip lead on the defending champ.

At this point in the tournament, the blinds were $10,000 and $20,000. Chan was first to act on each betting round. The flop was Q♠ 10♦ 8♦.

Chan checked. Seidel bet $50,000. Chan called. The turn card was a complete blank, and both men checked. The fifth and final card was another blank. Chan checked.

Seidel held a queen in his hand, giving him top pair, albeit with a weak kicker. He thought for a moment that Chan might have a queen with a better kicker. But by checking on the turn and on the river, Chan passed up his final chance to bet!

Seidel then pushed all of his chips into the center of the table, certainly a sizeable enough bet to cause Chan to release any slightly better hand in the event that Seidel had misread him. Seidel thought his all-in bet would prevent Chan from calling with hands such as a queen with a better kicker, or two small pair.

Seidel had, in fact, misread Chan. And not by a little, but by a lot. Chan smiled as he turned over his hand. Chan had flopped a straight with the J♣ 9♣.

Had Chan not bluffed, more than likely Seidel would have folded in the face of a bet from his adversary on the turn or the river. But Chan did bluff. In fact, he did it twice, once on the turn and again on the river and he reaped a handsome reward: his second consecutive World Championship.

Chapter 9

Money Management and Recordkeeping

· ·

· ·

*O*ld paradigms, like old soldiers, never die. Some never even fade away. At one time, people believed the Earth was flat and the sun revolved around it. Some of us still "knock wood," whistle when walking past a graveyard, avoid walking under ladders, believe black cats are bad luck, and patiently await the next harmonic convergence. Others — poker players, mostly — are enamored with the idea of money management.

What Is Money Management Anyway?

Money management is one of those concepts that should have died long ago but didn't and still makes its way into far too much gaming literature. Part of the definition, the up side, is based on the timeless adage, "Quit while you're ahead." After you win a predetermined amount, get up from that poker table and leave the game a bit richer and happier than you were when you walked in.

The down side tells you not to lose more than a predetermined amount (a *stop-loss limit*) at any one session. (See the section "Should you quit while you're ahead?" in this chapter.) Once you've reached your money limit, it's time to quit. "Give it up and go home," say the high priests of money management, "you won't make it back that day. Come back tomorrow. Lady Luck cold-shouldered you, and you ought to know better than to chase your losses."

Does money management make sense?

Consider these questions:

- Does following a money-management plan make any sense?
- Is it correct to quit while you're ahead?
- Should you quit once you've lost some predetermined amount?
- If you quit when you're ahead, as well as when you're losing, should you play only when your results are contained within the boundaries of your stop-loss limit on the negative side, and a stop-win point if you've had a fortunate day?

Even money-management adherents usually agree that a poker game theoretically never ends (at least in card clubs), and it makes no difference whether you play four hours today and four hours tomorrow, or play eight hours just today. If that's the case, what *is* the logic behind money-management theories?

Should you quit while you're ahead?

If you take the quit-while-you're-ahead approach, proponents say, you get to take your profit out of the game and not *give back* money you've already won. If you think about it, though, this makes sense only if you decide to quit poker entirely. If you know you'll never play again and you're ahead in today's game, then quitting does allow you to permanently put today's profit into your pocket.

But if you quit as a winner today and lose tomorrow, are you any worse off than if you simply played on and lost what you had won earlier in the session? The answer, quite obviously, is no. You're not worse off; you simply pocketed those winnings for a few more hours.

If you are only an occasional player, then walking away as a winner may be the wise move so that you have some extra cash to spend.

Should you quit when you reach a stop-loss limit?

Leave the game if you are losing (taking the stop-loss approach); ask yourself whether you plan to play tomorrow — or even next week, for that matter. If you answer "yes," then ask yourself if you think you can win. If you plan to play again and believe you can win, is there any real difference between quitting now or continuing to play?

If you regularly play in a game where you are not a favorite, you can expect to lose money — and it makes no difference whether or not you practice money management. If you are a favorite, however, playing makes sense regardless of whether you are ahead or behind at any given moment.

The Truth About Money Management

Here's the only facet of money management that's true: If the game is good and you are a favorite to win, you probably ought to continue playing. If the game is bad and you are an underdog, quit! Never mind whether you're winning or losing.

Of course, a game can be terrific and you may not be a favorite for any number of reasons unrelated to skill. You may be tired; upset because you argued with your spouse, kids, or boss; physically ill and not able to concentrate; or stressed out from work, freeway gridlock, or any other assault on the sanctity of the human condition that might put you off your best game.

You'll save lots of money over the course of your poker-playing career by following this simple rule: If you're not playing at your best, go home. If you quit the game, it will still be there tomorrow, but if you stay too long at the dance, your money might be gone.

Having a positive expectation

Consider this: Gambling successfully is predicated on putting yourself into situations where you have a positive expectation. That's why there aren't any professional craps or roulette players. In the long run, there is no chance of winning when the odds are not in your favor. Any reasonably skilled poker player can find games where he or she is favored to win. While favorites can and do get beaten, they show a profit in the end.

Quick tips on betting and stakes

Okay, here are three pointers for you to consider regarding betting and stakes:

✔ **Take a break if you feel yourself losing emotional control.** Players call this feeling *going on tilt,* an expression that harks back to losing your hard-earned quarters by hitting the pinball machine too hard. Having a bad beat or two can make you do crazy things in an effort to win back your losses right away. If you feel that urge, take a ten-minute break and catch your breath.

✔ **Play at stakes comfortable for you.** Make sure the stakes you are playing at are appropriate for your level of skill. As you get into higher stakes games, you can lose money very quickly.

✔ **Make sure that you can afford a loss.** No one wants to lose, but it is inevitable in poker. Just try to limit your losses to a reasonable amount. Don't let a poker game envelope your life, and never bet the rent or grocery money.

Game selection and money management

One of the key concepts to winning at any form of poker is game selection, so why would you voluntarily take yourself out of a good game simply because you have won or lost some arbitrarily predetermined amount of money? If you've suffered a number of *bad beats* (hands where you had the best of it until someone caught a miracle card to beat you) and nothing seems to be going right, you might want to quit even though the game is good. Quitting is okay in that case — but only if you can't assure yourself that you'll continue to play to the best of your ability.

Never quit just because you've reached a stop-loss limit.

What if you're in a good game and you're $1,000 ahead? Should you really quit when you're ahead? If the game is that good and you have no other pressing commitments, why not keep on playing? After all, you're a favorite. Chances are you'll win even more money.

But whether you win or lose from that point on, your future results are always up for grabs, regardless of whether you keep playing or pack it in and return to the game tomorrow. The game goes on, and the segments of time during which you're playing are only arbitrary measures.

The Importance of Keeping Records

If you don't keep records, how do you know if you're successful or not? Without accurate records, you never know how good a player you are. Many poker players — even good ones — don't keep accurate records.

If you are serious about poker, treat your game like a business or a profession. Every business keeps records. Without them, a business owner has no idea of what it costs to make, sell, or inventory product, and no way of knowing whether his or her bottom line is written in black or red.

Perhaps it's easier for the majority of poker players who don't keep records to avoid looking truth in the face. But if you plan to win money when playing poker, you must be aware of the results you're achieving.

Fortunately, the kind of records you need to keep as a poker player are a lot simpler than the records that business owners have to keep.

What kind of records should I keep?

Every poker player should be concerned about two basic statistical measures:

- ✔ *Win rate* indicates how much money you're winning — or losing — aggregated on an hourly basis.

- ✔ *Standard deviation* measures short-term fluctuations. Standard deviation measures variance — or luck. Good luck or bad; it makes no difference in this equation.

How to keep records

You don't need to be a statistician to keep these records. In fact, you can do this without knowing anything more than grade school arithmetic. It's easy. The next time you play poker, take along a small notebook and record the amount of money you use to buy into the game. Then record the following information on an hourly basis:

- ✔ Amount won or lost during the previous hour

- ✔ The game you're playing in (for example, $2–$4 Hold'em)

- ✔ Total number of hours played that session

When you get home, you can add the preceding information to your record of previous sessions so that you have cumulative statistics, as well as a record of how well you did each time you played.

Go ahead and calculate

- ✔ The amount won or lost for the entire year.
- ✔ The total number of hours played during the year.

Keeping up with recordkeeping

One of the psychologically difficult things about keeping records is simply keeping up with it. After a tough loss, it can be very difficult to record that loss in your record book and have it stare you in the face each time you glance that way. Nevertheless, if you don't keep records, you'll only delude yourself about the results you've achieved at the table.

If you are playing just for enjoyment and don't care whether you win or lose, then, excuse yourself from the drudgery. If you are a winning player, or aspire to be one, you must record and analyze your results.

How to Figure Your Win Rate

Computing your win or loss rate is simple: Divide the amount of money won or lost by the number of hours you've played.

This calculation shows you the average amount won or lost per hour played. In statistics, that figure is called the *mean*. If you play in different games, you might want to keep records on a game-by-game basis (to determine whether you're doing better at Hold'em, Lowball, or Omaha) as well as on an overall basis.

All averages are not created equal

Knowing how much you are winning or losing on an hourly basis is important. But it is also important to know whether the mean is representative. In other words, is the mean a good indicator of the data it represents?

If this concept seems confusing, here's an example to clear things up. Let's say San Francisco and Omaha each have an average annual temperature of 65°F. But San Francisco rarely gets very warm or very cold, while Omaha is very hot in the summer and bitterly cold in winter. While the mean temperature might be the same for both cities, there is greater variability in Omaha than in San Francisco. San Francisco's average temperature of 65°F is more representative, because it's probably closer to the actual temperature on most days than it would be in Omaha.

In poker, two players might win an average of $15 per hour. One of these players might be very aggressive and win large sums of money some days and lose quite a bit on others. A more conservative player might have more modest winning days — and more modest losing days, too. Both of these players, however, could have the same average.

The player who can achieve that win rate while putting less of his money at risk is better off. To measure these fluctuations, you need to know more about those *observed values* (the amount you won or lost each hour and recorded in your notebook) that were used to calculate your average wins or losses. Once you know that, you can easily measure just how well the mean *represents* those observed values. That measure helps *describe* the mean — that's where standard deviation comes in.

Standard deviation for the mathematically challenged

If you haven't taken a class in statistics, the term *standard deviation* might seem awfully frightening and foreboding. It's not, because you're about to discover a very easy way to calculate your standard deviation. After all, standard deviation is simply a way of indicating a typical amount by which all the values deviate, or vary, from the mean.

Think of the standard deviation as though it were an adjective modifying a noun (your hourly win rate).

Here's an example: "She's wearing a dress." Dress, of course, is the noun. You can modify that sentence by adding any one of the following adjectives: "She's wearing a (blue, businesslike, grandmotherly, revealing, designer, hideous) dress. See how substituting one adjective for another can radically change the meaning of that sentence? It's much the same with the relationship between the standard deviation and the mean.

Before we begin playing with examples, think about your own style of poker-play, and whether it encourages or discourages dramatic fluctuations. In other words, are you a *gambler?*

Do you usually have big swings from session to session, and are you happy with it? There's no right or wrong answer. Each player has an inherent amount of risk he or she is willing to tolerate. By monitoring their standard deviations as well as the average amount won per hour, players can choose to slightly reduce their hourly average winnings while substantially reducing their fluctuations.

How the standard deviation works

If there were no fluctuation (or *dispersion*) at all in a group (or *distribution*) of observed values, all of the values would be the same. No observed value would deviate from the mean. If, for example, it was exactly 72°F for six days in a row, the mean temperature would be 72 degrees for that period, and there would be no variance between high and low. Observed values usually deviate from the mean — some by a little, others by a lot.

Which of these sets of values would you expect to have a *larger* standard deviation?

Column A	Column B
(Mean=36)	(Mean=116)
6	111
24	114
37	117
49	118
64	120

(The right answer is Column A, and we show you why.)

Calculating the standard deviation

The values in Column A are more dispersed (they *deviate* more from the mean of 36) than those in Column B (with a mean of 116), so we can expect the standard deviation to be larger in Column A. Take a look at how this works out:

Column A		Column B	
Value	Deviation from 36	Value	Deviation from 116
6	−30	111	− 5
24	− 12	114	− 2
37	+1	117	+1
49	+13	118	+2
64	+28	120	+4

(Each Deviation column indicates the difference between the value and the mean.)

We can't simply take an average (arithmetic mean) of the deviations because they will always add up to zero — the negative deviations cancel out the positive. To overcome this difficulty, *square* each deviation by multiplying it by itself. This gets rid of the minus (negative) sign, because a negative multiplied by a negative equals a positive.

So for Column B, we have:

Deviation	Deviation squared
−5	25
−2	4
+1	1
+2	4
+4	16

The mean of the squared deviations is called the *variance*:

$$\text{Variance} = \frac{25 + 4 + 1 + 4 + 16}{5} = \frac{50}{5} = 10$$

The variance is a measure with uses of its own. However, it has a big disadvantage for everyday use: If the original values were in *dollars* (as they would be when you're calculating your hourly winnings or losses in a poker game), then the variance would be in *dollars squared!*

To get those theoretical (but hardly practical) "dollars squared" back into regular dollars, you need to take the square root of the variance. This result is the standard deviation.

The standard deviation of the distribution shown above equals 3.16228. (If you multiplied 3.16228 by itself, you'd get 10.)

The same calculations for the distribution in Column A yield a variance of 399.6, and a standard deviation of 19.99.

If you don't have a calculator handy, Table 9-1 is a handy guide of square roots to use. (You'll have to do a bit of estimating to come up with precise answers for numbers that fall between those listed on the table.)

Table 9-1		Square Root Quick Reference			
Number	Square root	Number	Square root	Number	Square root
1	1.00	14	3.74	90	9.49
2	1.41	15	3.87	100	10.00
3	1.73	16	4.00	110	10.49
4	2.00	17	4.12	120	10.95
5	2.24	18	4.24	130	11.40
6	2.45	19	4.36	140	11.83
7	2.65	20	4.47	150	12.25
8	2.83	30	5.48	160	12.65
9	3.00	40	6.32	170	13.04
10	3.16	50	7.07	180	13.42
11	3.32	60	7.75	190	13.78
12	3.46	70	8.37	200	14.14
13	3.61	80	8.94	300	17.32

Calculations made easier

Now that you've walked through the process of calculating a standard deviation and understand the process, here's how to simplify the calculations. Get a pocket calculator containing statistical functions. For less than $20, you can eliminate these time-consuming arithmetical steps.

Better yet, if you have a personal computer, use any of the popular spreadsheet programs to store your data. Set up properly, all you'll have to enter are your hourly winnings or losses. You then use the spreadsheet's statistical capabilities to calculate your average hourly results (the mean) and standard deviation on a cumulative basis.

Using standard deviation to analyze your poker results

When you begin to analyze your poker results, you'll see that you're really trying to maximize your hourly winnings while minimizing your standard deviation. In other words, you'd like to win as much as you possibly can while subjecting your bankroll to the smallest possible fluctuations.

Life on the edge: What's your risk tolerance?

From a statistical viewpoint, when you live on the edge you are flying in the face of minimizing your standard deviation. Because of this, you must come to terms with your own risk tolerance and how much of your bankroll you're willing to risk in order to gain some marginal boosts in earnings. If you're not comfortable at a certain level of risk, or you are playing on a short bankroll, you'd be better off minimizing your standard deviation than trying to maximize your winnings.

That situation, of course, is a real conundrum. If you choose to take the risks required to maximize winnings — such as getting all those extra bets in whenever you believe you have the best hand — you also tend to increase bankroll fluctuations simply because you're not going to come out on top in every one of those marginal situations.

In fact, because they're all very close calls, you'll probably wind up losing a lot of those confrontations. Let's face it, whenever you make a full house or some other equally monstrous hand, it's never a close call. You're going to get all the money you possibly can into the pot, because you're going to win the vast majority of those hands.

When you're out there on the edge, however, you're bound to lose nearly as many hands as you win. You're hoping, of course, to win more often than not, in order to maximize your winnings. But you're bound to experience fluctuations as you navigate this precarious path.

How to Reduce Fluctuations in a Poker Game

By avoiding marginal situations that require you to put additional money into the pot when it's a close call, you can play with a smaller bankroll. If you're a winning player, you'll eventually win just as much money. It will just take more hours at the table to reach your goals.

There is no right or wrong way to put money at risk in a poker game. Some people are comfortable with a high level of risk and have the bankroll to accommodate the fluctuations, which inevitably accompany this kind of play.

Others aren't so comfortable with high risk. In fact, you'll frequently hear players bemoaning the fact that they are at a table full of *live ones* (weak opponents who call too frequently). "I wish there were two or three good players at the table," they're likely to say, "because they bring more stability to the game and my good hands tend to hold up."

From a statistical perspective, this comment is a cry for a smaller standard deviation, along with an expression of those players' willingness to accept the slightly smaller win rate that goes along with it. Even without a knowledge of statistics, these players have learned that when you operate on the edge, the price you pay for an increased win rate is usually a significantly larger increase in the fluctuations you can expect.

As the win rate increases marginally, the standard deviation tends to fluctuate dramatically.

What does this mean to you as a player? Do you live on the edge, or seek whatever safety nets might be available? As long as you can afford to play the game you're in, this becomes a matter of personal choice. Remember:

- ✔ Only you can decide how much uncertainty you're comfortable with.

- ✔ If you elect to push every advantage, no matter how small, you can expect significantly higher fluctuations than you'd experience if you were willing to trade off that win rate for a bit more stability.

- ✔ If you elect to maximize your win rate, then you'll need a larger bankroll to play the game.

How Big Should Your Poker Bankroll Be?

How large a bankroll do you need to outlast any bad run of cards and ensure that you'll never go broke? This question comes up repeatedly whenever poker players start talking.

While "How big a bankroll . . ." is a complex issue that can't be resolved by applying a rule or formula, there is one fact you *can* bank on with absolute certainty: If you are not a winning player, your bankroll will never be large enough. To eliminate the possibilities of ever going broke, losing players need a big enough bankroll to outlast their life expectancy. Without one, they'll find themselves regularly infusing their playing stake with fresh cash.

A good rule for a reliable bankroll is 300 bets. If a bankroll of $6,000 to play $10–$20 Hold'em seems like a shockingly high number, we recommend reading *Gambling Theory and other Topics* by Mason Malmuth. It's an amazingly insightful work into some of the statistical realities that surround poker.

You'll find out how the ups and downs of fate can produce some extreme results over the short run, and even $6,000 may be a conservative estimate for that game.

But 300 big bets is not the whole story. If you were an outstanding player in a regular game composed of absolutely horrendous, extremely passive players (who seldom raised but always called until all hope, no matter how small, was completely dissipated), we're certain you could play on a much smaller bankroll without the risk of going broke. But few among us have been lucky enough to find a regular game filled with players who are that bad.

Even when you're a favorite in your game, you're probably not a prohibitive one. Here are some tips:

- ✔ If your opponents are generally good players, you probably need more than 300 big bets to hedge against going broke

- ✔ But for the average working professional player — the guy who plays every day trying to win between one and one-and-a-half big bets per hour — the conventional wisdom of a 300 big-bet bankroll makes good sense.

A fool and his money . . .

Some players really *do* have bankrolls that can outlast their life expectancy. In Southern California, where there's always lots of loose money at play in card casinos, these players have the derisive nickname "trust-fund pros." Many play every day and will swear to you that they are long-term winners. Trust-fund pros seldom deceive their opponents no matter how strongly they claim to be winning players. They delude only themselves, and their opponents know it.

The price of self-deception, however, can be high. Consider a 40-year-old trust-fund pro who plays $10–$20 and loses an average of one big bet per hour. If he plays 2,000 hours a year and lives to be 85, he can expect to lose $1.8 million by playing poker. Outside of a very select few, that's a lot of money by anyone's measure.

Suppose this particular player is not really *that* bad and loses only $3 per hour. He'll still run through $270,000 in the course of his playing lifetime. It's not as bad as $1.8 million, but still a stack of jack for most folks.

The best thing you can say about this player is that he did a good job of financial planning if he started with a $270,000 bankroll and spent his last dollar on his last day of life. (If he did a *perfect* job of financial planning, he'd work it so close to the nub that his check to the undertaker would bounce.)

Why many poker players wear hats

Players who are new to the poker scene might be puzzled by the sight of many players wearing hats (or sunglasses) at the poker table. For example, Amarillo Slim Preston probably wouldn't be recognized without his trademark Stetson. He, and many other top players, routinely wear hats — including baseball caps, sun visors, and cowboy hats — while playing poker.

The explanation usually has nothing to do with presenting a certain image, as much as it is a tactic geared toward fending off "tells" (tell-tale indications).

"I wear a big-brimmed Stetson so people won't see my eyes," Amarillo Slim explains. "See, a man's eyes usually give off what he's thinking. So, I keep my head down and my eyes hidden so I can keep 'em guessing."

Most players supplement their playing bankroll. While there are more than a few trust-fund pros out there, many players underwrite their poker with their paycheck. Poker, for the majority of players, is recreation — just a hobby — and if they lose today, it's no big deal. They can supplement their bankroll on payday, and as long as their losses do not exceed their discretionary income, they don't need to concern themselves with having an adequate bankroll.

For all the players who are not lifelong winners (and estimates suggest that 85 percent to 90 percent of all players do not beat the game), an adequate bankroll means either a trust fund big enough to sustain a lifetime of losses, or a paycheck that can cover their losses from one payday to the next — without risking the rent.

How professional players maintain their bankrolls

How much money do you need to keep from going broke if you're a professional and poker *is* your paycheck?

A professional poker player should realize that every dollar she wins will not be added to her bankroll. After all, she has to pay rent and buy groceries just like anyone else, and her only source of income is her winnings. Lose, and she pays her bills the only way she can: by dipping into her bankroll. But there's a limit to how deeply she can dig without putting herself in jeopardy.

Reducing your bankroll converts *capital* into *income* — and that distinction is an important one. Change too much capital into income and you've eaten your seed corn.

When a professional poker player on a short bankroll hits a protracted losing streak, she has only a few choices:

- ✔ Get a job in order to build up her bankroll (in which case she is reversing the process and converts income to capital)

- ✔ Become a *horse* by playing on a backer's money. (But a horse takes only a percentage of her winnings.)

- ✔ Quit poker entirely — or at least until she rebuilds her playing stake to a sizeable amount.

None of these options is very desirable for working professional poker players.

Bleeding off capital is not limited to poker players either. Businesses do it all the time. When veteran airline company Pan-Am was on the rocks, it sold its flagship building in New York City. Therefore, Pan-Am's balance sheet made it seem like the company had a good year. But you can convert capital into income only once, and then it's gone.

A poker player's bankroll *is* his capital. When poker is your business, you don't need money to build factories, or buy office buildings, trucks, machine tools, or computers. Money — in the form of a playing bankroll — is your capital. Lose some of it and you'll probably have to drop down and play at smaller limits, put the screws to your personal spending habits, and grind out an adequate bankroll. If you lose too much, you'll be so undercapitalized that you'll be ill-equipped to even compete at all.

Moving Up to Bigger Limits

Can you still take occasional shots at bigger games? Sure — and you probably should — as long as the game looks good and you think you can win. If anything, it will help you prepare for the next move up the poker ladder, once your bankroll grows large enough to play there regularly.

Limit poker, after all, is like a job. As long as you're a winning player, the more hours you put in, the more money you'll earn. And if you give yourself a pay raise by jumping to a bigger game, you ought to earn more in the long run. Just make sure you don't take risks you can't afford — like playing on a short bankroll. Without a sufficient cushion, all it takes is a few big losses to find yourself terminally downsized.

As for using money-management concepts — like setting stop-loss limits and quitting once you've won some predetermined amount of money — and thinking they will shield you against the possibilities of going broke, forget about it.

Parting advice on money management

This is the last word on money management. To paraphrase the poet John Keats, "This is all ye know, and all ye need know."

✓ Quitting once you've won a certain amount of money will neither stop your losses in the long run if you are a losing player nor protect your profits if you are a winner.

✓ Poor players will lose their money no matter what they do. Good players establish an expected hourly win rate whether or not they quit after they've pocketed a certain amount of winnings.

✓ Playing fewer hours by quitting when you're ahead isn't always the right strategy.

✓ If you're playing in a good game, and you are playing your best, stay in the game unless you have other obligations.

✓ If you're in a bad game, get out of it now — never mind if you're winning or not.

✓ If you're emotionally upset, stressed out, fighting the flu, or otherwise not at your best, you're better off not playing since your maladies will ultimately take themselves out on your bankroll.

Part III

Computers, Casinos, and Cardrooms

The 5th Wave   By Rich Tennant

"It's jacks or better to open, and the low card in your hand is wild...until my Mom walks in, and then we're playing Go Fish, got it?"

In this part . . .

You can play poker in more places than just the smoky back room of your best friend's house. People are playing poker against computer-generated opponents, and what's more exciting is that you can now use the Internet to join games with real, live opponents from around the world. Video poker requires special strategies, which we discuss, and we also tell you what goes on in poker tournaments, including the World Series of Poker.

Chapter 10

Poker Tournaments

*P*oker tournaments provide the opportunity to invest a relatively small amount of money in order to win a big payout. Tournaments have shown a great increase in popularity, with the premier tournament events occurring at the World Series of Poker in Las Vegas.

While we can't give you all of the secrets to winning a world championship poker tournament (both of us have visions of winning that some year), this chapter does offer some of the basics of tournaments and practical tips.

To get really good at poker, and to have a shot at the World Championship, you need to get experience. So plan to enter a number of smaller tournaments before you invest $10,000 to enter the World Championship. Oh, and if you do get there and win, don't forget to credit us for giving you the initial insight! (Acknowledgments and cash sent to the authors will be graciously accepted.)

Why Play Poker Tournaments?

We can think of many reasons to play in poker tournaments, probably as many as there are players who enter them. Poker tournaments can be exciting, lucrative, and invaluable for gaining experience. What follows are reasons why you should consider entering tournaments.

The thrill of victory

First of all, tournaments are fun. There's nothing like the thrill of competition that gets our competitive juices flowing. Sure it's nice to play in a cash game and walk away a winner at the end of the day. It's a terrific feeling to stuff the pockets of your jeans with your winnings, and to live — even for a moment — that famous line from Walter Tevis's *The Color of Money*. "Money won," Paul Newman's character Fast Eddie says as he reveals an ageless truth to Tom Cruise, "is twice as sweet as money earned."

Learn new games inexpensively

Aside and apart from the competition and the fun factor, tournaments are a terrific way to learn new games. Here's why: The game you want to learn might not be offered at betting limits that are comfortable for you. In fact, in smaller casinos, the game might not be available at all. Without tournaments, how can you ever learn to play Omaha/8, or Razz, or Seven-Stud/8 in a card casino that has enough room for only a few Hold'em and Stud tables?

If you enter low-buy-in tourneys, you can get plenty of play for a limited amount of money. You might get to play two or three hours of Razz for a $25 buy-in. That's not enough time to let you master the game, but it will be sufficient to help you decide if you enjoy it, and whether you have a feel for the game. (For details about buy-ins, see the section called "Buy-ins and fees" in this chapter.)

Tournaments can be a powerful learning tool because your investment is limited to the cost of the buy-in; and without mounting losses to worry about, you can devote your time to becoming more knowledgeable and more proficient at a new game.

The game is "pure"

Not only are your costs fixed when you enter a tournament, the game is invariably a bit more pure and uncluttered than cash games. More of your opponents are prone to play by the book in tournaments because they realize that once they lose their buy-in, it's *finis* — at least as far as that event is concerned. Tournament players follow the rules closely, so it's a bit easier for new players to see how theory works in practice. In a cash game, by comparison, the proper way to do things frequently get skewed by someone with an unlimited bankroll and a hankerin' to gamble.

Take on the champs

Finally, tournaments are a way to match your skills with some of the best players in the world. You're probably not going to see world-class players — the kind you've read about in *Card Player* or *Poker Digest* magazines — entering a $25 buy-in tournament in a small riverboat casino in Middle America, but you certainly will find players of this ilk entered in $100 buy-in tournaments in Las Vegas, Atlantic City, Connecticut, Mississippi, and California.

Nothing does as much for the confidence of a beginner than sitting at the same table with a big-name opponent and finding out that that player also faces the same challenges that you do.

Hey, you might even get lucky, catch a card and knock one of these big names out of the event. Then you can point to his picture in one of the magazines and say to all your friends, "He wasn't so tough. Why, I eliminated him when my set filled up on the river and just destroyed that pathetic flush of his!"

Poker Tournament Basics

Tournaments come in all types and sizes. They can consist of Hold'em, Seven-Card Stud, Lowball, Omaha, or other games. Here, we give you the basics regarding cost, betting structures, and the prize pool.

Buy-ins and fees

To participate in a tournament, you need to pay an entry fee called a *buy-in.* The entry fee buys you a seat in the tournament, where each player receives the same number of chips to begin with. The fee can range from a small amount ($100 is common) to a large amount ($10,000 for the World Championship).

Some tournaments are structured so that once you have lost the chips in front of you, you are out of the tournament. Others are *rebuy tournaments,* where you can buy more chips (after your initial buy-in) during a designated period of time — usually during the first hour or two of play, or during the first few betting limits.

Betting structures

In typical tournaments, the betting structure starts out with limits of $15–$30 or $25–$50. Betting limits then increase regularly, either every 30 minutes, 45 minutes, or hourly. The betting increase is often double the bet from the prior round.

In flop games, like Texas Hold'em and Omaha, two players also have to put up a certain amount of money before the cards are dealt. (These bets are usually called a *small blind* and a *big blind*.) The blinds are usually put up by the two people to the left of where the dealer button is placed (the button, of course, moves counterclockwise each hand). And the sizes of those blinds go up each time the betting rounds go up. So even if you never play a hand, the blinds eventually destroy your chip stock.

In some tournaments, no-limit or pot-limit rules apply:

✔ **No-limit tournaments:** In these tournaments, players can bet any amount of money in front of them.

✔ **Pot-limit tournaments:** Here, a bettor is allowed to bet an amount equal to the pot.

The prize pool

The prize pool in tournaments depends on the size of the entry fee and the number of players. The larger the overall pool of money available for splitting, the more opportunities will exist for finishing "in the money."

For example, if you have a tournament with a $500 buy-in and you get 400 entrants, you might have the top 18 finishers winning money. Table 10-1 shows a representative split for such a tournament (although the exact split varies from tournament to tournament).

Table 10-1	Splitting the Winnings ($500 Buy-in, 400 Entrants)	
Place	*Percentage of Pool*	*Dollar Range*
1st	40%	$80,000
2nd	20%	$40,000
3rd	10%	$20,000
4th	6%	$12,000
5th	4.5%	$9,000
6th	5%	$7,000
7th	2.5%	$5,000
8th	2%	$4,000

Place	Percentage of Pool	Dollar Range
9th	1.6%	$3,200
10th – 12th	1.2%	$2,400
13th – 15th	1.1%	$2,200
16th – 18th	1.0%	$2,000

So, if you are lucky enough to take first place, you can walk away with a cool $80,000!

That big prize is why tournaments have become so popular; there's the potential of a big bang for a small buck. Think of it this way: If you were a successful $20–$40 player — one who wins an average of one big bet per hour — that $80,000 first-place prize represents 2,000 hours of play in a cash game. Yes, you really can win an entire year's worth of money in one day!

But it's not all glamour and glory, either. Even top-notch tournament players can go a long time — years, even — without winning. Because tournament pay structures are so top-heavy (unless you are good enough to come in either first, second, or third periodically), the entry fees can deplete your bankroll sooner than you might expect.

For the very best tournament professionals, who seldom play cash games but travel the world from one major tournament to another, they have the added expense of sustaining themselves on the road. While travel may be broadening and playing poker for big bucks may seem glamorous, airfares, hotel bills, and the relatively high cost of eating all your meals out quickly mount up.

Satellite tournaments

Satellites are essentially mini-tournaments. A satellite is usually a tournament composed of one table, and the victor typically wins a seat in the main tournament. *Super-satellites* are multitable events where several seats are awarded for the main tournament. Satellites are a good way to get the feel of a game without committing as much money as would be required for the main tournament.

So check out playing in a satellite before jumping into the main tournament.

Key differences between tournaments and cash games

There are some very important differences between regular poker and tournament poker. Keep the following in mind if you want to successfully navigate the tournament landscape.

✔ **No right to buy more chips.** In most poker tournaments (except for tournaments that allow some "rebuy" of chips), you make do only with the chips you bought in with at the beginning. You don't usually have the option of replenishing your stack as you do in regular poker.

✔ **You can't walk away in the middle of the game.** Unlike a regular poker game, you can't pick up your chips and cash in your winnings if you get tired or feel like keeping some profits. The only way to win in tournaments is to be one of the finalists.

✔ **The players tend to be better in tournaments.** Players who enter tournaments, especially higher stakes tournaments, tend to play better than the players you might ordinarily find in cash games. And players who participate in tournaments often have entered a number of tournaments and have some relevant experience.

The Relationship Between Blinds and Betting Structure

One of the key differences between tournament poker and cash games is the relationship between the blinds and the betting structure. This difference is so significant, that many of the strategies that are employed in tournaments are directly derived from this difference.

Take a look at cash games first. If you were going to play $20–$40 Hold'em, you'd probably buy in to the game with approximately $800 in chips. That's common. Some players will enter the game with $500 and others with $1,000, but $800 seems to be typical. That $800 is the equivalent of 20 big bets and provides the opportunity to play quite a few hands before having to reach into your pockets for an additional buy-in.

In cash games, the blinds and betting structure remain fixed, and you can buy more chips anytime you're not involved in a hand.

The escalating blinds

In tournament poker, you can't buy more chips at any old time. Unless it's during a tournament's rebuy period, once your chips are gone, so are you. If that's not enough, the blinds (or antes, as the case may be) escalate at fixed intervals.

If the blinds and antes did not escalate at fixed intervals, tournaments would take days to complete. After all, most players would wait for outstanding hands before entering a pot. And what fun would that be? It would make poker the equivalent of watching paint dry, and nobody wants that.

Because blinds and antes escalate, one is forced to play. When a player's chips have been depleted, and she will be facing the blind in a hand or two, it may be the best course of action for her to go all in with as little as ace-anything (an ace plus whatever else is in the hand). After all, if she doesn't, she'll have to risk going all-in with the random cards she'll receive in the blind.

In the early stages of a poker tournament, the structure is similar to a cash game. Suppose 200 players buy into a tournament and each receives $500 in chips. The betting limits during the first round might be $15–$30. Under these conditions, if a player flops a *four flush* (four cards of the same suit), he can afford to take the chance and draw for it.

In the later stages of a tourney, however, taking such a chance often isn't worth the risk. Suppose you are one of the last eight remaining players. Since 200 players bought in initially, there was $100,000 in tournament chips in play. If you divide that equally among the remaining eight players, the par value is $12,500. In other words, if a player has precisely $12,500 at this stage of the tournament, he is *average* by definition.

The end game

So let's say you are one of the last remaining participants of the orginal 200 entrants in a tournament. By then, the blinds might have escalated to $1,000–$2,000. Even though our hero might have precisely $15,500 in chips, he has only 6¼ big bets left — a far cry from the 16⅔ big bets he had when he began the tourney with $500 in chips at the $15–$30 betting limits.

Now flush and straight draws become dicey propositions. In most cases you don't want to risk elimination on a speculative hand. If you are to be eliminated, you want to have *something* that stands a chance of holding up. Even a mediocre pair can do in a pinch. A flush draw or a straight draw that does not hold up will not win very many pots.

The Hal Fowler story

On any given day, a rank amateur can defeat a great player, even a world champion. It's happened several times — particularly, in poker tournaments. An amateur player even won poker's world championship once.

In 1979, an unknown poker player from California named Hal Fowler seemed hopelessly overmatched in experience and skill as the final day of play at the *World Series of Poker* began.

Fowler received a fortuitous string of favor at several critical stages of the tournament that left the poker elite shaking their heads in stunned disbelief. Time after time, Fowler hit inside straights, made second pairs, and completed flushes until he finally eliminated his last opponent. Fowler won the world championship and remains the only amateur player ever to win poker's most coveted title.

If you are very short-stacked (that is, you don't have a lot of chips left), the Hobson's choice that you're confronted with is either to go all-in of your own volition with a hand like A-4 of different suits, or be forced to go all-in on the blind — when all you will be holding are random cards.

Be extremely selective; be very aggressive

Two opposing forces are at work here in late stages of tournaments, and they are both caused by the changing nature of the relationship between the inexorably escalating blinds and the betting structure: One force is a push that says, "Be aggressive! You have to take a stand because you don't have very many chips left." The countervailing measure is pulling at you, saying "Be selective. You can't afford to be eliminated without a good hand."

The eternal problem, of course, is that you seldom know with any certainty whether to wait for a better hand, or make your stand with the cards you've been dealt. Therein lies the art of tournament poker. But it's the continuing escalation of the blinds and their relationship to the betting limits that makes tournament poker what it is.

Key Mistakes Made in Poker Tournaments

Players make numerous mistakes in poker tournaments. The action can be fast and you may encounter new situations and difficult decisions. This section highlights some common mistakes.

Trying to win too early

Some players gamble aggressively early on, hoping to get a major chip advantage, and then keep playing aggressively to win it all early. But gambling too much, rather than changing gears and slowing down, can often cause you to crash and burn.

Defending your blind too much

Many players try to defend their blinds too much. If you have just a mediocre hand, consider folding it instead of matching the bet and getting tied to a seemingly cheap hand.

Playing too tight

While you generally shouldn't be super aggressive in late stages, it's also a mistake to play overly conservative just to hang on for a final table finish. Playing too tight can unnecessarily erode your stack of chips because in the later stages of a tournament, the blind structure is usually very high in relation to the number of chips in play. And if you play too tight in the early stages so that you survive, you probably won't end up with enough chips in later hands to be a serious contender.

Playing a marginal hand after the flop

Don't feel that you have to play a marginal hand after the flop. Even if in Hold'em you flop a pair, but your kicker card is weak, consider laying it down if a solid player bets into you.

Being unaware of other players' chip stacks

As you get near the end of a tournament, it's a huge mistake if you are not carefully paying attention to the stacks of chips that other players hold. Knowing their chip position can help you make key decisions, such as whether or not to even play a hand.

For example, assume there are only eight players remaining and you have a medium number of chips, and two players have very low stacks of chips. At this point, you may very well want to play very conservatively and let those two players get knocked out ahead of you. Remember, each player who is eliminated promotes you one rung higher on the pay ladder. Don't forget, however, that the big payoff is for first place, so be willing to take reasonable shots.

Tournament Tips from a World Champion

Tom McEvoy, the 1983 World Champion of Poker, has numerous tips for playing winning tournament poker. Here are 10 tips from Tom's great book, *Tournament Poker*.

✔ **You need to adjust your play throughout the tournament.** There is more than one winning style of tournament play. You need to keep in mind the stage of the tournament and your stack of chips. For example, while you may play loose early on and accumulate a lot of chips, you should consider slowing down later on to preserve your chip lead and let other players get knocked out.

✔ **Always be aware of the chip counts of your opponents.** Particularly in later stages, you want to know where you stand relative to the other players. You may want to push someone with a short stack all-in, or you may want to let other players knock each other out for a while.

✔ **You need to play the player and his stack.** Even with a big stack, you must still use judgment and choose your spots. Be aware of which players have loosened up and those who have tightened up to survive to the final table. Short stacks will sometimes raise with less than premium hands, so you can comfortably call them if you have a big stack.

✔ **Never leave a short stack with only one or two remaining chips when you can put him all-in.** In the later stages of a tournament, a few chips can multiply quickly because of the high limits, so don't be nice and not put a player all-in when you have the opportunity to do so cheaply. Be cruel!

✔ **You must make correct decisions in the blinds.** Correct decisions on your blind hands can often spell the difference between success and failure in a tournament. Playing the blind correctly requires extreme prudence and discretion.

✔ **Take advantage of tight play.** When everyone else is playing tight in the later stages of a tournament you can take more chances and be more aggressive.

- **Bluffing is an important weapon in No-Limit Hold'em.** Bluffing can be very powerful in No-Limit Hold'em. The larger your stack, the more intimidating your bluff.

- **Study your opponents.** You must study your opponents especially when you are not actively involved in the hand. You want to get a sense of how loose or tight they are and how they play, for future reference.

- **Learn to survive.** Learning how to survive long enough to give yourself a chance to get lucky is essential. Anyone who has won a tournament has gotten lucky *during* various stages of that event. But in order to maximize your opportunity to get lucky, you must hone your survival skills.

- **Stay calm, cool, and collected.** You are going to get some bad beats in a tournament. You must maintain a tough mental attitude and not go on tilt. Many players lose a few hands, and then both their discipline and their stacks begin to crumble. Don't be that type of person, and do take advantage of that type of player.

A Johnny Moss story

At one time, poker legend Johnny Moss was flat broke. As fate would have it, there was a big poker game in town and Moss wanted a piece of it. Determined to get into the game, he went to a local bank to borrow money to play.

Moss strolled into the bank and asked to speak with the loan officer. Within no time, a young man came out from behind a big fancy desk and asked how he could be of assistance. Moss asked the loan officer for a $10,000 loan — a small fortune in those days, especially in 1950s west Texas.

"Tell me Mr. Moss, what type of collateral do you have?" the loan officer asked.

"None, except for my skill," Moss said.

"And what skill is that?" the loan officer asked, his interest piqued by such an incredible request.

"I'm a professional gambler," Moss replied.

The loan officer was stunned.

"Let me get this straight. You mean, you want to borrow $10,000 from the bank — to gamble with?"

"That's right."

At that very instant, one of the bank's most influential men, who was on the board of directors, walked in and immediately recognized Moss. The bank official had played with Moss many times and knew Moss was as honorable as they come.

"Are you doing business with us, Johnny?" the bank official asked.

"This man wants $10,000 to gamble with," the loan officer explained.

"Give him $20,000 if he wants it," was the bank official's reply.

Moss received the loan and paid it back soon thereafter.

Cutting a Deal at the Final Table

Often, the survivors at the final table of a poker tournament cut deals. For example, if there are only four players left and the payouts are first place, 40 percent; second place, 20 percent; third place, 10 percent; fourth place, 5 percent; and the remaining places, 25 percent, then the last four players could agree to a different cut no matter how the tournament officially ends.

Deals are usually made when there are huge differences between the prize money and when the chips are all reasonably close.

Should you cut a deal? Well, you need to assess the following:

- ✔ The quality of the remaining players
- ✔ The relative chip counts
- ✔ Your experience level in tournaments versus the experience levels of other players
- ✔ The type of deal offered

Making a deal can make a lot of sense, guaranteeing you a good win. But it does limit your upside. How much of a gambler are you?

The fairest way to cut a deal

When there are just two of you left, you can easily cut a deal that's fair for both parties — regardless of how many chips each player may have. Take a look at the prize pool structure in Table 10-1, where the winner walks away with $80,000 and second place wins $40,000.

Just suppose you're in that situation. From a starting field of 400 entrants there are only two of you left. After hours and hours of play, you've come this far. Regardless of whether you win it or finish second, you can count on a nice payday.

But wait, there's a big, big difference between the first-place prize of $80,000 and the second-place payout of $40,000. And unless you have an insurmountable chip lead, things can change very rapidly in the end game of a tournament.

The blinds are likely to be extremely high in relation to your chip count — yes, even if you're leading — and because of it, you are forced to take chances. When you're playing for very large sums of money, and your skill has thus far enabled you to best all but one of your opponents, the last thing you'll probably want to do is gamble.

Here's the easiest way to cut a deal that's fair to both players. Remember that you are each guaranteed a payoff of $40,000, since with just two players remaining, neither of you can finish worse than second.

There's $120,000 in prize money at stake, and each of you has locked up $40,000. You're now playing for the difference between first and second place, which is also $40,000. Let's assume you have 55 percent of the chips in play, and your opponent has the remaining 45 percent. To be fair, all you have to do is prorate the $40,000 that's being contested by the relative chip counts:

> 55 percent of $40,000 is $22,000. Add that to the $40,000 you have already locked up, and the chip leader should receive $62,000.

The person in second place, who holds 45 percent of the chips in play, should receive $18,000. When added to his $40,000 in *lock-up* money, it amounts to a $58,000 payday.

When the chip count is identical

When the chip count is identical or nearly identical, players often agree to take an even share of the money after cutting out a small portion to play for. If you and your opponent each had the same number of chips, you might agree to lock up $55,000 each, and play it out for the remaining $10,000. This way each player hedges his bets and is ensured of a $55,000 payday. The winner, of course, will receive $65,000.

No, it's not quite as attractive as an $80,000 payday, but it's a whole lot better than taking home $40,000 because lady luck gazed unfavorably on you that day.

When more than two players make a deal, the mathematics becomes quite complicated. When this happens, deals are usually struck by negotiation rather than computed arithmetically.

Issues with Payoff Structures

There's always been a lot of discussion in the poker community about the relatively top-heavy nature of tournament pay structures. Ask a tournament poker player which she prefers, and she'll invariably say something like, "Let's keep it like it is, and reward the winner."

The ethics of deal making

Some in the poker community are concerned about the perception of impropriety that surrounds deal making. After all, you don't see PGA golfers making deals prior to the final round on Sunday, do you? Others in the poker community are of the "So what; it's our money, isn't it" school of thought. And they're right. Poker tournaments don't have sponsors like the PGA tour. Poker players *do* put their own money at risk, and what's wrong with hedging a risky proposition anyway?

Still others say that poker will never attract corporate sponsorship unless they eliminate deal making at the final table, because even the mere perception of impropriety will send sponsors fleeing like a herd of stampeding cattle.

Expanded payoff structures

Professional poker player Mike Sexton, who founded the Poker Tournament of Champions, is a man who would love to see corporate sponsorship of tournament poker. He decided to attack the questions of deal making and top-heavy payout structure head-on.

Entrants in the 1999 Tournament of Champions were asked to vote on whether they would prefer to see the traditional payout format — the one we used for an illustration earlier in this chapter — or an expanded payout structure put in place. The expanded structure would award 35 percent to the first-place finisher instead of 40 percent. The second- and third-place finishers would also receive slightly less, but in return, the payoff would be extended and more players would be paid.

When the votes were tallied, the expanded payoff structure was the overwhelming choice, by a nearly 65 percent–35 percent result. Maybe the fact that deal making is forbidden at the Tournament of Champions is what led the majority of entrants to hedge their bets by weighing-in on the side of an expanded pay structure. Perhaps it's just a signal of changing times in the poker community. Or maybe the majority of players have all come to realize that corporate sponsorship — and there's not a player out there who wouldn't want to be playing for someone else's money rather than his or her own — won't come about until the winner is decided by competition rather than negotiation.

Where to Find Information about Tournaments

Poker tournaments are all over the place. You can find them in major casinos, on cruise ships, and at local card clubs. Here are a few places where you can find out current information:

- ✔ *Card Player Magazine:* This magazine, which comes out every two weeks, has extensive listings and advertisements concerning poker tournaments. You can subscribe by writing *Card Player*, 3140 S. Polaris Ave. #8, Las Vegas, Nevada 89102, Phone: (702) 871-1720. Web address: www.cardplayer.com. *Card Player Magazine* is distributed free in many card rooms.

- ✔ *Poker Digest Magazine:* This magazine comes out every two weeks, and contains poker tournament information and advice. You can subscribe by writing *Poker Digest*, 1455 E. Tropicana #300, Las Vegas, Nevada 89119, Phone: (702) 740-2273. Web address: www.pokerdigest.com. *Poker Digest Magazine* is distributed free in many card rooms.

  Poker Digest and *Card Player* are published on alternate weeks, so there is always some fresh reading material for those who are interested in improving their poker.

- ✔ www.pokersearch.com: This Web site has listings of upcoming tournaments with useful hyperlinks to additional information.

- ✔ rec.gambling.poker: This site contains the premier message board for postings about poker. It often contains timely information about poker events and current activities occurring in poker tournaments.

If you really want to hone your tournament skills, or even just think about the World Series of Poker, check out the following books.

- ✔ *Tournament Poker,* by Tom McEvoy (Cardsmith Publishing). Tom McEvoy, a former World Champion in the World Series of Poker, wrote this insightful book with special tips on Hold'em, Seven-Card Stud, Satellite Strategies, and Frequently Asked Questions About Tournaments.

- ✔ *Sklansky on Poker,* by David Sklansky (Two Plus Two Publishing). David Sklansky, the noted poker expert, has a special section in this book on tournament play. The book has some particularly insightful sections on freeze-outs, general concepts, implied odds, Hold'em situations, and playing Razz.

✔ *Championship No-Limit and Pot-Limit Hold'Em,* by T.J. Cloutier and Tom McEvoy (Cardsmith Publishing). This book has some excellent advice on winning major no-limit and pot-limit tournaments, setting up and trapping opponents, betting strategies, when to fold, and getting inside of your opponents' heads.

✔ *Poker Tournament Tips From the Pros,* by Shane Smith (Cardsmith Publishing). This book is subtitled, *How to Win Low-Limit Poker Tournaments,* and that's exactly what it's about. If you're new to poker tournaments or even if you are experienced but play primarily in low buy-in events, this book is filled with tips that author Smith gathered from some of the best known tournament players in the business.

T.J. talks

T.J. Cloutier, one of the premier tournament players in the world, was once asked a question: "What do you think the great tournament players have in common?"

"I think they're all different," Cloutier replied. "What works for me might not work for somebody else. (But) total concentration and knowing the players — they all have that."

(From *Championship Omaha,* by T.J. Cloutier.)

Chapter 11

Video Poker

*B*y now you have digested most of this book, and you've vastly increased your skills at the poker table. Now you're ready to apply all of that newly gained poker knowledge to video poker. Right?

Sorry! The first thing you need to understand about video poker is that it is *not* poker. Although some similarities exist between the on-screen game and the traditional cards-in-hand version, important differences make video poker attractive to anyone who doesn't want to work so hard to gain an edge.

But everyone occasionally loses a big pot that he or she expected to win and needs a diversion to regain composure. Why not a *profitable* diversion? Also, many poker players are accompanied by their spouse or a friend who blows their money on the slots while waiting. Why not make *their* time profitable (or at least cut the expected losses to a minimum)? For many people, video poker fits the bill perfectly, and it may even become your next gambling love.

This chapter shows how anyone can become a winner at video poker. What's that? You say you hit a royal flush just last month? Of course, and almost everyone hits an exhilarating jackpot occasionally, but over time most have a net loss. (So how did you think the casinos pay for the bright lights?) With just a little effort, however, you can be a winner. By seeking out the good machines (defined later in this chapter) and following a few simple playing rules, you can greatly reduce your expected loss rate, and in some cases, you can gain a real edge over the casino and have an expected win rate instead.

The Basics of Video Poker

Video poker shares some of the characteristics of a slot machine. The gambling gear itself is housed in a similar cabinet, and most have a coin slot and a payout hopper. Many have a slot-club card reader and/or a bill acceptor. The important difference is that on a reel slot you just pull the handle and hope for the best, but video poker involves an element of skill.

To the novice player, the main attraction of video poker is the prospect of pitting wits against the machine in fast action with a chance at a big jackpot. To the skilled player, however, the appeal is that some games offer an opportunity for a long-term profit. Just as in a live poker game, you can expect a considerable amount of risk and luck involved in the short term, but a player's skill can make the difference between a winner and a loser in the long run.

Unlike the no-brainer reel slots, the maximum payback of any video poker game can be ascertained from the game's payoff schedule. No, you don't have to do any math; just compare the payoff schedule shown on the glass or the screen of every machine with the tables below. A game's rated *payback* — the statistically projected return on money played — generally assumes perfect play. But leave perfection to the pros; we won't even attempt it here, yet we will easily get very close to the rated payback for a much higher return than is possible on any other low stakes casino game. The rated payback of each game is discussed in the individual sections that follow in this chapter.

Getting started

First, find an attractive game by comparing its payoff schedule with Tables 11-1 and 11-2. Then, insert your player's card. The slot-club rebate may make up a significant portion of your expected win rate, or it may even turn a negative expectation game into a positive situation. If the casino has a slot club and you don't have a card, you should get one before you begin playing.

Nearly every casino has a slot club, and membership is free. Before playing, go to the slot-club booth, fill out an application, and get your card. You may want to ask for two cards so you have a spare in case you leave one behind, or if you want to play two machines at once. In some casinos, your friend or spouse would be on the same account, and in others each of you would have a separate account.

Slot clubs have a variety of inventive names, but they all serve the same purpose of enticing you to play more at that casino by offering comps (compensation) and/or cash rebates for your play. Check out the club brochure for information on what you can get for your loyalty to that casino.

Playing hands

Now you're ready to play. To begin a hand, insert the number of coins you want to play. Although most machines accept from one to five coins, some accept only three or four, some accept eight or ten, and a few accept up to 100 coins. Always play at least the number of coins required to qualify for the full per-coin payoff on all jackpots (five coins on most machines).

After inserting the coins or pressing the Max Bet button, the machine "deals" your first five cards. Most machines immediately tell you if you have a dealt paying hand by beeping and displaying the type of hand. Select the cards that you want to keep by pressing the Hold buttons. There is one Hold button for each card on the screen. On most machines, you can press the same Hold (or Hold/Cancel) button again to deselect a card. The word HELD appears on the screen above, below, or across the center of each card selected.

Some of the newer machines have touch-sensitive screens, enabling you to select which cards to hold simply by touching their images on the screen. You can also touch the screen for the Bet and Deal functions, but most serious players speed up the process by using the buttons for all functions.

You can sometimes break up a paying hand that's been dealt. For example, you may choose to break a dealt flush or straight in favor of a four-card royal flush draw — most of the strategy depends upon the actual game.

When you're satisfied with your selection, press the Deal/Draw button to replace the discards in an attempt to make a winning hand (or to improve an existing winner), just as you would do in a live draw poker game. The game is then over. If you end up with a winning hand, the machine automatically pays according to the payoff schedule.

Most modern machines provide for credit play. That is, your wins step up a credit counter on the screen instead of automatically dropping coins, and you may bet from those credits rather than insert coins for your next play. If you are playing at over 100 percent expected payback, your average win rate is in direct proportion to your playing speed. So, always use credit play for maximum speed. Some machines feature Max Bet buttons for playing the maximum number of coins, or Replay or Deal buttons for requesting the same number of coins as for the preceding play. In either case, the deal for your next hand begins when you press one of the buttons.

The ranking of hands in video poker

For basic video poker games, the ranking of hands is the same as we describe for live table poker throughout this book. The only differences are in Deuces Wild where five-of-a-kind, the wild royal flush, and four 2s are defined as additional hand types inserted between the straight flush and natural royal flush. See "Deuces Wild" later in this chapter for details about these additional hand types.

Video Poker versus Regular Poker

Video poker uses the same 52-card deck (or 53 cards with the joker) as table poker, and most video poker games deal the cards pretty much like the (almost extinct) table game of five-card draw. Also, the hand ranks and the card combinations that make up those hands are generally the same, but the similarity ends there.

So just how is video poker different? Consider the following:

✔ In video poker, the house is banking the game, yet the machine is not trying to beat your hand. The mechanical game is more like solitaire. Attempting to bluff or to "read" your opponent is pointless because no other players are involved.

✔ In live poker, the distinction between a straight flush and a royal flush is slim. Except for rare cases in Hold'em, either flush is almost certain to win the entire pot every time, but a royal flush in video poker pays at least 16 times as much as a straight flush.

✔ In live poker, aces up (two pair) is a much stronger hand than 7s up; in video poker all two pair hands pay the same.

✔ In live poker, any four-of-a-kind always beats a lower four-of-a-kind. In some video poker games, four 2s, 3s or 4s pays more than four 5s through four kings. Of course, special cases are exceptions, such as four 2s in a Deuces Wild video poker game.

✔ You can't get a *bad beat* in video poker. Your flush can't lose to that full house on another player's machine. It will always win according to the payoff schedule.

✔ Some plays that may be correct in table poker become costly mistakes in video poker. (See "Six Mistakes to Avoid in Video Poker" later in this chapter.)

Video poker myths

There are many myths surrounding all gambling games, and video poker is no exception. Here are some of the most common myths about video poker, and the truth behind each myth.

Myth: Look for a machine that hasn't hit recently. It's probably due for a jackpot.

Fact: You may have heard that a royal flush occurs about once per 40,000 plays, but that doesn't mean that a machine can be "due" to hit. No matter now recently or how long since a machine has paid a jackpot, the random number generator used to shuffle the cards has no memory, so the probability of a royal on the next play is always about 1 in 40,000. Yes, any game can run "hot" or "cold" for short periods but there is no way of knowing ahead of time when any such streak will begin or end.

Myth: The machines are set for a specific payback, so the way you play doesn't matter.

Fact: This is only a lazy player's excuse for not learning how to be a winner. You may as well say it doesn't matter how you play live table poker since the cards are shuffled, thus giving everyone an equal chance at a good hand. Skill is a big factor at video poker, just as in live table poker, and the good games can exist only because the majority of players give up about 2 percent of the potential payback by not learning an accurate strategy. As Mark Twain said: "Let us be thankful for the fools. But for them, the rest of us could not succeed."

Myth: Because the machines are random, you can't possibly beat the games.

Fact: "Random" and "beatable" are not synonymous. For example, suppose you were banking a craps game with honest dice. The outcome of each event would be random, but the house edge would assure that you would be a winner in the long run. Some video poker games give you the same opportunity to bet on the winning side of the game.

Myth: Okay, so the machines are random, but what if they were biased so that high cards or wild cards come up a bit less often than expected?

Fact: You may find that sort of stacking in foreign casinos, on cruise ships, and so on, but Nevada and Louisiana regulations mandate that each unseen card in video poker must have an equal probability of appearing just as if the cards were being dealt from a well-shuffled, real deck. This makes it possible to work out an optimum playing strategy and to determine the expected payback using that strategy. For some games, that expected minimum payback exceeds 100 percent, so the game is beatable. Because most manufacturers want to be certified in Nevada, all of their machines shipped anywhere almost certainly meet these requirements.

Myth: If you want to bet only 25¢ total, play five coins on a nickel machine rather than one coin on a quarter machine.

Fact: That is good advice if the 5¢ and 25¢ games have the same payoff schedule. Often, however, you're confronted with full-pay quarter machines but only short-pay nickel games. You give up about 1.5 percent of the long-term payback by playing only one coin (since you don't qualify for the big royal jackpot), but a short-pay schedule is usually even more costly. If you're going to play anyway, it's better to play one quarter on a full-pay machine than five nickels on a short-pay machine. In any case, video poker is almost always better than the reel slots, but it's best to always play five coins on a full-pay game.

These characteristics primarily make video poker a big winner for the casino, even on games that offer over 100 percent payback. The following sections show just how easy it is to keep the house edge to a minimum. You may even gain an advantage over the house with the prospects of being a long-term winner.

Jacks-or-Better Video Poker

The first step in winning takes place before you even start to play. Only a small percentage of the wide variety of games can be beaten in the long run, so you must first figure out how to recognize those games. Differentiating between full-pay and short-pay games is extremely important. Table 11-1 shows the five-coin payoff schedule for full-pay Jacks-or-Better Draw poker.

Table 11-1	Payoffs in Jacks-or-Better Video Poker
Type of Hand	*Payoff in Number of Coins*
Royal flush	4,000
Straight flush	250
Four-of-a-kind	125
Full house	45
Flush	30
Straight	20
Three-of-a-kind	15
Two pair	10
Pair of jacks or better	5

We note only the five-coin payoffs because you don't qualify for the full 4,000-coin (800-for-1 odds) payoff for a royal flush with fewer than five coins, thus cutting the long-term payback by up to 1.5 percent. You typically get only 250-for-1 odds ($62.50 for a royal for one quarter, compared to $1,000 for five quarters).

This machine is commonly called a 9/6 machine because of the 9-for-1 payoff for a full house and 6-for-1 for a flush. The most common type of short-pay game is an 8-to-5 payoff schedule. That is, the payoff for a full house is reduced to 8-for-1 and the payoff for a flush is reduced to 5-for-1, thus cutting the game's payback to only 97.3 percent. Some casinos are more subtle, cutting the payoff elsewhere, so check the whole payoff schedule before starting to play. This game offers 99.5 percent or higher payback and is currently available in many gambling areas in 5¢, 25¢, 50¢, $1 and higher denominations.

Knowing how to play Jacks-or-Better accurately is just as important as finding a full-pay machine. The good news: the game is much easier than live poker to play skillfully.

Here are a few rules to live by when playing Jacks-or-Better:

- ✔ **Rule #1:** Never break any made pay of two pair or better, with one exception. Break anything but a pat straight flush for any four-card royal.

- ✔ **Rule #2:** Break a high pair only for a four-card royal or any four-card straight flush.

- ✔ **Rule #3:** Break a low pair only for K-Q-J-10, any three-card royal, or any four-card flush or straight flush.

- ✔ **Rule #4:** Break a four-card flush or straight draw for any three-card royal.

- ✔ **Rule #5:** If you have both a four flush and a four straight, go for the flush.

- ✔ **Rule #6:** Break A-K-Q-J only for three suited high cards.

- ✔ **Rule #7:** Break any three of A, K, Q and J for any two suited high cards.

- ✔ **Rule #8:** Hold all high cards (jacks through aces), but discard the ace from A-K-Q, A-K-J, or A-Q-J.

Always follow the first rule that applies to the cards dealt. For example, if you are dealt Q♠J♣10♣Q♣8♣ (in any order), you have a high pair (queens),which is a made payoff. You also have a three-card royal and a four-card inside straight flush draw. Rule #2 says to break a high pair for *any* four-card straight flush. Rule #4 says to break a four-card flush or straight for a three-card royal, but it doesn't say anything about breaking a four-card straight flush, so the best play is to hold everything except the Q♠. If the other four cards are not all suited, hold the pair of queens. (Daddy told you never to draw to an inside straight, didn't he?) If the 8♣ were any lower club, you would have only a four-card flush rather than a straight flush draw; this would make the three-card royal better than the flush draw (Rule #4), but still not as good as the pair of queens (Rule #2).

Just how does 99.5 percent payback affect this situation? Subtracting from 100 percent, we see that we can expect to lose 0.5 percent of our bets. If you are playing a five-coin quarter machine at 500 hands per hour (a fairly typical rate), you are wagering $1.25 X 500 = $625 per hour. In casino lingo, this is your "action." On average, you can expect to lose one-half of one percent of that, or $625 X 0.005 = $3.125 per hour. But, of course, it's impossible to lose fractional cents, or anything other than a multiple of $1.25 for that matter. In the short run, your actual results will fluctuate widely above and below that figure, but if you play long enough you can expect an average loss rate of a little over $3 per hour.

Although we simplified the strategy a bit for this book, the strategy rules will yield close to 99.5 percent payback on a game with the payoff schedule shown in Table 11-1, thus cutting a hunch player's loss rate by as much as 80 percent. A good slot-club rebate or comps can turn this into a net winning situation. Even with such simple rules, your expected payback is very close to the theoretical maximum, and much better than most other games in the casino.

If you want the complete strategy that can increase your odds of winning, check out the book *Video Poker — Optimum Play,* by Dan Paymar (see "Further Readings" at the end of this chapter).

Deuces Wild: The Best Game for Beginners

Deuces Wild is the most widely available game that offers significantly over 100 percent long-term payback, giving you the opportunity to actually make a long-term profit when playing video poker. As a bonus, the game features the four 2s mini-jackpot that can be expected about once per ten hours of play. Table 11-2 provides the five-coin payoff schedule for full-pay Deuces Wild.

Table 11-2	Payoffs in Deuces Wild Video Poker
Type of Hand	*Payoff in Number of Coins*
Royal flush	4,000
Four 2s	1,000
Wild royal flush	125
Five-of-a-kind	75
Straight flush	45
Four-of-a-kind	25
Full house	15
Flush	10
Straight	10
Three-of-a-kind	5

Many people avoid Deuces Wild because there's no payoff for a high pair or even for two pair. Don't let this scare you away. With four wild cards, three-of-a-kind occurs more often than a high pair in Jacks-or-Better or other games with no wild cards. The number of final hands with no payoff is almost exactly the same (roughly 54 percent) in both games.

Note the 25-for-5 payoff for four-of-a-kind *(quads)*, which is very important because fully one-third of the total payback of this game comes from quads. Cutting the quads payoff only one unit (to 20-for-5) cuts the payback by 6 percent; with rare exceptions, increases elsewhere in the schedule never make up for this shortfall.

Many players find Deuces Wild easy to learn because the strategy is broken down according to the number of 2s in the dealt hand. Table 11-3 offers strategies for winning in Deuces Wild.

Table 11-3	Strategies for Deuces Wild Games
Number of 2s	*Draw to the 2s Alone, Except Hold . . .*
4	Since a hand with four dueces cannot be improved, we recommend holding all five cards to minimize the chances of an error.
3	Wild royal flush; five-of-a-kind
2	Any four-of-a-kind or better made pay; any four-card royal, or any suited 6-7, 7-8, 8-9, or 9-10
1	Any made pay, except always draw to any four-card royal flush or any suited 5-6-7, 6-7-8, 7-8-9, 8-9-10, or 9-10-J; any four-card straight flush (including inside draws); a three-card royal flush (but not with an ace); any suited 6-7, 7-8, 8-9, or 9-10
0	Any made pay, except always draw to a four-card royal flush; any four-card straight flush (including an inside draw); any three-card royal flush; one pair (discard a second pair, it doesn't matter which); any four-card flush or fully open-ended four-card straight; any three-card straight flush (including all inside draws); Q-J, Q-10, or J-10 suited; any four-card inside straight (except A-3-4-5)

With Table 11-3 in mind, remember these suggestions:

✔ Never discard a deuce. This includes holding a one-deuce wild royal flush rather than drawing one card for the natural royal flush. The 2s are included in the hand names. For example, 2wK♥10♥ is a three-card royal flush. "2w" means "any deuce" because the suit of a wild card is immaterial.

✔ Always hold the card combination according to the first rule that applies to the dealt cards. If you don't have any of the combinations described in Table 11-3, then you must redraw all five cards.

For example, if you are dealt 2wQ♣6♣2w7♣, look under the two-deuce rules. You have a made flush, but that's not even listed since it would be a waste of the two deuces! The best play is to hold everything except the queen, giving you a fully open-ended straight flush draw. If the 7 had been an 8 (leaving a gap between the 8 and 6), if the 6 and 7 weren't suited, or if it were 5-6 or lower instead of 6-7 or higher, then you should hold only the deuces.

✔ Many people get confused about inside straight flush draws with a wild card. A hand such as 2w7♣8♣10♣ is an inside draw even though you could consider the 2 to be the 9♣. Only six cards will complete the straight flush, whereas with a fully open-ended draw — such as 2w7♣8♣9♣ — seven cards (5♣, 6♣, 10♣, or J♣, or any of the three remaining 2s) will complete the straight flush. Note that any straight or straight flush draw whose highest card is less than 7 is effectively an inside draw.

✔ Pay close attention to that very last rule in Table 11-3. (Well, I didn't say that Daddy was *always* right.) This is just one example of the necessity for a different strategy for each game. In this game, eight cards can complete an inside straight, making it just a little better than a five-card redraw. You're facing a losing proposition either way, but it's kind of like hitting a hard 16 against a dealer's ace in Blackjack; you've been dealt a bad hand, and you have to play it out the best way you can. In the long run, you stand to lose less by drawing to the inside straight than by drawing five cards.

If you want the complete strategy that can increase your odds of winning, check out the book *Video Poker — Optimum Play*.

Enhanced games

Some machines have a progressive jackpot on the royal flush. The jackpots almost always appear in banks of eight or more tied into a common jackpot counter. Some lower payoffs are usually reduced, and part of the shortfall is returned to the players by incrementing the jackpot. A five-coin 8/5 Jacks-or-Better (that is, one that pays only 40-for-5 for a full house and 25-for-5 for a flush) returns only 97.25 percent. With no other changes, the royal on a quarter machine would have to be $2,400 to reach 100 percent expectation. Each additional per-coin cut in the full house requires an additional $575 in the jackpot to compensate for the loss.

The main problem with such games is that the short-term payback has been cut to feed the progressive jackpot, so you experience a greater loss rate on your way to that jackpot.

A better kind of enhanced game can be found at the Stratosphere in Las Vegas where they have some Jacks-or-Better Draw poker machines that pay extra on a flush or full house. Either of these enhancements adds about 1.1 percent to the payback, making the game very attractive. Also, a few casinos offer full-pay games with a progressive jackpot.

Tips for Becoming a Better Video Poker Player

Here are some general pieces of advice that you should take to heart when playing video poker:

✔ **Play intelligently:** Learn to recognize and play only the better games, and learn an accurate strategy for each game you play. To do otherwise is just donating your money to the casino.

✔ **Look for competitive casinos:** Nevada regulations set the minimum payback for slot machines at 75 percent, but statewide statistics show average paybacks in the 90 percent to 98 percent range.

Most casinos understand that players come back to lose more when their money lasts longer. Most casinos advertise that their machines are "loose," but that's just hype. (In most cases, dropping one "o" from "loose" makes a more realistic statement.) You can compare the payoff schedules of video poker games yourself. Do it!

✔ **Consider maximum payback:** No upper limits exist on game paybacks in Nevada, but many newer gaming jurisdictions set a maximum payback at less than 100 percent. The reason usually given is to prevent "skimming" (extraction of casino winnings by feeding them to a crony), but in any case, it's to assure that the state will get its tax revenue. Save your money for a trip to Las Vegas.

✔ **Go where the good games are:** It doesn't do much good to learn the strategy if you can't find any good games. Several Web sites are available to keep you up-to-date on good video poker all over the country. You can find links to several such sites from `www.vegasplayer.com/video-poker.html`.

✔ **Find out when the good games are available:** Because machines are limited, you may have trouble getting on the most attractive games in the evening or on weekends. Try weekdays and early morning hours.

✔ **Join the slot clubs:** In many cases, the comps and/or cash rebate from the slot club make a situation attractive. Besides the benefits shown in the club literature, most casinos send out special offers in the mail, often worth more than the slot club itself. Join the club and play at least one roll of quarters in every casino you visit.

Six Mistakes to Avoid in Video Poker

Steer clear of the following goofs:

- **Playing an unknown or short-pay game**: Most players pay little attention to the payoff schedule. We often see someone playing a short-pay game while a full-pay machine sits idle nearby. Avoid any game that does not match the payoff schedule shown with a published strategy.

- **Holding too many cards:** The most common playing error is holding a useless card (a *kicker*). In live draw poker, you can occasionally hold a kicker. For example, holding an ace along with a pair gives the possibility of making aces up, which is a pretty good hand in draw poker, and it has the deceptive value of making some opponents think you have trips. In video poker, two pair pays the same regardless of the ranks, and deception is futile. Holding that kicker merely reduces your chances of making three-of-a-kind or four-of-a-kind. Just remember that every card held means one less chance of catching a desirable card. Some people just refuse to draw five new cards, yet a significant part of your payback comes from those five card redraws.

- **Playing with money you can't afford to lose:** This is a symptom of compulsive behavior, and the dangers apply to all forms of gambling. If losing that next bet means that you won't be able to pay the rent, then you are doomed to lose. All intelligent gamblers take risk of ruin into account. Each bet should be only a very small percentage of your gaming bankroll. If you don't have some discretionary funds that are not needed for necessities, then you shouldn't be gambling at all.

- **Playing hunches:** Many players think that they see patterns in the cards, but human nature may coax us in the direction of seeing order in chaos, much as we see faces in the clouds. The machines are random, and hunches cost you money by leading you to deviate from the correct strategy.

- **Following "tips" instead of a real strategy:** Many general gambling books and other publications offer brief guidelines written by someone who may be an expert at other forms of gambling, but not video poker. Most of these sources contain some serious errors and misconceptions. Use a real strategy from an acknowledged authority on the subject.

- **Not optimizing your play:** Your expected gain obviously will be reduced by using too simplified a strategy (or foregoing a strategy altogether). What many serious players don't understand is that it may also be reduced by attempting to use a strategy that is too highly detailed. If a strategy is too complex for you to memorize, it slows your play and leads to unintentional deviations. Optimum play means using an accurate strategy that is simplified just enough for fast action without deviations, but without significant loss of expected payback. The best goal is to maximize your expected hourly win rate without overplaying your bankroll.

Further Readings

You bought *Poker For Dummies* because you wanted to get started winning at poker. Perhaps you found that most other poker books are either worthless or are too complex for you. Well, most video poker books are filled with myths and errors, or else they are so simplified as to be worthless. Others are so full of special considerations such as penalty cards (don't ask) that most players will get lost in the details. Again, optimize your play with publications you can understand.

Below are some worthwhile publications to review.

- ✔ *Video Poker – Optimum Play.* Everyone who likes video poker should begin with this best-selling book. In it, you get the complete Precision Play rules for Jacks-or-Better, Deuces Wild, Bonus Deuces and Joker Wild (Kings-or-Better), plus lots of information on slot clubs, bankroll requirements, risk of ruin, and much more. Great as a gift or to convert a slot player to these higher payback games.

- ✔ *Video Poker Times* is a newsletter that has been published bimonthly since 1994. The data in this 4–8-page newsletter are invaluable to all players seeking a profit at video poker. Each issue contains at least one feature article, typically covering the strategy for an attractive game, risk of ruin, promotions, tournament play, banking slot games, and other subjects directly related to being a winning player. The regular Tidbits and other columns keep you up-to-date in the rapidly changing world of video poker. No fluff. Only $45 per year (six issues) by first-class U.S. mail.

- ✔ *The Best of Video Poker Times.* All the currently useful data from back issues of the newsletter have been collected in the two *Best* volumes. Volume I covers issues 1.1 through 4.3 ($19.95 plus $2 S&H), and Volume II covers issues 4.4 through 7.2 ($24.95 plus $2 S&H). Save even more by getting both volumes for only $40 plus $3.50 shipping & handling.

- ✔ *Video Poker Anomalies & Anecdotes.* This little booklet is not about winning play. Instead, it's a collection of the best stories I've heard about video poker.

- ✔ *Cue cards.* Highly optimized, laminated, shirt-pocket-size cue cards (hand rank tables) are available for the most attractive games, as follows: Jacks-or-Better, Stratosphere Jacks-or-Better, Deuces Wild, Loose Deuces, Sam's Town Bonus Deuces, Stardust Deuces Deluxe, Double Bonus, All American, Double Double Jackpot, Flush Attack, Joker Wild Kings-or-Better, Joker Wild Two Pair, Atlantic City Double Joker Wild, Las Vegas Double Joker Wild, Pick'em Poker and Pick Five. Cards are $4, and five or more at $3.50 each (mix or match) or any ten or more at $3 each. Add $1 per order for shipping and handling.

You can obtain these publications at the following locations:

- ✔ **Web:** www.vegasplayer.com /video-poker.html
- ✔ **Telephone:** Gamblers' Book Club, 1-800-522-1777

(This chapter was written by video poker pundit Dan Paymar. He has over 42 years of experience in computer programming and has been playing video poker since 1989. Dan has been writing about the game since 1991; his books have been best-sellers since 1992. You can reach him by e-mail at vptimes@wizard.com. Further information on video poker is available at www.vegasplayer.com/video-poker.html.)

Chapter 12

The World Series of Poker

*E*ach year, from late April through mid-May, the world's best poker players converge on Binion's Horseshoe in downtown Las Vegas (also known as "Glitter Gulch") to compete in the World Series of Poker. (For a closer look at Binion's Horseshoe Casino, see the sidebar "Real gaming at Glitter Gulch.")

The World Series of Poker comprises more than 20 separate events — each costing between $1,500 and $10,000, and anyone with the buy-in is welcome to enter. The play generally begins daily at noon and continues until all but nine players are eliminated. The game reconvenes at 4:00 p.m. the next day and continues until one player wins all the chips.

There's only one event for low rollers, and it's free: the Press Invitational. This event is designed to provide members of the working press a first-hand World Series experience without putting any of their own money at risk. But risk and reward are closely related in poker, and the $1,000 prize paid to each year's winning journalist pales in comparison to the $1.5 million that the winner of the main event takes home. (Up until 1999, the big prize was $1 million.) That main event is a $10,000 buy-in, No-Limit Texas Hold'em tournament. It's the Big Kahuna of all poker games, played out over four days in mid-May, and the winner is regaled as poker's world champion for the next 12 months.

How It All Got Started

The World Series of Poker began in 1970 as a small gathering of top poker professionals invited to the Horseshoe by its owner, Benny Binion, to play a few friendly games of poker at very high stakes. When the dust cleared, the assemblage cast votes for the player to be named world champion. Johnny Moss, who passed away in 1996 and was still a competitive force among poker players in his 89th year, was chosen. Moss was a fitting choice, for it's Johnny Moss and his old friend Benny Binion who can take most of the credit for popularizing poker in Las Vegas.

Moss, the Grand Old Man of Poker, was an old-time Texas road gambler; a breed made redundant by the proliferation of casinos and legalized poker rooms. Back in 1949, however, Nevada was the only state that offered legal gaming. That's when legendary gambler Nick "the Greek" Dandalos came to town. The Greek wanted to play no-limit poker, and he wanted to play against a single opponent. Binion agreed to host the game, and there was no question in his mind about the man for the job. He immediately called Johnny Moss, who caught the next plane from Dallas, took a cab to Binion's Horseshoe, and sat down to a friendly game with Nick the Greek.

Binion positioned the table near the casino's entrance, and the crowds — intrigued by the biggest game the town had ever seen — stood five- and six-deep to watch. The confrontation between Moss and Dandalos lasted five months, punctuated by breaks for sleep every four days. In the end, Nick the Greek, who had broken all the gamblers on the East Coast (including mobster Arnold Rothstein), stood up from the table, smiled, and said: "Mr. Moss, I have to let you go." Over that five-month period Johnny Moss had beaten Nick Dandalos for more than $2 million.

1970: The First World Series of Poker

In 1970, Binion decided to recapture that magic by inviting the top professionals to play in public. Five games were played at the inaugural World Series of Poker, and Johnny Moss won them all. He won again in 1971; and when he captured the title a third time in 1974, the legend of Johnny Moss and the World Series of Poker were forever linked.

Since its relatively modest beginnings, the World Series of Poker has grown exponentially. From five events in 1970, it's become a 20-plus event tournament. The grand finale, the $10,000 buy-in, No-Limit Hold'em tournament, attracts more than 400 participants each year, creating a prize pool that exceeds $4 million in the process.

The 1997 winner, Stu Ungar, a professional poker player from Las Vegas, who also won it in 1980 and 1981, walked away with a cool $1 million. The remainder of the prize money was distributed to the top 27 finishers according to their order of finish. Since that time, each winner has received a first prize of at least $1 million.

Real gaming at Glitter Gulch

If the World Series has grown by leaps and bounds, so has Binion's — and downtown's Glitter Gulch along with it. Once a shabby, dark, narrow, incredibly noisy casino, Binion's expanded a few years ago to keep up with its growing clientele. Binion's is always crowded. It's just that now they can pack more customers inside their expanded digs.

If Las Vegas has become more family-oriented in recent years — Disneyland with gaming — Binion's is what it's always been: a gambling hall where there's no upper limit on your bets and no ersatz pirate ships or erupting volcanoes to distract serious players.

Binion's formula obviously worked because the casino expanded while most of downtown stagnated. Expansion was easy. The Binion family purchased the Mint Hotel and Casino located next door, tore down the walls and doubled their capacity overnight. In addition, the downtown casinos — together with the City of Las Vegas and the Las Vegas Convention and Visitors Authority — jointly financed construction of a latticelike archway that runs the length of Fremont Street. During the day, the archway tames the desert sun. At night, more than 2 million lights, controlled by 121 computers and 208 speakers, create an extravagant light and sound show every half-hour.

High-Roller Tournaments Made Affordable

When gaming expanded to Atlantic City, Connecticut, Mississippi, and much of the Midwest, Las Vegas kept ahead of the curve by continuing to reinvent itself — and the World Series of Poker was no exception. The tournament's early years were restrictive, since one had to be a high roller to enter. Democratization came in the 1980s with the advent of satellite tournaments. (See Chapter 10 for details about these mini-tournaments.) Satellite tournaments give everyone an opportunity to compete in big buy-in events. Not only is it possible to parlay a $220 satellite entry fee into victory in the main event, it's been done. In fact, when Tom McEvoy defeated Rod Peate for the title in 1983, it marked the first time two players parlayed satellite victories into a shot at the championship. "It's like taking a toothpick," said 1972 champ Amarillo Slim Preston, "and turning it into a lumber yard."

But the tournament events are not the entire story: non-stop side games exude high energy and big money. Betting limits of $400–$800 are common. Surrounded by smoke, green felt, cards, the clacking of chips riffled through the fingers of some 600 players, you realize that this is poker's equivalent of a feeding frenzy: games 'round the clock, contestants playing at double and triple their usual stakes, and top pros from all over the world competing against each other in Las Vegas's biggest games. After all, when you're a professional poker player who's been knocked out of today's tournament event, what are you going to do until tomorrow? You're gonna play poker. What else?

The biggest poker tournament in the world

Just how big has the World Series of Poker (WSOP) become? By the end of the last century, more than 4,000 entrants were entering annually to contest more than $12.25 million in prize money; and new records for the number of entries were being established regularly. (The WSOP is composed of about 20 events, with an average of 200 entrants per event. The prize money for the main event totals almost $4 million.)

The internationalization of poker became overwhelmingly apparent at the 1997 World Series, with 12 of the 21 events won by foreign-born players. In 1999, the last World Series of Poker to be played in the 20th century, the $10,000 buy-in No-Limit Texas Hold'em tournament — the main event of the World Series — had 393 entrants.

Noel Furlong, who won the 1999 World Championship, hails from Ireland. So do Padraig Parkinson, who finished third, and George McKeever, who was seventh. Chris Bigler, the fifth-place finisher, is Swiss. With Europeans capturing four of the first seven places in the main event in 1999, it's clear that poker is truly an international game. In addition to the Irish and Swiss finalists, final-table finishers in other events that year hailed from England, Germany, Italy, and Australia.

It's not just a guy thing either. Women have also come into their own as formidable competitors. Three women — Linda Johnson, Maria Stern, and Susie Isaacs — won open-event titles in recent years. Maria Stern is also part of another unique record: She and her husband, Dr. Max Stern, are the only couple in World Series history to both win titles; they did it in 1997. After each won a title, Dr. Stern captured a second event for good measure. Isaacs won the Women's World Championship two years in a row and wrote her own poker book, *MsPoker*.

No-Limit Texas Hold'em — the Cadillac of Card Games

Popularized in part by the World Series of Poker, Texas Hold'em was always the game of choice for Southern road gamblers. Now, most poker players prefer Hold'em. Part of the popularity of Hold'em is that it's faster than Stud, there's more action, and there's no need to rack one's brain memorizing exposed cards and folded hands.

Hold'em is a deceptively simple game. Two players to the dealer's left must post blind bets — before seeing their hands — and each player is dealt two cards face down. Acting in turn, players may either fold, call, or raise the blind bet.

Three cards are turned face up in the center of the table, and another round of betting takes place. These face-up cards are communal cards — called the *flop* — and players use their two private cards in conjunction with the communal cards to make the best possible poker hand. Two more communal cards — the *turn* and the *river* — are dealt face up, with a round of betting after each. When a hand is concluded, the dealer position and blinds rotate clockwise around the table.

In tournaments, blinds increase at prescribed intervals to stimulate action and to adjust to the higher chip count of the remaining players.

Most Hold'em games are played with betting limits. In a recreational $3–$6 game you may bet or raise in $3 increments before and on the flop, and bet or raise in $6 increments on the turn and river. If you are raised, it will cost another $6 to call.

But No-Limit Hold'em is altogether different. Each entrant at the World Series starts with $10,000 in tournament chips and can bet any amount at any time. Imagine *yourself* in a no-limit game. You might bet $100 only to confront a raiser who pushes his entire stack of chips toward the center of the table. If his chip count is equal to or greater than yours, you must move *all-in* to call. Fold, and you've relinquished any claim to the pot. Call, and it's all over until next year if your hand is beaten. It's a daunting decision. No-Limit Hold'em is both a game of cat and mouse — each player trying to trap an opponent for all his chips — as well as a game of well-timed bluffs and aggression.

Suppose the pot contains $500 and your opponent bets $2,000. What does that mean? Does she have the goods or is she bluffing? Does she have an unbeatable hand and is betting in hopes that yours is *almost* as good? Or is it a naked bluff? Certainty is rare in No-Limit Hold'em — and that's why the great Hold'em players all tell you that heart is more important than knowing odds and working the numbers. In No-Limit, everyone tries to steal the pot — you really can't win in the long run if you don't — but the best pull it off adroitly. The mediocre are routinely caught — *snapped off*, as they say at the table — and left to stagger away talking to themselves.

In a limit game, by comparison, all it will cost is a single bet if you are raised, and because you know that, your risk is predictable. In no-limit, your entire stack of chips is always in jeopardy. At the end of four days each year's world champion may have made a mistake or two over the course of this tourna-ment but was lucky enough to draw out on his opponents, or — and this is much more likely — he outplayed them at critical junctures.

Let's Get Ready to Rumble: The Latest Battles at the World Series of Poker

The main event is what draws the crowds to Las Vegas, and the 1997 and 1998 World Series of Poker were more dramatic than most. One event is the thrilling yet ultimately sad tale of an incredible comeback, the other a quin-tessential American success story.

Stu Ungar: The Comeback Kid

A dozen former world champs competed in the 1997 event, including two-time winners Doyle Brunson, Johnny Chan, and Stu Ungar, along with 27-year-old defending champion Huck Seed. Formerly an engineering student at Cal Tech, Seed took a year's sabbatical to play poker and never returned.

When Norway's Tormod Roren was eliminated late on the evening of the third day of competition, only six contestants remained, setting the stage for the final table, to be played outdoors on Fremont Street the next day. Stadium seating for the general public was erected under the curved, lattice-like space frame of the Fremont Street Experience. Bleachers had also replaced card tables in Binion's tournament area, and crews were laying cable and wheeling in big-screen TVs to provide additional viewing for the main event.

The six remaining contestants for poker's biggest prize took their seats at the table shortly after 10:00 Thursday morning, and ESPN colorman Gabe Kaplan conducted short, "up-close-and-personal" interviews with each finalist:

- ✔ Peter Bao, the man with the shortest chip count, was a 26-year-old college student majoring in computer science who moved to the United States in 1988 from his native Vietnam.

- ✔ John Strzemp, president of Las Vegas's Treasure Island Hotel and Casino, enters poker tournaments only occasionally and had never finished in the money at the World Series of Poker before this year.

- ✔ Mel Judah, who was 49 years old, is a savvy, well-regarded tournament player from London, England. He had finished in the money at the World Series of Poker 15 times in his career.

- ✔ Bob Walker is a former college mathematics professor and, like Judah, a professional poker player. But Bob, according to Kaplan, specializes in cash games, and this marked the first time he had entered a major poker tournament.

- ✔ Ron Stanley, 44 years old at the time, was dressed for the occasion in a tuxedo — with black-and-white baseball cap to match. He is a Las Vegas pro who had accumulated World Series earnings of more than $326,000.

- ✔ Stu Ungar completed the field. Once known as "The Kid," he stunned the poker world in 1980 and 1981 when, as a 27-year-old, he captured the title two years in a row. Coming into this event he had already won more than $1 million at the Horseshoe's annual poker tournament, and he was once regarded by knowledgeable insiders as one of the top poker players in the world. In addition, he was generally acknowledged to be the best gin rummy player in history. But tough times, drug addiction, and health problems beset Ungar in recent years, and this tournament marked a comeback of sorts for him.

The generally accepted wisdom among the punters was that Ungar — who began the day with a chip lead of almost $400,000 over Ron Stanley, his nearest competitor — would sit quietly and let others eliminate themselves before moving into the fray with guns blazing. But Ungar's reputation was not built on passivity; it centered on two critical skills: Unrelenting aggression in suitable situations, and an uncanny ability to read his opponents and know with near certainty what cards they were playing. When Ungar was on top of his game, it almost seemed like his opponents were playing their cards face up — while his were disguised and unfathomable.

Ungar attacked early and often. His opponents frequently folded. Tournament poker differs from normal games in one very significant way: *You're not wagering money in a tournament so much as you are betting a portion of your total equity in the game.* For Ungar, with his huge chip lead, a bet of $20,000 represented only 2 percent of the $1 million or so in chips that was stacked on the table in front of him. For the short-stacked Peter Bao, $20,000 represented ten times that amount.

No one wanted to be the first player eliminated. The sixth place finisher would receive $127,200 — not a bad payday, but substantially less than fifth place, which would be awarded $162,120. Fourth place would earn $212,000, while third place was worth $371,000. Second place paid $583,000, while the winner was slated to walk away with a cool $1 million. At each fork in the road, staying alive was a far better alternative than elimination, and survival meant avoiding a confrontation with Ungar, the chip leader.

At one point Ungar raised seven hands in a row. No one called. Was he bluffing? Of course he was — some of the time. Everyone knew that. But no one knew when. Every contestant hoped one of his opponents would be eliminated first. It didn't matter which one. Every time someone was knocked out, the surviving players climbed another rung on the pay ladder. Ungar knew that.

Ungar's mastery of the table seemed palpable. He was a shark among a school of fish, and he sensed blood in the water. Bao, short on chips the entire day, was the first to fall — eliminated by Judah. By 1:30 p.m. Ungar had more chips than his remaining four opponents combined.

Ungar's biggest competitor was fellow Las Vegas pro Ron Stanley, sitting in second place. But five minutes later an incredible event took place. Stanley raised Strzemp, putting him all-in. Stanley had a pair of kings; Strzemp a pair of 10s. The flop helped no one, and Stanley was a huge favorite to win that pot. But the turn brought forth a miracle card, one of the two remaining 10s in the deck, giving Strzemp trip 10s. The river card was a blank, and Stanley stared at the table in shock. When Judah announced that he discarded a 10, Stanley knew he suffered what poker players call a *bad beat.* Only one card remaining in the deck could have won the hand for Strzemp and he caught it. After the flop, with two cards to come, Strzemp's chances of catching the lone remaining 10 were less than 5 percent. He faced elimination as a 22-to-1 long shot and survived!

By 2:00 p.m. Ungar held 60 percent of all the chips in play, and his aggression showed no signs of relenting. None of his opponents appeared willing to settle for a fifth place finish, since fourth place paid $50,000 more. Fifteen minutes later the stalemate was broken when Judah's humble pair of 2s proved strong enough to eliminate Bob Walker, who flopped four to a straight and four to a flush. But neither hand materialized, and the war of attrition claimed another victim.

Shaken from the bad beat that Strzemp administered — as well as an earlier incident when Ungar bluffed him out of a $200,000 pot and then flipped his cards face up on the table as if to show the world just what he was capable of doing — Stanley was eliminated when he ran into Strzemp's full house. Three contestants now remained at the final table, but only for a moment. Dangerously low on chips, Judah was eliminated when he lost a pot to Ungar.

After a short break it was Ungar against Strzemp — heads-up (just two players). During the break, Jack Binion, accompanied by eight very large security guards, carried a box filled with $1 million in hundred-dollar bills to the table, to await the outcome of the final confrontation. Ten minutes later Strzemp made a big bet. Ungar deliberated for what seemed like an excessively long time. He riffled chips through his fingers. He glanced furtively at Strzemp, peering over the tops of his bright blue sunglasses, trying to read him, trying to catch any sort of sign — or *tell,* as poker players call it — that would provide the clue he was looking for. Suddenly he snapped erect and pushed his chips toward the center of the pot, putting Strzemp all-in. Since there could be no more betting, both players turned their hands face up. Strzemp held A-8; Ungar A-4.

The dealer turned the flop over. It was A-3-5. Each player had a pair of aces, but Strzemp's side card put him in the lead. The turn was another 3. Now each player had two pair: As and 3s. But Strzemp's hand was A-A-3-3-8, while Ungar's side card was redundant.

Everyone knew the odds. If the last communal card was a 5, 6, or 7, Strzemp would win the pot since his side card would be bigger than the unpaired card on the board. He'd also win if the last card was an 8, since it would give him As and 8s to Ungar's As and 3s. If the river card was a 9 or higher, the pot would be split since both side cards — Ungar's 4 and Strzemp's 8 — would be obviated by the higher communal river card. Ungar could win only if the river card was a 4 — giving him As and 4s against Strzemp's As and 3s — or a 2, which would complete his straight.

The river card was a 2. Strzemp seemed crushed, and Ungar elated. Stu Ungar, now 43 years old and no longer "The Kid" who won it two years running in 1980 and 1981, captured poker's biggest prize for the third time. In doing so, he dominated a field of world-class professionals and top-notch big-money players from North America, Europe, South America, and Asia in the process.

Another Stu Ungar story

Stu Ungar, a three-time World Series Champion, was always youthful-looking for his age. He stood only 5'4" and weighed barely 100 pounds. Once, Ungar went into a bar and ordered a drink. Skeptical of his age, the bartender asked Ungar for identification to verify he was old enough to order an alcoholic beverage. Because Ungar never carried identification, the bartender refused service. Unwilling to take no for an answer, Ungar was determined to prove his age. He reached deep into his pockets and pulled out two hefty stacks of one-hundred dollar bills wrapped in $10,000 bundles and slammed the money on top of the bar.

"There!" Ungar said. "Now tell me, what kind of kid carries around that kind of money?"

The bartender gazed at the $20,000 and paused for a moment. "You've got a point," the bartender finally replied. "What'll you have?"

But Ungar's day in the sun was short-lived. A few months later a lifetime of bad habits caught up with him. The man acknowledged as the best gin rummy player in history, and quite possibly the best no-limit poker player of all time, was found dead in a Las Vegas hotel room. Too many years of drug use and attendant health problems had taken their toll, and a man with talent as big as the mountains would never make another comeback.

Scotty Nguyen: An American dreamer

To win the 1998 World Series of Poker, Scotty Nguyen, a seasoned professional poker player who was used to competing in big money games against very tough competition, had to overcome a field of some 350 players. Each competitor ponied up $10,000 to enter this tournament, a four-day event that guaranteed the winner a cash payment of a cool million dollars. Nguyen had done well earlier in the World Series. After placing third in the $2,000 No-Limit Hold'em event, he vowed that " . . . you'll see me at more final tables here in the Horseshoe."

At the moment he defeated runner up Kevin McBride after some 3½-hours of heads-up play, Nguyen — once given the nickname "The Prince" — became poker's king.

But it wasn't always bright lights, million-dollar payouts, and all the glitz of poker's premier event for Scotty Nguyen. Flash back to 1979. A 17-year-old Thuan Nguyen and his younger brother decide to escape from the Vietnam war zone he was raised in. The decision to flee was, by far, a bigger gamble than any he'd encounter at a $10,000 buy-in poker tournament, and one that almost cost the brothers their lives. He recounts the story of near death in the ocean, of running out of gas, and nearly running out of food, his younger brother so near death that 17-year-old Thuan — not yet "Scotty," and not quite "The Prince" — had to hand-feed him to keep him alive.

Then the miracle at sea occurred. The boys were picked up by a Taiwanese boat and placed in a refugee camp. They finally got a sponsor and then entered the United States. After a year in Chicago, which young Thuan found too cold for his liking, Nguyen relocated to Orange County, California, the West Coast's center for Vietnamese immigration.

Now 19 years old and a recent graduate of Costa Mesa High School, Nguyen and some friends went to Las Vegas on a lark. Nguyen decided the town was for him. Not one to waste a minute, he walked up to the manager of the restaurant where they were eating and said, "I need a job; I'll do anything."

Asked if he could start tomorrow, he did not even return to California to pick up his belongings. Instead he found a room to stay in. It wasn't the Ritz by any means. At times there were five to seven others staying there too. He borrowed clothes, slept on the floor and then on a couch, which " . . . finally broke in half after a year." An inauspicious beginning to be sure, but it is the stuff American dreams are made of. An immigrant boy becomes very much the American and makes good. It was during his bus-boy, crash-pad days that he became "Scotty." The restaurant manager, who couldn't remember Nguyen's real name, pinned "Scotty" on him. Nguyen liked it; the name stuck, and he's been "Scotty" ever since.

In his spare time Scotty studied poker. He read books and watched the big money games that were then held at the Stardust. By now he had moved into his own apartment, but found the career of a busboy financially limiting. He took his developing love of poker and enrolled in dealer's school. In 1983, shortly after his twenty-first birthday, Scotty began dealing poker.

Scotty learned poker from watching the big-money games at the Stardust. Vowing not to make the same mistakes he saw other players make, he quit his job and began playing poker full time. He was now a full-time poker player and a winner from the start. He played daily. He won a big tournament but couldn't handle the success. He gave money away and lost the rest at the craps table. By 1988 he was broke and had to take a job dealing poker at the Golden Nugget.

This time, however, there was a silver lining in Scotty's black cloud and her name was Dawn. "The first time I laid eyes on her I fell in love," said Scotty. The feeling was mutual. The romance blossomed, the couple married, and today are the parents of Anthony, Brittney, Courtney, and Jade.

But life was a financial roller-coaster ride for the Nguyens. Scotty would win. Scotty would go broke. Dawn gave him money and friends helped out when times were tough. But Dawn believed in Scotty and he believed in himself. After all, he had conquered much more than poker in just getting to America, and he was determined not to fail now. He worked at his game. He studied. He persevered. His game improved. Gradually he became a consistent winner.

Nguyen began playing in small tournaments and by 1995 he cashed in his first World Series of Poker, when he placed thirteenth in a $2,500 limit Hold'em event. The following year he won two events at the Queens Poker Classic, where he was nicknamed "The Prince" by one of the tournament employees.

"The Prince" is a nickname that's as prophetic as it was popular with Scotty, for today he's counted among poker's royalty. But it wasn't easy for him. It never has been. The *Big Kahuna,* the $10,000 buy-in, No-Limit Hold'em championship is never a walk in the park, not even when you've gone from rags to riches. It's never easy, even when your life's experiences include very nearly dying at sea as a 17-year-old in a mad dash to freedom. It's never easy when you come to America and find yourself sleeping seven-to-a-room while laboring as a bus boy. Dealing poker isn't easy either, and neither is playing professionally — particularly when you go broke regularly and have to rely on your wife's earnings and the kindness of friends to keep you afloat.

But overcoming struggle is the defining characteristic of the American immigrant. It's the fuel that energized our nation and forged our character in a crucible of dreams. And, ultimately, it was that strength that enabled Scotty Nguyen to win the 1998 World Series of Poker. But it wasn't easy.

The championship is a four-day marathon, not a sprint. Three-hundred and fifty players entered. By the start of the last day all but five had been eliminated. Scotty Nguyen was the chip leader, with $1,184,000, trailed by newcomer Kevin McBride with $873,000. T. J. Cloutier, *Card Player Magazine's Player of the Year* for 1998, was in third place with $829,000. Dewey Weum, a veteran of the poker wars from Monona, Wisconsin, and San Diego's Lee Salem trailed with $376,000 and $240,000, respectively.

Short on chips, Salem and Weum are eliminated within two hours. Now the game is three-handed. Cloutier, a former professional football player considered by many to be the best tournament player in the world, has yet to win the big one. He won't this year, either.

On the 157th hand of the final day, McBride raises $40,000 from the small blind. Cloutier reraises $120,000 and McBride calls. The flop is 4♠5♦7♠. Cloutier bets his remaining $400,000. McBride ponders, but calls. Since Cloutier is all-in, the players turn their cards over. Cloutier holds K♦Q♣. McBride, incredibly, has just called a $400,000 bet with J♠9♠ — only a flush draw. The next card is a J♦, giving McBride a pair of jacks. But Cloutier still has hope. A king or a queen that does not make McBride's flush will win it for T. J. But the river card is the 2♥ — a complete blank — and Cloutier is eliminated.

Now it is heads-up, and McBride, with $2,207,000 to Scotty's $1,293,000, has 63 percent of the chips in play. It's a big lead, but not insurmountable, and McBride's chip lead is, to some degree, offset by Scotty's extensive tournament experience. McBride, after all, is a newcomer. He's a rags-to-riches story himself — at least as far as this tournament is concerned. He entered a $220 satellite, won a buy-in to the main event, and now finds himself heads-up — with a chip lead — for the World Championship.

Scotty Nguyen, like most top-notch tournament players, has a reputation for aggressive play. But on this day the heads-up match is more like a chess game. Like two fighters with dynamite in their fists, they probe and parry — respectful, if not wary, of each other's punching power. They dart in and dart out — again and again — each unwilling to make an error that would severely cripple or knock him out of the tournament altogether.

They play heads-up for nearly four hours. It's a very long time by past World Series standards. Gradually, Scotty edges into the lead, only to lose it back on the 184th hand when a seemingly innocuous 3♠ on the last card gives McBride a full house. He now has $1.9 million to Nguyen's $1.6 million.

Sixteen hands later Nguyen is in the lead again. The chip count stands at $2.5 million to $1 million. But McBride is a warrior and it's not over yet. On the 251st hand, both men call. The flop is 3♣4♣A♦. Scotty bets $30,000 and McBride calls. The turn card is the 4♠. McBride calls Nguyen's $80,000 bet. The last card is the 9♥. When Scotty bets $200,000 McBride raises $386,000. He is now all-in. He immediately gets up and leaves the room. Five minutes later he returns from his pit stop.

"It's all over if I read you right," says Nguyen. But Scotty reads him wrong and McBride, who is holding 4♥5♦ in his hand is back in the chase after his trip 4s skewers Scotty's A♥Q♠. But Nguyen makes no more mistakes, and after letting his opponent back in the game, he rebuilds his stack of chips to $2.9 million — while McBride labors with $600,000.

On the 268th hand, with the blinds at $25,000 and $50,000, the end comes. McBride raises $50,000 before the flop and Nguyen calls. The flop is 8♣9♦9♥. Scotty checks and calls McBride's $100,000 bet. The next card is the 8♥. Nguyen checks, and McBride, who is holding Q♥10♥ and has a draw to a straight flush, bets $100,000. Scotty calls. When the 8♠ falls on the river, Scotty moves all-in saying, "If you call, it's gonna be all over."

Kevin McBride later stated that Scotty's comment was what got him to call. He thought Scotty was using table talk in an attempt to get him to relinquish his hand. This time, however, it was McBride who read Nguyen wrong and called with the remainder of his chips, saying, "I'm playing the board." But Scotty Nguyen, holding J♦9♣ won the pot, and the 1998 World Series of Poker, with nines full of eights (9-9-9-8-8).

It was nearly 5:00 in the evening as the 35-year-old immigrant from Vietnam posed with Jack Binion in front of what was now his: $1 million.

World Series of Poker: The Winner's Circle

Here's a quick look at the best of the best: the men and women who have won the $10,000 buy-in, No-Limit Texas Hold'em championship at the World Series of Poker.

1970: Johnny Moss

1971: Johnny Moss

1972: Amarillo Slim Preston

1973: Puggy Pearson

1974: Johnny Moss

1975: Sailor Roberts

1976: Doyle Brunson

1977: Doyle Brunson

1978: Bobby Baldwin

1979: Hal Fowler

1980: Stu Ungar

1981: Stu Ungar

1982: Jack Strauss

1983: Tom McEvoy

1984: Jack Kellar

1985: Bill Smith

1986: Berry Johnston

1987: Johnny Chan

1988: Johnny Chan

1989: Phil Hellmuth, Jr.

1990: Mansour Matloubi

1991: Brad Daugherty

1992: Hamid Dastmalchi

1993: Jim Bechtel

1994: Russ Hamilton

1995: Dan Harrington

1996: Huck Seed

1997: Stu Ungar

1998: Scotty Nguyen

1999: Noel Furlong

Chapter 13

The Computer: Your Shortcut to Poker Mastery

In This Chapter

▶ Finding out how a PC can help you master poker

▶ Choosing the right computer for poker practice

▶ Understanding advantages of interactive practice

▶ Creating a comprehensive, interactive self-study course

▶ Using interactive poker software games to practice and improve

▶ Discovering how you can try out interactive software for free

*I*f you're serious about improving your poker skills — especially if you're a beginner — you need to get cozy with a personal computer. Here's why:

The union of poker and computer technology offers an opportunity to jump-start your poker progress and move up the learning curve with ease. Playing poker on your PC will also save you money: Dump those beginner boo-boos before they cost you dearly in real games!

Today's poker students can use a personal computer as the cornerstone of a comprehensive, interactive self-study course in poker. If you study poker books *and* use a computer to practice your newfound skills, you can leapfrog past the anguish and expense of gaining experience the old-fashioned way (by losing your greenhorn's money to the sharks).

With a PC you can try out your fledgling poker skills in games against surprisingly tough computer opponents. On the Internet you can play against *human* opponents for play-money or even real money, gaining valuable experience for live casino play.

Once online, you participate in the newsgroup `rec.gambling.poker` (RGP) and other sites dedicated strictly to poker. Here you will find stimulating discussions to sharpen your thinking and deepen your understanding. You'll receive feedback from more experienced players, including experts, and you'll be able to get information about games anywhere in the world.

Choosing the Right Computer for Poker Study

What, you don't have a computer yet but are thinking of taking the plunge? Do you have an old computer and wonder if you can get by? If you don't have a computer, now is the time to get one. Anyone serious about becoming a consistent winner in poker is handicapped without a PC. Whenever you sit in a game for cash stakes, you'll be facing opponents who use computers for poker study.

Some of those players are even doing computer simulations to discover the *lifetime* results of playing the same hand several different ways. The latest PCs can handle this chore in less time than it takes you to watch a movie — and we're talking about *three million* hands or so! Do you *really* want your competitors to have this kind of resource at their fingertips when you don't?

Getting by with a used computer

Okay, we've convinced you — you need a computer. But remember, it can't be just any PC. The dinosaur your brother-in-law dumped on your front lawn ten years ago when his pizza business went under just won't make the grade, nor will most computers that are more than a few years old.

Realistic computer poker has arrived, but you have to meet it head-on with the right equipment. Advances in computers in just the past year or two have already left earlier models dead in the water, matching the astounding advances in poker software step for step.

Computers just aren't like cars. An old, well-maintained PC may be okay for your bookkeeping, but it won't have the pickup and speed you need on the Internet superhighway, nor will it have "the right stuff" to cope with the complex graphics of quality poker programs. Assigning an old computer to handle these tasks is not like putting an old car on the freeway, but more like putting a hay wagon out there! Trying to get somewhere on the Internet? You may get there, but you won't like the bumpy ride!

Face it. If you're serious about improving your poker skills and have a computer more than a few years old, you probably need to replace it, unless you're a computer whiz who is capable of doing lots of fancy upgrades. Keep your blood pressure somewhere beneath the stratosphere by turning it in for a new model.

Our final word: Buy new if you possibly can. The ease, speed, and convenience offered by the latest computers are worth it. Most new computers will have most — if not all — of the following accoutrements already built-in, but it doesn't hurt to check.

For the computer activities we recommend in this and the following chapter, you'll avoid problems by having at least . . .

- ✔ **The Windows 95 (or higher if you're buying new) operating system.** (Poker program designers love Windows. In fact, many poker programs won't work with anything but Windows. Don't try to swim upstream by buying a Macintosh!)

- ✔ **A Pentium-class (or equivalent) processor incorporating MMX technology** (which improves a computer's ability to run complex stuff like videos and the sophisticated graphics of today's realistic poker programs).

- ✔ **64 megabytes or more of RAM (random access memory).** Poker programs are greedy — they eat up lots of computer memory space, especially when you're playing on the Internet.

- ✔ **A modem with a minimum speed of 33,600 bits per second (bps).** 56,800 bps is even better. (A modem is a device that enables a computer to send and receive data through an ordinary phone line.)

  Note: You may see the numbers written as 33.6Kbps or 56Kbps, with the K standing for kilo (thousand). The faster your modem connection, the easier it will be to use the Internet.

- ✔ **A sound card** so you can hear neat things like the clacking of chips when the pot is pushed to you; the warning beep when it's your turn to act and you're buried in the sports pages; or the canned laughter of your opponents when you do something dumb.

- ✔ **A CD-ROM or DVD drive** for installing poker software and other programs, and for playing cool music to calm your nerves when the poker god is smiling everywhere but in your direction.

Using a Computer for Interactive Poker Practice

In the past, you could learn the nuts and bolts of poker quickly, but you could get experience — that old beginner's bugaboo — only through the school of hard knocks. There was no comprehensive, integrated poker course for beginners. You just had to run the gauntlet of costly errors at the tables and take your lumps. Period.

Then poker books came on the scene, making things a lot easier for those willing to study them. By using this book and others we recommend in a continuous cycle of reading, studying, playing, and thinking, you'll have a real leg up on the competition. Videos and seminars will help, too. And do discuss your play with experienced friends!

Still, poker, like musical performance, is a hands-on activity. No matter how much you study and prepare for it, you must actually play to improve. There's just no way around it.

You must interact with other players, too. Poker is, after all, an interactive activity. In music, you can become a big-shot soloist superstar, playing merrily away in the limelight, generating big bucks by your lonesome. To become a poker star, you must constantly interact with other players while monitoring and adjusting your own play. That's how you improve!

The best poker books and other learning aids can give you a solid framework for winning play. They *cannot* give you the extensive hands-on, interactive game experience you need. A computer *can!* A PC can provide three types of interactive play:

✔ In interactive poker software games, a computer functions simultaneously as instructor/guide, practice opponent(s), and progress assessor. There's no financial risk, and you can practice to your heart's content at no cost beyond the initial cost of the software. Most importantly, you'll improve constantly.

(Don't think you'll have it easy playing against the computer opponents, either. Some are even tough enough to give experts a run for their money!)

✔ Linked to the Internet, your computer can bring you play-money games in which you will compete against live opponents. The other players will be much like you, just wanting to learn and have fun. You'll be able to "chat" with them as you play by typing messages on your keyboards back and forth. There are no financial risks, but there may be a nominal fee for using the Internet site. (And some sites are absolutely free.)

✔ Your computer can link you to Internet poker casinos where you can play against *real people* for *real money!* Keep in mind that this is *no longer practice*, but *real poker!* Consider the pros and cons of this carefully before getting involved. (We help you take a hard look at this option in Chapter 14.)

An Interactive Self-Study Course

Interactive computer software games and Internet play-money poker games are the heart of a comprehensive self-study course. They get your head out of poker books and get your game off the ground.

But wait! You don't get to abandon those books — ever! You'll be reading and rereading them throughout your poker career. They'll also be valuable while you cut your teeth on computer poker games. Nobody will see you sneak a peek at a hand-ranking start chart or look up the chapter that tells whether you really should have reraised with four players yet to act behind you. Keep those books handy.

Be creative! Mix it up! Read a paragraph, play a hand. Walk the dog. Think about the hands you just played. Get some coffee. Think some more. Read that chapter on short-handed play, then set up a short-handed game. Play some hands. Reread the chapter. Play more hands. Get the idea?

Think of your self-study course as a three-legged stool:

✔ From a choice selection of poker books you can learn everything from the bare-bones essentials of poker to advanced theories. That's one leg.

✔ The second leg is a quality computer poker software program in which you'll play against computer opponents and work on specific problems.

As a supplement, you can play in mock games for play-money against *human* opponents on the Internet (whenever you just have to know there are real folks out there).

✔ The final leg is the lively interchange of ideas and opinions you'll find in an online newsgroup dedicated to poker. By participating frequently in `rec.gambling.poker` (RGP), you'll grow by leaps and bounds in your understanding of the theoretical and psychological elements of poker. You'll even have a ready-made audience whenever things aren't going well!

Take a look at each of these three essential components. (This chapter introduces you to the extraordinary learning opportunity of interactive software. We examine Internet poker games and RGP in the next chapter.)

Interactive Poker Software Programs

Computer poker programs have come of age. The best programs offer interactive learning opportunities that were unavailable only a few years ago. Improved versions are hurtling down the pipeline at warp speed, each leaving its predecessor light-years behind. The realism of contemporary programs has largely negated statements made by poker gurus only a few years ago:

"I suspect poker is just too difficult a game to program reasonably well," wrote one expert in 1996. At about the same time, another expert wrote that computer opponents were unable to learn from events in previous hands when making decisions, something a human player always does (or should).

To do the most good, your practice sessions should be done under conditions approaching real play. The latest poker software offers the realistic game context you need to improve. Computer opponents have evolved, and so have other features.

Reviewers are now saying — half seriously — that they'd like to put some of the computer opponents in real games for real cash.

These new cyberopponents — with their ability to bluff and semi-bluff, slowplay and checkraise, can do all of the following:

- Make adjustments for position and number of players
- Alter strategy when checkraised
- React to events in prior hands
- Take their share of pots and leave you muttering

No doubt that they'll prepare you for real games.

Finding the best software

Tracking down the best software is easy. Just check out the highly regarded Turbo Poker series by Wilson Software. Poker experts and satisfied customers almost unanimously praise this software series for its realism and overall quality. Wilson Software offers these games:

- Turbo Seven-Card Stud
- Turbo Omaha High Only
- Turbo Omaha High-Low Split
- Turbo Texas Hold'em
- Turbo Stud 8/or Better
- Tournament Texas Hold'em

All of these games require the Windows operating system (sorry, Macintosh users). For more information on the offerings by Wilson software, visit its Web site at www.wilsonsw.com or call 1-800-735-4430.

Using the offerings from Wilson Software

Program installation is remarkably easy and takes only a few minutes. You don't even need to restart your computer.

The games are user-friendly. After a simple and speedy installation process that all but directs itself, you can be absorbed in a game within minutes. Feel free to plunge in!

Once you start a program, you can simply click the Help button at the top of the screen. It will bring up an index to detailed instructions, including how to start a game.

At the top of the program screen you'll find five or six buttons. Click the button called Game Setup, and familiarize yourself with the options you find there. You'll be able to structure each new game as you see fit: number of players, toughness of computer opponents, blinds or antes, betting limits, number of raises permitted per round, and many other variables. It's well worth your while to explore all these options thoroughly. Type in your preferences and then start your first game. Get those cards in the air!

One option deserves special mention if you lose interest in any hand. Click Modify Game Settings⇨Game Setup⇨Always zip to the end. By "zipping to the end," you immediately see the showdown result each time you fold. Then click Deal and you're on to the next hand!

You can also zip manually by clicking on Zip at the bottom of the screen. Don't like your hand after the flop? Zip! Missed the flop again? Zip! More lousy cards? Zip, zip! Fun, isn't it?

Hmmm . . . should you call or raise? Need some advice here? Just click Advice. A disembodied voice accompanied by onscreen hand analysis steers you in the right direction. You get a warning if you make a play that the advisor doesn't like (unless you turn off this feature before you begin).

Want to know the odds against making your hand? You guessed it — click Odds for a detailed analysis. Think you misplayed the hand and want to see what would have happened if you had raised? Click Replay. Play it again, Sam!

The latest versions of the games offer "tips," which pop up automatically when you start a program. Read them carefully. It's a good idea when you're first starting out to read a group of them by clicking on Next at the bottom of each tip in turn until you've read as many as you can absorb for that session. These tips will give you a good idea of the program's scope and possibilities. Once you start a game, you can return to reading tips at any time by clicking on the Tips button at the top of the screen.

A comprehensive user's guide typically comes with each program. Don't be intimidated — you don't have to be a rocket scientist to glean what you need from it. If you're a poker greenhorn, your objective is to just get playing, which you can do simply by using the Help and Tips buttons. (Be sure to read the manual. Just don't get bogged down in the technical stuff when you're first starting!)

Getting lots of practice quickly

Here's another fabulous timesaver available in some of the Wilson Software programs. Once you set up a game and click to start it, a screen instantly pops up to ask whether you want to be dealt random hands, hands worth at least a call, or strictly raising hands. (Now don't you just wish you could do *that* in a real game?)

The zipping and hand-skipping features enable you to play 60,000 hands — the equivalent of a full year's play in a live game at 30 hands per hour, eight hours per day — in a quarter of that time (or less). It's a lot like typing; you'll get faster and faster as you practice. How many hands can you play per hour? Except for those hands you elect to play out, your speed will be limited mostly by how fast you can click that mouse.

Playing at a higher level

When you're comfortable playing poker on the computer, tackle these techniques — and tackle them sooner rather than later because they're not difficult:

- ✔ To see how well you're doing, click Stats at the bottom of the screen. On the list of options that appears, click Play Evaluation to see colorful charts that assess your overall play and your play at each betting level versus the play of the programmed advisor. If there are clear areas of weakness in your game, you can pinpoint them here. Then explore the garden of informative charts, graphs, and tables tucked behind other Stats options.

- ✔ Over the course of an hour or so, play only A-A, say, in Hold'em or play A-K-Q-J in Omaha High, or a hidden high pair in Stud by clicking Game Setup⇨Stack the Deck. You'll gain experience in a variety of situations — experience that might take you a year or more to accumulate in real games. In each practice session, work on different hands. Keep a chart of acceptable starting hands handy and work methodically through it over a number of sessions.

- ✔ Like to practice playing only the big blind, small blind, or button? Find yourself calling too often in early position? To toughen up your play where it's weakest, click Modify Game Settings⇨Freeze the Button to indulge yourself in an orgy of same-position play.

- ✔ Combine the Stack the Deck option with Freeze the Button. Play A-K in the big blind for only several rounds, then on the button, and so on. (Create parallel situations in Omaha with four cards.) You can also stack the flop, turn, and river cards (and opponents' hands, as well) to replicate hands from books you study, or to replay the hands of your worst nightmares.

- ✔ Most beginners would rather sit in a full-handed game than play short-handed. Learn to profit from shorthanded games the easy way — make them a staple of your practice sessions. Don't forget to reduce the rake (the portion of each pot taken by the house)! (Yes, you can do that, too!)

✔ Figure out how to modify the preprogrammed computer opponents, create new ones, and use both in combination with high-speed simulations to do your own poker research.

Dealing with computer opponents

Here's where you can really be creative! Remember the fun you had mixing paints or building blocks or modeling clay when you were a kid? There was always a thrill in creating something new, wasn't there?

Using the options available under Profile in most programs, you can do the following:

✔ You can modify playing styles of the 40 or so imaginatively and often humorously named cyberopponents.

You can also create new ones by blending preprogrammed profile characteristics of the originals. (The originals are never lost, however — just temporarily altered or borrowed. They revert to their natural selves whenever you give the word.)

✔ You can name your new creations and put them in action at a virtual table. When you do this, you are "loading" them into the "lineup" — your selected group of players for a game.

Although you can use entirely preprogrammed lineups if you wish, take advantage of the more open-ended options to mimic players in your favorite live game. Or create a player profile that plays like you do and toss it into different lineups to see how it performs.

✔ You can arrange to have players entering and leaving randomly every couple of rounds, just as they would in a real casino poker game.

To find out how to use the Profile and Lineup options, first read the pertinent tips. (Clicking the Tips button brings up a handy list.) Click the Help button if necessary. Digest the comprehensive manual in small doses, and remember that you can contact Wilson software anytime for more assistance. Don't be afraid to experiment!

Running simulations

Simulations are very high-speed tests in which the computer does *all* the playing so that you can learn something. If you want to test something concerning your own strategy, you can customize a player profile to mimic your playing style and load it into the lineup for your test . The computer "sits in" for you while it plays out the equivalent of a yearlong (or longer) game with the rest of your chosen lineup, then presents you with the game statistics. You'll know how much you won — or lost — to the penny.

In a "smart" (computerized) simulation — the only kind that won't give you misleading results — the computer plays its usual strategic game for each cyberopponent you've loaded. It simply does so at lightning speed. The resulting statistics summarize what happened under realistic game conditions in which bets, raises, reraises, and checkraises force opponents to either fold or pay dearly for their mistakes.

The games from Wilson Software do only smart simulations unless you specifically set up a "dumb" or "shutdown" simulation that simply deals out cards to see who wins, and then records the results. Dumb simulations produce misleading results, and you really won't find them helpful in improving your game.

Modern computers handle such tasks in an amazingly small amount of time. You might be able to grab a soda and check the sports scores while the computer plays a million hands of whatever situation you've set up! That's right — a *million* hands! (You can even run a test for three million or more — the equivalent of a lifetime of poker — while you watch a football game. Your computer should have the test results ready for your review by halftime!)

(This chapter was prepared by Kathleen K. Watterson. Kathleen has a B.S. in newspaper journalism from the S.I. Newhouse School of Public Communications at Syracuse University. She is particularly adept at challenging games such as chess, Scrabble and poker.)

"Test driving" poker programs

Like to try these programs out for free first? If your computer is already linked to the Internet, head for the Wilson Software Web site at www.wilsonsw.com, where you can download mini-versions of some of the programs. You'll be able to play only 25 hands. After that you'll be treated to the same cycle, over and over. So there's no free lunch here, but do try these yummy appetizers!

At the same site, you'll find recent reviews of the programs (neatly arranged in adjoining links), detailed descriptions of program features, and a user-friendly e-mail form.

You can also search out other software poker programs described on the Internet by using keywords, such as **poker software**, on any of the following search engines:

✔ www.yahoo.com

✔ www.altavista.com

✔ www.excite.com

✔ www.google.com

✔ www.askjeeves.com

Chapter 14

Internet Poker

• •

• •

Sometimes you simply have to know that you're playing against, well, real people — not against computer creations. When the computer opponents of interactive software games have you talking to yourself and longing for human adversaries to gripe about, what can you do?

Just as you can find almost anything else on the Internet, you can find poker games. These cybergames have no physical location, but you can summon them up from your personal computer at any time. Like genies in a bottle, they await your command — all it takes is a few clicks of your mouse!

Internet Play-Money Games

If you're not ready for cash stakes, you can play in mock games for play-money on the Internet. Your opponents may be anywhere in the world. They won't be in the same room with you, but they're real folks looking for a game.

You'll have to make a few adjustments when you move into online playing. Internet poker games take place in *cyberspace,* the universe of electronic connections that is at once everywhere and nowhere. At first it's a little disconcerting to hear a disembodied voice ask for your blind, or to have your cards yanked away by invisible hands instead of folding them yourself!

The Internet game designers have done all they can to simulate the sights and sounds of a real poker game:

✔ You see yourself represented in pictogram form, seated at a virtual table with other pictogram players, whose real counterparts may be anywhere in the world.

✔ Your player name or "handle" and the amount you have in play are listed above or beneath your virtual representative.

✔ Vibrantly colored cards, tables, chips, and player costumes mimic the visual elements of real casino poker.

✔ An invisible dealer announces bets and raises and declares winning hands. (However, he doesn't accept tokes.)

✔ You hear the sounds of cards being shuffled and dealt, and chips clacking when the pot is pushed to the winner.

✔ You "converse" with other players in the "chat window" by typing messages back and forth on your keyboards.

✔ To check, bet, or raise, you click on-screen choices with your mouse. Help and hand history are easily summoned by clicking other options. Want to leave the game or go to another? Click!

But it isn't real poker, is it?

Internet play-money poker isn't real poker, but it's not supposed to be. *Real poker* is played for *real money*. Even so, you can practice many skills in these cybergames. For instance, you can brush up on

✔ Evaluating hands

✔ Reading hands

✔ Folding, betting, calling, raising, and reraising

✔ Categorizing opponents

✔ Figuring pot odds

As in most free (or nearly free) things in life, there are some inherent limitations when you play in online play-money poker games:

✔ You won't be able to watch for *tells* (the involuntary physical and emotional slips that often give away a player's hand) unless you're psychic. The opportunity to fire in a raise because you've seen fear in an opponent's eyes is an experience you won't have in Internet games.

✔ You won't be able to practice tricky strategies. You'll probably have to "show down" a real hand after all the cards are out — forget fancy moves and bluffs. Players will usually call with anything when no money is involved.

✔ The games are generally slower than live games and much slower than interactive software where you play against computer opponents. Many people play in the games while doing other things, or they may have slow computers or problems with their Internet service providers (ISPs).

What the games are like

Most Internet play-money games are loose action games. (That's putting it mildly!) Players enter pots with guns blazing, firing bets and raises at will. Much of this activity is just smoke and mirrors, but when the smoke clears, someone will have made a hand. Don't expect to win a pot without a struggle!

There are many *family pots* (pots in which all players participate in the action), and you won't find many wallflowers sitting on the sidelines hand after hand. Betting is frequently *capped* (when players put in the maximum number of raises allowed). Hang on for the ride — *if* you have a hand.

You'll see players call or even call raises with cards they should have folded without a moment's hesitation. You'll see people calling with a bottom pair, with backdoor draws, even with as little as one overcard — hoping to get lucky. After all, it's fun to play and no fun at all to fold! Your challenge in these games is to keep from joining the party!

At a good play-money site you will find at least Texas Hold'em and Seven-Card Stud. Omaha is another popular offering, and if you're lucky you'll have a choice between Omaha High-Only and Omaha/8. The trend is toward a wider selection of games. You can also find tournaments.

Game menus change with popular trends, and even game sites themselves come and go. To find out what games are currently available, post an inquiry at the Internet poker newsgroup `rec.gambling.poker` (RGP). (We tell you all about RGP later in this chapter.)

How these games help you to improve

You'll be playing with people who, like you, are learning the game or have limited experience. But *unlike* you, most of them will be playing strictly for fun. Those folks will be mired in bad habits because they either don't care or just don't know any better, while you'll be playing seriously in order to improve. That's right, *seriously!* Play as though it's for keeps, as though your chips in cyberspace will be cash in your pocket when you win. Oh, you lost? Oops, there goes your bankroll! Better keep your day job! You can't refrain from playing when you get a streak of bad cards? Better get a second job while you're at it — you're going to need it.

Think playing cyberpoker is going to be easy? Maybe for the first 30 or 60 minutes. After that you'll be fighting the 4F trio: frustration, fatigue, and the *fun factor* — the tendency to join in the loose play to have a better time. So lick temptation *now*, while there's no cost.

Make these sessions count. Keep records. Determine when your break point occurs: How long can you play without yielding to the temptation of playing inferior hands? Of calling when you shouldn't? Of getting emotional when a poor player draws out on you? Remember that the hardest victory in poker is conquering yourself!

If it's hard to take an Internet play-money game seriously "when it really doesn't count," remember this: For you, the game really *does* count. It counts as preparation, and when you sit in a game with real stakes, you'll face many of the same factors you face in these cyberspace games. Here's why:

- ✔ Unless money is no object, you'll be playing your first cash games for low limits. In many places, low-limit games are of the loose, "no fold'em" variety. Even though there's real money at stake, many players in low-limit casino games will be playing with a devil-may-care attitude. In fact, they'll be betting and raising as though they're risking nothing but play-money!

- ✔ If you can keep your discipline even in a play-money game, you are even more likely to keep your gambling gremlin in check when there's real money on the table. (What's a gambling gremlin? Why, it's that little voice — and we all have it — that keeps popping up to urge us to stay when we should fold, or to see one more card when we know the odds don't justify it.) Keep this in mind: Losing players indulge their gambling gremlin. Winners don't!

The Best Internet Play-Money Sites: Internet Poker Casinos

Online poker casinos offering real-cash games often offer introductory play-money games. These are a great place to start. Here's why:

- ✔ Because they are meant to get clients used to the graphics and procedures of cash stakes games, these play-money games are user-friendly by design. You're a potential cash client, and the online casino hopes to expand its business by making you feel welcome and comfortable.

- ✔ Although the games are remarkably easy to use, the programming and graphics are highly sophisticated — they're identical to those used in the money games. Overall, the games are far superior to games offered at Internet sites intended strictly for entertainment.

- ✔ Players will be somewhat more serious than those you'll find at sites meant strictly for fun. (Notice we say "somewhat more serious." You'll still see seven out of ten players calling the flop. But at least it won't be ten out of ten!)

- ✔ You can watch the game of your choice before you play, and then select your seat to give yourself a positional advantage.

If you wish, you can watch the cash games. If the procedure for doing so isn't clear, don't hesitate to ask about it. Ask other players by typing in the chat window or send an e-mail to the designated helper to get directions.

At Internet poker casinos that offer real-money games, you won't have to pay to practice in the play-money games. You may have to go through the motions of setting up an account, though. (Setting up an account doesn't mean you have to provide a credit card number, but you will probably have to give your name, address, e-mail address, and telephone number when you register.)

Getting started

First, you need to download the game site's program files to your computer.

You then supply a user name or *handle* by which you'll be known in the games. Some people use their first name or initials, or an amalgam of parts of their first and last names. Others adopt imaginary, literary, or humorous names — feel free to be creative here.

Once you choose your handle, you may not be able to change it easily, so choose carefully. (Your handle is the only way opponents will be able to identify you to remember how you play, so it wouldn't be fair to keep changing it.)

Finding games

Your ISP may offer play-money poker games. These less-sophisticated games make fewer demands of your computer. If you have questions or problems, send an e-mail and ask for help. Most game sites respond promptly to inquiries.

If you're already using America Online (AOL) as your ISP, you can play Seven-Card Stud, Hold'em, Omaha High, and others (including tournament games), for a small fee per hour. Hours and minutes are meticulously posted to your account, which is available for your inspection at any time. The total accumulated time is simply billed to you with your regular fee.

AOL has made it easy to find and use the games. To learn about them, use keyword **AOL: HOW TO PLAY GAMES ON AOL.** To get to the games, simply go to keyword **POKER.**

If you're not on AOL, your ISP may offer play-money poker games under the categories Entertainment or Games. If not, or if you don't like the games, try Gamestorm at www.gamestorm.com.

Looking for serious play-money games

If you're serious about poker, not afraid of a challenge, and have some quality time to put in, you might like to participate in IRC Poker. (IRC stands for *Internet Relay Chat*.) IRC Poker is a real-time network poker game community offering heavy-duty poker games and tournaments played for imaginary "etherbucks."

What's heavy duty and serious about that? Plenty. IRCers are highly competitive, motivated, and serious about their games. Even expert players participate — they enjoy the challenge. IRC Poker offers pot-limit and no-limit games and tournaments, as well as limit tables, giving players on short bankrolls the opportunity to test their skills in high-limit poker with virtual dollars. In short, most IRCers can flat out play, so listen up, pilgrim. Playing here will definitely improve your game, but don't expect anything about it to be easy. You won't get fancy colored graphics, sound effects, or kid-glove coddling here!

IRC game screens are anything but inviting, and if you tarry too often, you may find yourself unceremoniously dumped from the game by the IRC poker police (longstanding dedicated players who get to enforce the rules).

To play, you need to download the necessary programming, which is called "Greg's Poker Client," at `http://webusers.anet-stl.com/~gregr`. Once you have the program installed and are online, starting the program will automatically take you to `IRC.POKER.NET`, the game server.

At this point, we'll leave you to your own ingenuity, but with one parting tip: Once you've dipped one toe in IRC Poker, get your feet wet at the Internet newsgroup `rec.gambling.poker`. Post a message at the RGP site to the effect that you're new with IRC Poker and need help.

Participating in the Future of Poker at rec.gambling.poker (RGP)

Think of the Internet newsgroup `rec.gambling.poker` (RGP) as your one-stop poker newspaper, discussion club, information bureau, and personal advisor. Like all Internet newsgroups, RGP is a global, interactive electronic bulletin board serving thousands of people interested in the same subject — in this case, poker.

As with other bulletin boards, you can read messages already there, respond to them (using either private e-mail to the author or a public message called a *post* that is meant for all RGP readers), or create your own messages.

RGP is not a chat room; you cannot conduct real-time discussions in news-groups. Also, expect a slight delay between the time you post a message and when it actually appears onscreen. (Newsgroup messages are relayed through a series of servers before reaching the site that appears on your monitor.)

Finding RGP

RGP is located in the part of the Internet called Usenet News, or Usenet. Usenet is like a huge electronic bulletin board hanging in cyberspace. It has thousands of subdivisions called *newsgroups*.

Newsgroups are organized into categories called hierarchies. You can find RGP under the *category* or *hierarchy* called "rec" (short for recreation), under *subcategory* "gambling," and is devoted to the *specific topic* "poker."

As you can see, newsgroups have nothing to do with the daily news. On AOL, they are found under keyword: **Newsgroups.** Once there, click on the follow-ing: Add Newsgroups⇨rec⇨gambling⇨poker. You will have the opportunity to add **rec.gambling.poker** to your "Favorites" list, where you store sites that you return to again and again.

Other ISPs handle newsgroups much the same way. If you don't find RGP easily under "Newsgroups" from your ISP's home page, try typing **rec. gambling.poker** into the Internet address window and click on Go. (You don't have to put the cumbersome `http://` first when going to a newsgroup.)

Benefiting from RGP

RGP represents the future of poker because it represents the entire poker community, from experts to rank beginners. As an open forum where one can exchange ideas, theories, opinions, and personal experiences, it is like a healthy extended family whose members agree to disagree sometimes. All members learn from each other's mistakes and experience.

Regular participation in RGP is the third leg of your comprehensive self-study course in poker. (The other two are interactive poker software games and Internet play-money games.) Here are some of the key ways RGP will help you become a better player:

> ✔ If you're looking for specific information, someone in your extended poker family either will have the answer or know who does. Looking for a game in Missoula, Montana; Marblehead, Massachusetts; or Magnolia, Mississippi? Want to find out which Internet poker casinos are the most reputable? Seeking info on the best games in your area or an upcoming tournament? Just post a new message and ask.

✔ If you give an opinion or propose a theory, you're likely to get a cheerful little earful of the opposing view (just like you would at home). This causes you to think through your ideas to define them clearly enough to defend them, and to benefit from counter-arguments and the experience of other players.

✔ In the course of defending their own viewpoints, in answering questions, or just as a service to the rest of the group, members will include links to other Internet poker sites in their posts. (The text of these links, called *hyperlinks,* usually appears underlined and in a different color than the surrounding text. When you rest your mouse pointer over a hyperlink without clicking on it, the pointer will change into a tiny hand.) Explore these sites and record or bookmark their addresses.

✔ Many game-specific and/or hand-specific situations are described in detail by players looking for feedback. You can participate in these discussions or just read any responses posted by experts, who often respond to the most interesting posts.

Posing an interesting question or theory in a new message may spawn a lengthy *thread* (the initial posted message plus its trail of responses). If the subject is interesting or controversial enough, the thread may go on to weave a life of its own, generating responses from responses to the point where everyone from world champions to railbirds chimes in with his or her two cents. You'll wonder how in the world your seemingly innocent little post wound up causing such a fuss!

Such "superthreads" are the crown jewels of RGP posts. By following their strands from message to message, you'll reap a whirlwind of poker knowledge, insight, and vicarious experience — three factors that translate into profits when it's time to cash out your chips at the cage!

Virtual Poker for Real Money: Internet Cash Stakes Games

Using state-of-the-art computer technology, thousands of people play poker online for real money. By linking their computers to the Internet, players living as far apart as New York, London, and Tokyo are able to play together simultaneously in computer-generated poker games — for real cash.

Until recently, such games weren't feasible. The challenge was to invent poker software that would enable strangers to play against each other in live games from different locations — and with enough confidence to back their mouse clicks with cash.

Without real money at stake, online casinos cannot make profits. (They take a *rake* — a fixed percentage of each pot — just as a real casino poker room does. The only difference is that it's taken electronically rather than by a human dealer.)

Milestone advances in computer graphics, sound, and programming made Internet cash games possible. On January 1, 1998, Planet Poker was the first Internet poker casino to offer poker for cash stakes. Others followed.

But is it legal?

The answer as to whether such games are legal depends on which side of the business you're on — supplier side or client side — and also on where you live.

If you're thinking of starting an online poker casino, you'd better get out of Dodge! In the United States, you may be prosecuted for operating such a business, since they are likely prohibited by federal law.

Seeing a potential gold rush of almost unlimited client demand, foreign entrepreneurs rushed in to fill the void. Internet poker casinos are based in countries where laws are more lenient, such as Costa Rica.

The clients, however, may live anywhere. In some areas, it is against the law to place bets on the Internet. Depending on where you live, it may be illegal to play poker for cash stakes online.

Our advice to you

You're in a gray area of the law if you place bets on the Internet. Our advice is to stay abreast of new developments in federal and state laws by inquiring about them regularly on `rec.gambling.poker`. Then, let common sense dictate.

You also need to be concerned about your legal rights — or, rather, your lack of such — if you play for cash in online casinos.

Consider the following:

> ✔ **If an overseas-based casino goes bankrupt, you could lose any money you have on account without recourse.**
>
> *Our advice:* Check out an online casino's reputation with the Internet poker newsgroup `rec.gambling.poker`. Once you start playing, keep good records and cash out your wins frequently. Leave no more on account than you can afford to lose.

✔ **Be alert for collusion.** Dishonest players may play in the same game while using cell phones, instant messages (real time "chat" typed back and forth from computer keyboards by people who have set up this capability in advance), or even adjacent computers. *In any of these ways, cheaters may be sharing information unfairly against you.*

Our advice: The best online casinos have extensive programming that monitors and tags unusual betting patterns that indicate collusion. Choose a well-known online poker casino, and before you sign up, ask questions about what steps are taken to thwart colluders. Also, if you're a beginner lacking the necessary experience to detect unusual betting patterns yourself, *stick to the lowest limits available.* (Cheaters usually play for higher stakes.)

✔ **The easiest way to open an account at an online casino is to use a credit card to make a deposit.** You should be concerned any time you submit credit card numbers and other personal information on the Internet. Carefully monitor your credit card statements each month.

Our advice: Take the time to check out the poker Internet newsgroup `rec.gambling.poker`. Look for threads (groups of messages listed by subject headings) concerning online poker casinos. After you've read the related threads, start a new one by asking if anyone has had problems with an account at casino X.

If you're still not comfortable making a credit card deposit, arrange to wire the money or send a cashier's check or money order. Even a personal check may be acceptable. (When in doubt, ask. Send an e-mail inquiry to the casino you have in mind.)

(This chapter was prepared by Kathleen K. Watterson. Kathleen has a B.S. in newspaper journalism from the S.I. Newhouse School of Public Communications at Syracuse University. She is particularly adept at challenging games such as chess, Scrabble and poker.)

Part IV
More Poker Fun

The 5th Wave   By Rich Tennant

"Sure I'll play FanTan with you. If you match cards like you match shirts with ties, this should be an easy win."

In this part . . .

This short part contains some information that didn't really fit in the previous parts. In Chapter 15, we pull together all of the poker terms, slang, and myths that you're likely to encounter. And in Chapter 16, we provide you with many resources for honing your poker skills.

Chapter 15

What's Behind the Sayings, Terms, and Myths

Sayings, myths, and slang abound in poker, conjuring up visions of the Old West, glittering casinos, or Saturday nights at a buddy's home — take your pick! Some sayings contain elements of truth, while others are hogwash. In this chapter, we define some of those sayings and myths, and poke fun at others.

Poker Sayings

The colorful quotations you hear in poker can be based on real events or just made up from long ago. Here is a list of some popular quotations along with our version of what a person *really* means when he uses the quote:

Phrase	Translation
"I'd rather be lucky than good."	Typically said by a player who is neither lucky nor good. This player often believes that he should play more hands than reasonable and that he can get on a lucky streak by doing so. In the long haul, when all the luck is bled out of the equation, it's skill that separates winning players from losing players.

(continued)

Phrase	*Translation*
"You've got to know when to hold'em, know when to fold' em."	Typically said by a Kenny Rogers fan or someone who has no clue as to whether he should continue playing the hand or fold.
"Sheesh, what a bad beat."	This refers to when a player loses a hand where, mathematically, she was a big favorite. Most players have a bad beat story.
"If you can't spot the fish at the poker table, then it's you."	This refers to the fact that, if you can't read players or their abilities very well, you will probably be the sucker at the table.
"Hey Joe, bring us a live one."	Often said by a player at a card club, asking for a new sucker player to be brought to the table.
"I'm down a little."	I'm down a lot.
"Boy, he is a tight player."	Boy, is he anal-retentive and conservative.
"Read 'em and weep."	Look at my big hand that beats all of your puny hands, suckers.
"I was drawing to a double belly buster."	This is a draw to two different straights, such as 3-5-6-7-9. A single belly buster is drawing to an inside straight.
"Sheesh, things can't get any worse."	Usually said by a poker player who has gone on a losing streak, and the streak is about to get worse.
"Trust everyone, but cut the cards."	Means trust no one, and cut the cards as a way to try to prevent cheating.
"Any two will do."	Refers to the concept that any two cards in Hold'em can *theoretically* win the hand. Used as a justification to play truly wretched starting cards. However, we all know that good starting hands are the key to winning at poker in the long run.

Poker Slang

Some of the colorful terms you hear in poker are intuitive — where the meaning is clear. For others, the proper response should be, "Huh?" If you want to sound like a pro, then take a look at the following list of common terms and definitions:

Slang	*Translation*
All-in	Having all of your chips in the pot. A player who is all-in can't be forced out of the pot, but can win only that portion of the pot that she is eligible for. A side pot for extra bets is created.
Ante	A bet required from all players before a hand as a requirement to being able to play in the hand. This money seeds the pot. Pronounced "AN-tee."
Bad beat	A good hand that is beaten by a better hand, usually through a lucky draw of cards by the winner.
Bet	To put money into a pot, as in "I bet."
Big Slick	Not Bill Clinton. This refers to an ace and a king as your hole cards in Texas Hold'em.
Blind	A mandatory bet by a player or two sitting to the left of the dealer button before each new hand is dealt. The button rotates and, thus, the blind rotates.
Bluff	A bet or raise without a good hand, in the hope that the other players will fold.
Board	The cards showing and available to be seen by all players.
Boat	Not a cruise ship or paddle boat. Refers to a full house (three of a kind plus a pair).
Bug	Not a cricket or ant. Refers to a wild card joker. Most often used in Lowball.
Bump	To raise the pot. Often phrased as "Bump it up." Not to be confused with speed bumps on the road of life.
Buy-in	The minimum amount of money necessary to buy into a poker game. For example, in a $20–$40 Texas Hold'em game, the minimum buy-in is usually $200.
Call	Not a phone call to your mom. Refers to placing the amount of money into the pot by another player in order to keep playing the hand. Often stated as, "I call your bet."

(continued)

Slang	*Translation*
Cards speak	Not a freak of nature. Refers to the best hand being determined by every player turning his cards face up, without any declaration.
Check	Not anything to do with the "check is in the mail." Refers to declining to bet when it's your turn to do so.
Checkraise	To check when it's your turn, and then when someone else bets, to raise that person.
Crying call	Calling a hand reluctantly, on the belief that you will likely lose but will be tremendously pleased if you win.
Cut	To divide the deck in half prior to the dealing of a hand, in an effort to keep the dealer honest and by spoiling an attempted stacked deck. The person to the right of the dealer cuts the deck.
Declare	In high-low games (usually home games), each person declares which way she is going: high, low, or both ways. This is typically done with chips in the hand, such as one chip for low, two chips for high, and three chips for both ways.
Down and dirty	Not mud in Australia. Typically refers to the last down card dealt in Seven-Card Stud.
Drawing dead	A draw where no matter what card you get, you are still going to lose.
Drop	To fold a hand, as in "This pile of horse-puckey is so bad, I'm dropping."
Family pot	Not marijuana for the whole family. Refers to lots of players playing in a hand.
Fish	A sucker or player who is either clueless or a very bad player.
Floorman/ floorperson	Not a guy who lays tiles on the floor. Refers to a person of authority in a cardroom who can arbitrate disputes or enforce rules.
Flop	Not falling on your face. Refers to Hold'em's first three common cards on the board.
Flush	Five cards of the same suit, but not in any particular order. Also refers to what happens to your face if you win a big hand at the World Championship of Poker.
Fold	Does not refer to laundry. It means to drop out of a pot rather than calling or raising a bet.
Forced bet	A required bet of a prescribed size. The alternative is folding the hand, but not checking it.

Slang	*Translation*
Free card	A card received at no cost, because no bets were made by the players on the prior round.
Gut shot	Not a bullet to the belly. Refers to drawing one card to an inside straight, such as to J-10-8-7.
Heads up	Playing up against a single opponent.
Hole	Refers to your first two cards dealt face down in Seven-Card Stud. Also known as *pocket cards.*
Kitty	Not your Aunt Betty's pussycat. Refers to the pot of money or chips in the middle.
Lock	See *Nuts.*
Lowball	A poker game in which the best low hand wins.
Misdeal	A hand dealt wrongly that requires a whole new redeal.
Muck	Folding your hand by throwing it into the pile of dead cards.
Nuts	Not what you think! Refers to an unbeatable hand, given the cards that have been played. Also referred to as a *lock.*
Omaha	A variation of Hold'em where each player receives four down cards and must use two (and only two) of those cards with three of the five common cards on the board. Can be played high only or high-low with 8-or-better low.
On the come	Needing to improve the hand to have a chance at winning.
Open	To start the betting round by making a bet, as in "I open."
Pat hand	In draw poker, a hand that doesn't need any cards drawn to, such as a straight, flush, full house, or four-of-a-kind. Sometimes players bluff by staying "pat," trying to represent a big hand.
Pocket pair	In Hold'em, two hole cards that are the same rank, such as J♥ and J♦.
Poker face	Having no expression that may give away what a player may be holding.
Pocket rockets	A pair of aces in your hand in Texas Hold'em.
Pot limit	A game where the maximum bet allowed is equal to the size of the pot at the time of the bet.
Quads	Four of a kind. (Four cards of the same rank.)
Rag	Not a dirty dishcloth. Refers to a worthless card or hand. "I have a rag hand."

(continued)

Slang	*Translation*
Raise	To call a bet and put an additional bet into the pot, forcing other players to put more money into the pot if they wish to stay in the hand.
Raiser	The player who raises.
Read	Refers to the act of determining whether a person has a good hand, a bad hand, or is bluffing.
River	The last common card dealt.
Rock	A very tight or conservative type of player.
Rush	A hot streak in poker hands.
Sandbag	See *slow play*.
Semi-bluff	To bet a hand that isn't necessarily the best hand, but has a reasonable shot at improving to become the best hand.
Slow play	Doesn't refer to dim-witted play. Refers to playing a strong hand weakly at first, usually done in order to keep players in or to set up future raises. This is sometimes referred to as *sandbagging*.
Street	The sequence of cards dealt in a poker hand. Specifically, when more than one card is dealt simultaneously, the last card in the sequence is the *street*. In Seven-Card Stud, each player initially receives three cards (two face down, one face up) and there is a round of betting. That betting round (the first round of betting) is said to take place on *third street*. The fourth card dealt is called *fourth street,* the fifth card is *fifth street,* and so on.
	"Street" isn't used in Draw poker and Lowball, which have only two betting rounds each.
String bet	An illegal act where one player puts in an amount to call a bet and then goes back to his stack to put more chips in to raise, without having orally declared a raise.
Stuck	Losing money at the table, as in "I am stuck $1,000 in the game."
Table stakes	Typically means that the amount of money available for a player to play in a hand is limited to the amount in front of her (meaning that she cannot pull out money from her pocket to play in the middle of a hand).
Tapped out	Broke. Without money left to play. Also referred to as *Tap City.*

Dead Man's Hand

Poker was very popular in the 1870s. Among the many poker players was James Butler "Wild Bill" Hickok. Wild Bill came to the town of Deadwood in the Dakota Territory, and in his leisure time, played poker in the saloon. Wild Bill had killed a great number of people, so he had a few enemies.

One night, he was playing Draw poker. His back was to the door, and an assassin came in and shot Hickok dead while he was in the middle of a hand. He was holding aces and 8s (two pair), which has now become known as the "Dead Man's Hand."

Tell	A telltale indication as to what type of hand you have, usually by a different mannerism of some kind. In the movie *Rounders,* the bad guy's tell was that he played with an Oreo cookie whenever he had a good hand.
Tilt	Not a pinball wizard term. Refers to someone who has started playing badly after a few beats. The player is referred to as *on tilt.*
Toke	A tip for the dealer.
Trips	Three of a kind. (Three cards of the same rank.)
Turn card	The fourth common card dealt face up in Texas Hold'em. Also known as the *turn.*
Underdog	A hand that isn't likely to be the winner.
Wheel	The best possible hand in Lowball poker, which is A-2-3-4-5 in most casinos.

Poker Myths

Knowing the difference between myth and truth can help you win at poker, so here's what you need to know:

The myth	The fact
The winner in poker is the one who wins the most pots.	The fact is that the winner is the one who wins the most *money.* Winning a lot of pots, but losing some great pots can lead to trouble.
You should quit when you're ahead.	If the game is good, you're playing well, and you don't need to be somewhere else, you should continue playing to win more.

Set stop-loss limits so that you don't lose too much at any one time.	This is the other side of "you should quit when you're ahead." If the game is good and you're playing well, however, you should keep playing. If the game is bad, cash out even if you're winning.
Follow Kenny Rogers' advice from the song, *The Gambler,* that goes, "Never count your money when you're sitting at the table, there'll be time enough for countin' when the deal is done."	In reality, if you don't count your money at the table, you'll never know how you stand. Most good players are always keeping track of their progress by counting their money. After all, how else can you keep score?
You need a real poker face to play winning poker.	Actually, you can be poker faced or highly animated, just as long as you don't reveal the strength of your hand.

Chapter 16

Learning More about Poker

*O*kay. Where do you go from here? While we sincerely appreciate the fact that you've purchased and diligently pored over every word in *Poker For Dummies*, it would be presumptuous on our part to believe that this book alone would allow you to master the game. Determinative mastery of poker — or most other things, for that matter — isn't easy to come by, and while we hope this book gives you a sound foundation, becoming a very good poker player is not going to happen overnight. You'll need more tools, along with a plan, if you want to become a good poker player. But at least you're on your way.

The Zen Poker Process

You can learn poker in lots of ways. Until recently, the best — in fact the only — way to learn poker was to attend the school of hard knocks. Someone showed you how to play, and then you sat down in a game and lost your money but hopefully acquired some knowledge in the bargain.

Some folks still learn that way. And while one can learn poker by the seat of the pants, many players who attend the school of hard knocks still make the same mistakes today that they've made over the course of their lifetime. While experience might be a good teacher, a substantial amount of poker theory has appeared in books and other media over the past few decades, and it's silly not to take advantage of it.

Learning poker has a Zen-like cachet about it. Imagine laying out all the poker theory ever developed in front of you like clothes you were planning to pack for a trip. Even if you could learn all the theory there is to know about poker, some of that theory would not mean much to you because there's always an underpinning of other knowledge required before you can make good use of each succeeding layer of thought.

That layered knowledge is one reason why learning the basics of poker is so critical. It provides a basis to understand and place all those juicy tidbits you've just learned in perspective. Knowledge, without a context, is not very useful. Poker, after all, is neither abstract nor theoretical. To the contrary, it requires the practical application of knowledge and theory.

The application of knowledge within a given context is generally called "know-how," and poker is a "know-how" game that's best learned by going through cycles of study, play, and reflection — again, and again, and again.

A Learning Plan

While all roads may lead to Rome, some are full of potholes and others fraught with detours. Do you want to jump-start the learning process? The best way to become a good poker player in a relatively short period of time is to follow the plan in this section. It's a full-immersion process. Study books, use your computer, play in simulated games, read the magazines and the Internet discussion groups, play in real games, and think about poker.

While this process will jump-start your learning, please realize that learning never ends. There's always something new to learn about this game, and to keep one jump ahead of your opponents you have to keep learning just as long as you keep playing. If you're not learning, you're falling behind, and your opponents will eventually pass you. After you master the basics of poker, it's the thinnest of lines that separates consistent winners from those who lose more often than they win. When the gap is narrow, you can't afford to give any edge to your opponents and hope to keep winning.

Read beginner-level books

There's no point in studying books aimed at advanced players without knowing the fundamentals first. You need to get the building blocks in place, and you made a good start by buying this book. After all, you learned arithmetic before algebra, and back in elementary school you were reading about *Dick and Jane* before you tackled *War and Peace*.

Read the magazines

The world of poker currently has two magazines devoted exclusively to it. The first, and oldest, is *Card Player Magazine*. The new kid on the block is *Poker Digest*. Both are published in Las Vegas and appear biweekly on alternate Thursdays. Because of this, you are assured of something new to read about poker once a week.

Because the magazines are distributed in some quantity to those casinos that advertise in their pages, chances are you can pick up each of these magazines for free if you live in an area that has a casino with a poker room. If you're geographically challenged, you can subscribe and keep on top of all the happenings in the poker world that way.

Use your computer

The computer is a great tool for learning about poker, and we devote a whole chapter to that electronic wonder. (See Chapter 13.) Not only is there software that can help you play better poker by simulating cash games, other software enable you to practice playing in a tournament environment, too.

You can also play IRC (Internet Relay Chat) poker. Although IRC poker is played only for bragging rights and not real money, you'll find the games and tournaments a great place to improve your game and chat with other players while you're at it.

In addition, the Internet newsgroup `rec.gambling.poker`, or RGP, as it's called, provides a forum for poker discussion. RGP is a great place to pick up tips from some of the top professional players who regularly participate in that forum.

In addition to RGP, there are other sites dedicated to poker discussion. Two Plus Two Publishing, which publishes the books of Mason Malmuth, Ray Zee, and David Sklansky, among others, maintains a moderated discussion group at `www.twoplustwo.com`. Many players participate in discussions on both sites; and frequently, a discussion that begins on one forum makes its way to the other.

Another site you might want to visit is `www.conjelco.com`. It's both a source of information, as well as an online bookstore devoted exclusively to gaming literature. ConJelCo publishes the works of Lee Jones and Lou Krieger, sells almost every poker book imaginable, and even offers an online newsletter to those who request it. This publication, called *The Intelligent Gambler,* contains articles by some of the most respected poker theorists in the world.

Play poker

To learn poker, you have to play it too. That's the reason behind all the study. But when you play it's important to be aware of what you've read and what you've experienced in simulated games. You won't be able to recall all you read and immediately bring it to bear in a real game. But if you can at least recall some of the theory you've studied and see how it applies under game conditions, you're well on your way to becoming a much better player.

Think about the game

When you get away from the table, take some time to think about the game. And when you think about it, don't think about the time that someone caught a miracle card and beat you out of a big pot. Think about how you played. Think about the things you had some control over. Think about some of the things you read in books and assess whether you played well or not. Figure out what you did wrong and make up your mind to rectify it next time.

Not all the elements of a poker game are within your control. Your opponent can do everything wrong and still get lucky. That happens, and nothing you can do will put a stop to it. In fact, you should be happy when a poor player sticks around when he really should have folded and wins with a hand that's a real long shot. After all, if he keeps playing that way, the money he won really isn't his; it's just visiting.

 Good players beat bad players in the long run, and you shouldn't lose sight of that just because you lost a pot you figured to win. You'll get it all back and more when you consider all the times a poor player will stick around with those long shots and not get lucky. It's never as dramatic, but in the long run, you'll come out far the better of it when you are the favorite and your opponents are the underdogs. Because poker has a large element of short-term luck associated with it, it doesn't matter whether any one effort is successful. What does matter is knowing when a positive expectation is associated with a given play.

All Kinds of Poker Books

There's enough recommended reading material in this chapter to give you an undergraduate degree in poker. Like any recent college graduate, however, you'll find the real world to be somewhat different, and education at an entirely new level begins at the table. Nevertheless, these books will provide the basics you need.

Moreover, they are books you'll probably reread many times. Some of the concepts and strategies in the advanced books are very sophisticated, and beginning players will not grasp all of their potential implications in one reading. In fact, the more one learns, the more applicable many of these books become. You'll find yourself reading and digesting them in a repeating process of "read, play, and think," and never stopping because the process of learning and thinking about poker should never cease.

Books for beginners

Recently there has been an explosion of poker books hitting the market. You picked this one, and it's a good start. Many excellent poker books have been written in the past decade — as well as a few that are really dreadful. Right now there is enough literature to build an entire poker curriculum, just as if we were going to construct a college reading list about poker.

Our intention in compiling this list is to not only identify worthwhile books, but to specify their order of study. To learn how to play well, and to do so quickly, you need a desire to learn and enough hours at the table to apply your new-found knowledge under game conditions. If you aspire to becoming a better player, there's more you need to read once you've thoroughly digested this book, and the reading list for our poker curriculum follows.

General poker theory

- ✔ *The Theory of Poker,* by David Sklansky. Originally published in 1983 under the title *Winning Poker,* this classic is an absolute requirement for any player who seeks a thorough grounding in poker theory. Sklansky discusses poker theory and strategic concepts against a variety of games and situations. No matter what game you might decide to specialize in, this book is one that you will often refer to.

- ✔ *Super System — A Course in Power Poker,* by Doyle Brunson. This is the bible of "how-to" poker books, covering most games you'll ever want to play. It was written by two-time world champion Brunson, along with selected experts such as Mike Caro, Chip Reese, David Sklansky, and former world champion Bobby Baldwin. In spite of changes in game structure that have occurred over the years, *Super System* is still the second book in your syllabus.

- ✔ *Caro's Book of Tells,* by Mike Caro. For a long time this was the only book available dealing with body language at the table. Now this book has been supplemented with a two-tape video package called *Caro's Pro Poker Tells.* If one picture is worth a thousand words, these videos are worth millions.

- ✔ *Sklansky on Poker,* by David Sklansky. This incorporates an earlier book titled *Sklansky on Razz* into a book full of solid, easily understood poker theory. Although not a *magnus opus* like *The Theory of Poker,* it belongs on the bookshelf of any serious poker student.

✔ *Improve Your Poker,* by Bob Ciaffone. Ciaffone, a *Card Player Magazine* columnist called "The Coach," presents sophisticated strategic concepts in such an easily understood manner that we decided to include this book in the recommended reading list for beginners. His advice on deception and bluffing, reading opponents, and tournament play is excellent, as are the sections on Hold'em, Stud, and Omaha poker.

✔ *Fundamental Secrets of Poker,* by Mike Caro. This book captures the most important concepts that Caro teaches at his popular poker seminars. (Caro takes his seminars on the road from time to time, but his home base is the Mike Caro University of Poker, Gaming, and Life, based at the Hollywood Park Casino in Inglewood, California.) This book provides sound advice on Seven-Card Stud and Hold'em, and contains tips on money management, tells, psychology, and tournament advice.

✔ *How To Win at Low Limit Casino Poker,* by Shane Smith, includes general strategies for low-limit play, and specific sections on Texas Hold'em, Omaha/8, Seven-Card Stud, and low buy-in tournament poker. It is well researched, well written and a good book for beginning players. Smith is also the author of *Omaha Hi-Lo Poker.* While *Omaha Hi-Lo Poker* is full of sound advice, we recommend that beginners become familiar with Texas Hold'em before venturing into an Omaha/8 game. But when you're ready to learn Omaha, Smith's book on Omaha should be your primer.

Hold'em books for beginners

The following books should keep the aspiring Texas Hold'em player busy for a while:

✔ *Hold'em Excellence: From Beginner to Winner,* by Lou Krieger

✔ *More Hold'em Excellence: A Winner For Life,* by Lou Krieger

✔ *Winning Low Limit Hold'em,* by Lee Jones

Actually, there is more than enough information in these three books to turn any newbie into a competitor who is far more knowledgeable than most beginning players. In fact, there's enough information in these books to make a winning player out of anyone willing to study and apply the concepts they learn.

Seven-Card Stud books for beginners

Two books can give beginning stud players a solid grounding in the game:

✔ *Seven-Card Stud: The Complete Course in Winning at Medium and Lower Limits,* by Roy West

✔ *Seven-Card Stud: The Waiting Game,* by George Percy

West's book is newer, easier to read, and broken down into lessons that make it easy for any beginner to get a good handle on the game.

Books for advanced players

It's probably not surprising that there are more books written for advanced
players than beginners, even though there are far more beginning players
than those skilled enough to consider themselves a cut above the beginner's
rung. Poker authors, after all, are not beginning players, and the natural
temptation is to write to one's own level of expertise rather than to write for
those who are not quite so advanced.

Once you've mastered the basics, here are some additional books you'll probably want to study to take your own game to the next level.

The "Championship" series

The Championship series of books, written by former World Champion Tom
McEvoy and a man generally regarded as one of the best tournament players
in the world, T. J. Cloutier, comprises the following:

- *Championship Stud*
- *Championship Hold'em*
- *Championship Omaha*
- *Championship No-Limit and Pot Limit Hold'em*

These books contain expert level advice from two highly regarded tournament professionals. The books are pragmatic and conversational in tone.
Reading them is almost like listening to a tape recording of a conversation
between two top players.

The "For Advanced Players" series

The "For Advanced Players" series of books is written by David Sklansky,
Mason Malmuth, and, on occasion, Ray Zee. The series includes:

- *Seven-Card Stud For Advanced Players*
- *Hold'em Poker For Advanced Players*
- *High-Low Split Poker For Advanced Players* (contains sections on
  Omaha/8 and Seven-Stud/8)

The For Advanced Players series and the Championship series are very different in tone, but it's that very difference that makes them complementary.
Sklansky, Malmuth, and Zee lean heavily toward theory that is based on
sound analytical and mathematical underpinnings. The Championship series
is much more conversational in tone, and takes you into the inner thoughts
of professional players in the heat of battle.

Tournament poker

We recommend two books for tournament players:

- ✔ *Tournament Poker,* by Tom McEvoy, is probably the best book of its kind. McEvoy won the World Series of Poker in 1983, and has played poker professionally for more than two decades. This is a 340-page compendium of poker tournament advice, geared for experienced players.

- ✔ *Poker Tournament Tips From the Pros,* by Shane Smith, is a good read for those new to tournament poker or for those seeking to enjoy themselves in smaller events (where the buy-ins are considerably less than what the big guns play for).

Other recommended books

A number of other books are worth reading, too. Bob Ciaffone's books, *Omaha Hold'em Poker* and *Pot-Limit and No-Limit Poker,* (the latter co-authored by Stewart Reuben), contain solid advice for experienced players, and both belong in the library of any serious player.

David Sklansky's *Getting the Best of It*, Mason Malmuth's *Gambling Theory and Other Topics*, along with his *Poker Essays,* and *Poker Essays — Volume II,* are also highly recommended. Another collection of essays is also worth reading — this one by long-time *Card Player* columnist and Las Vegas-based professional poker player Roy Cooke — titled, *Real Poker: The Cooke Collection.*

If you want to supplement all of this technical material with some books that give you the flavor of poker, we recommend *The Biggest Game In Town,* by A. Alvarez, which is about the World Series of Poker and its participants.

You might also enjoy *The Big Deal* by Anthony Holden. In this book, Anthony "London Tony" Holden, the author of two authorized biographies of Prince Charles, takes a year off to play poker tournaments and cash games in Las Vegas, London, the Isle of Man, and other exotic locales. Holden's perception, wit, and self-deprecating sense of humor make this book a real page-turner.

Beyond the Written Word

You need a lot more than book learning to become a successful poker player. Personal characteristics, integrity, strength of purpose, resiliency, willfulness, and dedication are all ladled into this stew. As in almost every other human endeavor, talent is nice to have, but character and the ability to stick with it count too.

Where to get the books: A buyer's guide

You can purchase many of the books we mention in this section at the major chain bookstores, but there are other sources that specialize in poker and gaming books:

✔ **ConJelCo:** In addition to publishing books, ConJelCo is also an e-based retail business located at www.conjelco.com. ConJelCo has a complete catalog of more than 100 books, software, and videos devoted to gaming. The Web site also houses detailed analyses of past World Series of Poker results and a lot of other information most poker players find fascinating. If you are not yet on the Internet, you can write ConJelCo at 1323 Radcliff Drive, Pittsburgh, PA 15237-2382 or phone 1 412-492-9210.

✔ **The Gambler's Bookshop,** located at 630 South 11th Street, Las Vegas, NV 89101, will send you a free, 72-page catalog if you call them at 1 800-522-1777. They've been around since 1964, and are probably the oldest and the biggest bookstore devoted to

gaming literature. Check them out on the Web at www.gamblersbook.com.

✔ **Card Player Magazine** and **Poker Digest** both do a booming business in book sales, and almost all of the books we discuss can be purchased there too.

Card Player is located at 3140 S. Polaris Avenue, Suite 8, Las Vegas, NV 89102, and their phone number is 702-871-1720. You can also reach them online at www.cardplayer.com.

Poker Digest is located at 1455 E. Tropicana Avenue, #300, Las Vegas, NV 89119; phone 702-740-2273. Their online address is www.pokerdigest.com.

At their Web sites, you'll also find links to other poker information, listings of tournaments and other upcoming events in the world of poker, and afford yourself an opportunity to read an abbreviated version of the magazines online.

Here are ten keys to success that hold just as true for life itself as they do for poker.

✔ **Know thyself:** An outrageous table image works for some people but not others. Some players are better suited to cash games, others to tournaments. Know yourself. Do what you do well.

✔ **Be responsible:** What you achieve is the product of your own play. If you can't hold yourself accountable for the results you achieve, you won't succeed.

✔ **Think:** Do your homework. Keep up with the current literature. Think about the game at the table and away from it. Analyze and modify your game. Repeat as needed.

✔ **Plan:** What is your goal as a poker player? Do you want to have fun and just break even? Do you want to be a top tournament player? Be the best $15–$30 player in town? If you don't have a plan of your own, you are most assuredly part of someone else's!

✔ **Set deadlines:** If your goal is to play 30 hours per week, then do it. If you want to read the latest poker book, then set a deadline and do that, too. A plan without a timetable is just so much wishful thinking.

✔ **Be realistic:** Set challenging but reachable goals. Keep trying. But don't expect to win the World Series of Poker next year if you've never before played no-limit poker.

✔ **Expect difficulties:** You'll succumb to all your flaws as a poker player while you're learning. Each top-notch player struggled to reach the level of success he or she has achieved. You're going to have to do the same.

✔ **Build on small accomplishments:** If you study hard, put what you read into practice, and integrate sound strategy into your own style of play, you'll improve. Success builds upon itself. Ignore small setbacks. If you play poorly, correct it next time. Focus on achievement. Taking the worst of it on a hunch, or simply for the fun of it, is nothing more than premeditated backsliding. Do it and you have only yourself to blame.

✔ **Persist:** You must sustain. Ninety percent of success is just showing up. Keep playing, practicing, and building on small victories.

✔ **Have fun:** Enjoy yourself. While there are lots of bitter pills that we all have to swallow in life, we ought to enjoy what we *choose* to do. If you can't enjoy yourself when you play, you might want to think about other outlets for your time and money.

Puggy's bus

Poker legend Puggy Pearson is one of poker's most endearing personalities. Never one to refuse a gamble, Pearson has a long-standing offer to play anyone, at any game, for real money. And, he puts it "in writing."

Emblazoned on the side of Puggy's giant motorcruiser, which he frequently drives on road trips across the country, the former world poker champion has stenciled a catchy proposal that has most certainly turned a few heads along American highways:

I will play any man — from any land,

Any game — that he can name,

For any amount — that I can count.

It's only when you get up close to the side of the bus and see in tiny letters underneath that you see the fine print:

As long as I like it.

"Gambling is just like running a business," Puggy says. "If I'm going to take a gamble, I want to make sure I have the best of it."

Part V
The Part of Tens

The 5th Wave   By Rich Tennant

EDWARD SCISSORHANDS AT A CARD PARTY.

"Actually Ed, if any of us had been thinking, we'd have asked you to pass on the shuffle."

In this part . . .

Every *For Dummies* book ends with top-ten lists, and this one is no exception. We offer you ten ways to read your opponents, and we also talk about the ten best poker players we know of.

Chapter 17

Ten Ways to Read Your Opponent

*P*oker is a brilliant blend of strategy and psychology — there is really nothing else like it. When compared with strategy, however, how important is *psychology* in poker? Well, you can beat poker without understanding psychology, but you can't beat poker without understanding strategy. Therefore, it's important to learn the fundamentals first. But wait! Now we're going to say something that — at first — seems to be contradictory: *Psychology can account for the majority of profit you will ever make in poker!*

That statement is true because *after* you master the fundamentals of poker, you're most of the way to becoming a good player as far as strategy goes. Sure, you can improve, but the difference between excellent strategy and perfect strategy won't put that much extra cash in your wallet or purse — unless you happen to be playing against all world-class opponents, which we don't recommend. What *will* put extra cash in your wallet or purse is getting inside your opponents' heads and making them call you when you have the best hand.

In this chapter, you find out about one extremely powerful aspect of poker psychology called *tells.* What's that? Tells are telltale signs from which you can determine, for example, whether or not your opponent is bluffing — just by noting her mannerisms at the moment. Watch your opponent's body language and listen for verbal clues, and you'll often know with surprising accuracy what cards your opponent is holding.

Tells come in two types:

✔ Those from opponents who are unaware that they are providing the tell

✔ Those from "actors" who know they are providing the tell and are doing so in an attempt to deceive you

So, first, you need to decide if your opponent is acting. If so, determine what that opponent is trying to get you to do and then you (usually) do the opposite.

Your opponents act because poker puts them in an unfamiliar arena. They know that they *must* act to conceal their hands, but they don't know how to go about it. Therefore, most weak and intermediate players just about give you their money by usually acting the opposite of the true strength of their hands. When they're strong, they pretend to be weak; when they're weak, they act as if they are strong.

No need for you to go to acting school to find out about revealing cues. Get into your opponent's head by taking a look at our list of the top ten tells.

Shaking Hand

Hands that shake is not an act. There's a homespun theory that goes with this one. The theory says that if you see someone suddenly start trembling when making a wager, that's a signal that this bettor is nervous about the bet and is probably bluffing.

That theory is just plain backwards. If ever a tell were almost 100 percent reliable, it's this one. Few players act in an effort to show nervousness, and genuine shaking is hard to fake. What most likely is happening is this: Your opponent has made a *very* strong hand. The hand is, in fact, unbeatable or *almost* unbeatable. What you're seeing is a release of tension following the suspense of waiting to see what will happen.

Some players are always nervous; they will shake whether or not they've made a big hand. The tell that I'm talking about is *sudden* shaking. I'm talking about a player who was previously steady but is just now starting to shake. This behavior is especially suspicious if the player seems to be trying to control the shaking, but can't.

This sudden shaking isn't a bluff, because players who bluff tend to bolster themselves. They force themselves to be unnaturally steady, and they hardly move. They tend to realize instinctively that anything they do might look suspicious to an opponent and trigger what we term the *calling reflex*.

The calling reflex is built into most players who have come to the poker table for the excitement of seeing a showdown and have a bias toward calling and against folding. They are looking for any excuses whatsoever to call a bet, and most bluffers instinctively realize this and do nothing to trigger that calling reflex. So, expect bluffers to be rock steady and seldom animated. Expect that sudden trembling is not an act, but an involuntary release of energy after a good hand is made. Unless you have an extremely strong hand, don't call.

Jittering

Jittering and fidgeting is usually not an act. Players can be impatient. Sometimes, you'll see a player drumming fingers rhythmically on the table. Now, he bets. The drumming of fingers continues. You reach toward your chips. The drumming stops!

What does this mean? It usually means the bettor is weak or bluffing and doesn't want the call. A player who really has a big hand will usually continue to be relaxed in the face of a pending call. When we have a close decision about calling or folding, we often use the technique of seeming to reach toward our chips to see what a jitterer's reaction will be. Whether it's drumming of fingers or fidgeting beneath the table, if that action stops abruptly, we call, believing the likelihood of a bluff is high. If it doesn't stop, we fold.

Shrugs and Sad Voices

WARNING!

Shrugs and sad voices are acts. Whenever a player shrugs, sighs, and says, "I bet" in an exasperated tone of voice, you need a big hand to call. This player is going way out of his way to convey sadness.

So, let us ask you a question: *Why is he doing that?* If he really had a weak hand or was bluffing, would he go out of his way to let you know it? Of course not! He's acting sad because he hopes that will make you think his hand is weak. But, remember, weak really means strong when they're acting. Shrugs and sad voices are key indications of strong hands.

Changes in Breathing

A change in breathing patterns is not an act. This unconscious tell is one of the strongest in poker. If you're seated near the opponent, you often will be able to hear this tell. But even if you're seated across the table, you sometimes can see it by the movements of the person's diaphragm.

The key here is that players who make strong hands tend to become excited and need to breathe faster. Players who are bluffing, on the other hand, tend to disguise their breathing and sometimes stop entirely. They fear that anything they do might trigger their opponent's calling reflex, so they become extremely unanimated and scarcely breathe.

Misdirected Bets

A misdirected bet is an act. If the action is three-way or more, expect your opponent to be most concerned about the player who appears to be the most threatening. If you seem to have the strongest hand, based on exposed cards and previous action, then *you* should be the main target.

What if an opponent, instead, stares down another player who doesn't seem to be the big threat? And what if the opponent then aims his bet toward that other player? What then? Then you have witnessed a misdirected bet and you have every right to think, "Hey, what about me?"

This misdirected bet usually means that the player is trying to convince you that he isn't really worried about your hand but about something he sees elsewhere that is even more powerful. But if you can't see that other threat, then you should usually conclude that the misdirected bet was all an act. You should not be intimidated into folding. In fact, if your decision would otherwise have been between calling and raising, you might lean toward raising.

Extra Emphasis

Extra emphasis on a betting motion is an act. This is one of the hardest of all tells to spot, and you need to train yourself to see it. We're not talking about conspicuously exaggerated bets. Those bets can be either a lure to entice your call, or a false warning not to call, depending on the opponent and the situation. What we're talking about is more subtle.

Watch the tail end of a bet. If the betting motion is smooth but is closed by a slight extra flare — perhaps a flick of the fingers releasing the chips — that's extra emphasis and it usually indicates weakness. The opponent is either bluffing or uncomfortable about the strength of his hand. The final flare happened because the player thought at the last instant that he wasn't making the bet seem strong enough. Why would he worry about that? Only if the hand was not powerful enough to make the bet comfortable.

So, when you see extra emphasis on the tail end of a bet, tend to call more often than usual.

Looking Away

Conspicuously looking away from the action is usually an act. A player looking away from you tends to be more dangerous than a player looking at you.

When you see a player gazing away from the action as if distracted, beware. There are only two possibilities here, folks. Either that player really isn't interested — so why risk a bet? — or the player is acting to deceive you. If the player is acting, then she's trying to make your bet comfortable. Don't be fooled. Unless you have a very strong hand, check and fold after the opponent bets. If you bet a medium-strong or worse hand, expect to be raised. And almost never bluff into a player who is gazing away from you.

Staring at You

When it's your turn to act, an opponent conspicuously staring in your direction is likely acting. This usually is a dare, an attempt to prevent your bet through intimidation. The opponent may call but will almost never raise. This means that you can bet any medium-strong hand with impunity, not fearing a raise.

So, instead of being intimidated by an opponent staring you down, simply consider that you can make more borderline bets for profit when you hold marginally strong hands.

Reactions after Looking at Their Cards

When opponents look at their cards, they are usually not acting at this point, because they don't think they're being scrutinized. Unless you'll slow up the game, it's silly to look at your cards while your opponents are looking at theirs. Your cards will still be there later, and if you look at them now, you'll miss out on some of the most valuable tells in poker.

See if your opponents quickly glance toward their chips after seeing their next cards. This tell usually means they liked what they saw and are planning to bet. This is especially true if they glance at their chips and *then* stare conspicuously away as if uninterested. This last part — staring away — is what they *do* think you'll see after you get done looking at your cards. Remember, players staring away usually have strong hands.

On the other hand, your opponent may not bother to stare away. It's the quick glance at the chips here that you'll miss if you're not watching. This is an especially powerful tell in Hold'em on the flop. Watch your opponents watch the flop. You don't need to see it yourself just yet. It won't go away. Also, watch when your opponents first peek at their starting hands. The longer they look, the more likely it is that the hands are weak and they're pretending to show interest. Conversely, if the opponent looks and recognizes a big hand, he will usually cover it quickly and then pretend to show no interest in pursuing the pot.

Reaching for Chips

Reaching for chips in anticipation of another person's bet is often an act. While weak players and beginners who hold strong hands may sometimes reach for their chips before it's their turn to act, more experienced players don't do this.

If you're thinking about betting a borderline hand, see if your opponent reaches for chips as you make a motion toward your stack. If so, there's a good chance that this was a deliberate act designed to prevent your bet. This means you can comfortably bet many borderline hands that would have been too risky had you not known that your opponent didn't want you to bet.

A Final Word

Here's one additional tip about learning to spot tells: Don't get frustrated. Most tells aren't 100 percent accurate. You need to use tells to add weight to the final decisions, just as you might take the exposed cards into consideration. Tells are just another factor to consider along with the strategic action that led up to the current decision — a very powerful factor, but just one factor.

Finally, don't concentrate on too many players at one time. We recommend that you focus on just a single opponent until you become comfortable reading tells. Trying to see *everything* can be so overwhelming that you end up seeing *nothing*

(This chapter provides tips from the legendary "Mad Genius of Poker" Mike Caro. Mike Caro is the founder of the Mike Caro University of Poker, Gaming, and Life Strategy, located at Hollywood Park Casino. Its online campus is at www.planetpoker.com. He is also the author of a number of poker books, including *Mike Caro's Book of Tells — The Body Language of Poker*.)

Chapter 18

Ten Poker Legends

*P*oker is the only popular game of skillful human interaction where it's possible on any given day to play against the world's best players. At any of the hundreds of major poker tournaments held in the United States or Europe every year, you could find yourself face-to-face against former world champions such as Scotty Nguyen, Phil Hellmuth, Jr., or Huck Seed. Ever heard of them? How about T. A. Preston? Name sound familiar? He's better known as "Amarillo Slim." If No-Limit Texas Hold'em is your game, you might get raised by none other than Johnny Chan, who appeared in the film, *Rounders*. Chan won two World Series of Poker titles back to back!

If you visit Las Vegas, you could go head-up against Doyle Brunson, also known as "Texas Dolly." Brunson has been called the "Babe Ruth of poker" — a fitting moniker among poker players that does as much for the late Bambino's image as Brunson's. He's a living legend and a two-time world champion. Just walk into casinos in Las Vegas, Los Angeles, Atlantic City, London, and places in between, and you'll see players who have electrified the game and thrilled millions of viewers on ESPN, the Discovery Channel, and in several championship poker videos.

What distinguishes a poker "legend" from other poker players who may be successful in their own right? Conferring legendary status means the player has reached a certain level of accomplishment in the poker world manifested in the universal respect of one's peers. Poker legends are widely respected because they usually win (or have won) the most money in years past. They also usually win (or have won) the biggest tournaments in their careers. Their play is feared and respected. They have a powerful public image, even a celebrity-like status in poker circles when they walk into a cardroom and sit down in a game. That's a poker legend.

In this chapter, we identify ten legendary poker professionals. It's possible you will encounter some of these names during your poker career, particularly the younger superstars who are now dominating tournament competition. At the very least, you will hear these names spoken around poker tables, so it's certainly wise to give yourself some background about poker's rich history and discover what makes these players truly special.

Stu Ungar

In the late 1970s, Stuey "the Kid" Ungar burst onto the Las Vegas poker scene with the full force of a firestorm. When it came to conventional poker strategy, Ungar didn't just push the envelope, he ripped it to shreds. Poker hasn't been the same since. From an early age growing up in New York City, Ungar was a savant at the card table. Before becoming a successful poker player, Ungar set the gin rummy world ablaze. His talent was so overwhelming that by the time Ungar was a teenager, he could no longer find opponents willing to play for money. So, at age 24 Ungar moved to Las Vegas and immediately jumped into the biggest poker games he could find.

Ungar won the World Series of Poker and the Super Bowl of Poker three times each. (No other player has won both events even once.) But the genius that made him also destroyed him. Ungar's lifestyle was as flamboyant as his rollicking character at the table, his eccentricities amplified by astronomical wins and devastating losses. As brilliant as he was at the poker table, Ungar was burdened with personal problems that were largely of his own making. This ultimately resulted in his tragic death in 1998, at age 45.

Most memorable quote: "I just want to destroy people at the poker table."

Johnny Moss

Johnny Moss was called "The Grand Old Man" for good reason. He played poker almost daily his entire life, all the way until his 89th birthday. Originally from Texas, Moss played on the famous underground circuit in illegal gambling halls and backrooms of the South during the Great Depression and eventually became respected as one of the best traveling pros in the world. Moss was the first to launch the concept of poker as a spectator event, participating in perhaps the greatest heads-up poker match of all-time, the 1949 duel on Fremont Street in downtown Las Vegas when he faced Nick "the Greek" Dandalos in a 21-week marathon of Five-Card Stud.

Moss later moved to Las Vegas and took over the Dunes poker room, which for many years was the mecca for high-stakes poker. Moss won the World Series of Poker three times (the only player other than Stu Ungar with as many victories). Had the World Series been initiated earlier — before Moss's advanced age — there's no telling how many more world championships he would have won. He passed away in 1997.

Most memorable quote: "If things get tough, you get tougher."

Jack "Treetop" Straus

Everyone called Jack Straus "Treetop" because he stood six-feet seven-inches tall and had a big bushy beard. He was a truly lovable man, a larger-than-life figure with a reputation for gambling every single dollar in his pocket on a daily basis. Straus carried around bundles of money, which often amounted to thousands of dollars, stuffed haphazardly into a brown paper bag. On more than one occasion, Straus lost the bag and was left flat broke. He usually dismissed these losses with a casual comment, "Such is life." Straus was a truly great No-Limit Texas Hold'em player, certainly one of the best of his day. He won poker's world championship in 1982. For many years, the Frontier Casino in Las Vegas held a major tournament in his name, which attracted poker's top players. He died of a heart attack in 1988 while in Los Angeles, fittingly while sitting in a high-stakes poker game. No doubt, Straus died with a smile on his face, doing what he loved best — playing poker.

Most memorable quote: "I have only a limited amount of time on this earth, and I want to live every second of it."

Benny Binion

One of Las Vegas's last true patriarchs, Benny Binion started out by running illegal bootlegging and gambling rackets in Dallas during the 1930s. Binion arrived in Las Vegas in 1946 (some insist to evade murder charges back in Texas) and bought the dilapidated Eldorado Casino. He renamed it Binion's Horseshoe, and it soon became the epicenter of gambling activity. The Horseshoe wasn't really built for common tourists; it was a place for real gamblers.

For more than four decades, Binion had a standing public offer: He would accept a wager of any size, from anyone who walked into his casino. More than a few eccentrics were entranced by Binion's willingness to take the ultimate gamble, and there are many stories in Binion's folklore (all true) of high-rollers with suitcases full of money riding on a single roll at the craps table. But Binion's first love was poker.

In 1970, Binion decided to try and duplicate the success of the Johnny Moss-Nick Dandalos match some 20 years earlier. He invited all of the top poker players to the Horseshoe for what he deemed would be the world championship. The World Series of Poker was born. Now, over 30 years later, the annual event at Binion's Horseshoe remains the preeminent poker event in the world and every serious poker player's dream. Binion died in 1989. The Binion family continues to operate the casino.

Most memorable quote: "Treat people right, and the rest will take care of itself."

"Amarillo Slim" Preston

Probably the best-known poker player in the world, Amarillo Slim's down-home style and natural charm have made him a household name. Thomas Austin Preston was, in fact, born in Arkansas and took his memorable appellation many years later when he bought a ranch in West Texas with his gambling winnings. In his younger days, Slim made most of his money not at the poker table, but as a pool hustler. During a stint in the navy, Slim won over $100,000 in cash (and five cars, according to one story) while traveling up and down the West Coast.

Slim's exposure to gambling introduced him to other legendary players of his day, including Doyle Brunson, Brian "Sailor" Roberts, and Johnny Moss. Slim won the World Series of Poker in 1972 and continued to be a dominant force in the poker world for a long time. Aside from his poker prowess, perhaps Slim's true genius has been marketing himself with colorful yarns and homespun quips that have entertained millions of viewers and turned new generations on to the excitement of poker.

Slim has appeared on *The Tonight Show* over a dozen times in addition to his numerous other television and radio appearances. Slim also organized what was for many years poker's second-largest tournament, the Super Bowl of Poker. Today, Slim lives in his namesake Amarillo and can be found at many of poker's biggest tournaments.

Doyle Brunson

"Texas Dolly" was born in the dusty West Texas town of Longworth in 1933. He earned a full basketball scholarship to Hardin-Simmons University and was scouted by the (former) Minneapolis Lakers. Just before the NBA draft, Brunson shattered his knee and the history of poker (and perhaps basketball, too) changed forever. Brunson, who went on and earned a degree in education, toured gambling's underground circuit in the South like many of his poker contemporaries — winning hundreds of thousands of dollars while dodging the law and getting robbed at least a dozen times.

Brunson won back-to-back world poker championships in 1976 and 1977. He also finished second in 1980. Brunson has won a total of six World Series of Poker events, including his most recent victory in 1998 in the Seven-Card Stud Razz event. (Razz is a version of Seven-Card Stud in which the lowest-ranked hand wins.)

In 1999, Brunson defied the odds again by making the final table at the inaugural Tournament of Champions, besting nearly 500 other poker players. Brunson is equally respected for his many contributions to poker's development. He wrote the book acclaimed by many as the "bible" of poker: *How I Won A Million Dollars Playing Poker,* (also known as *Super/System: A Course in Power Poker)* first published in 1978. He also wrote a popular column, *According to Doyle,* which ran in *Gambling Times* magazine for more than a decade. Today, Brunson lives in Las Vegas and still plays almost every day in the biggest games at the Bellagio.

Johnny Chan

Known as "the Oriental Express," Chan arrived in the United States from China when he was 9 years old. His parents, fleeing the horrors of the Cultural Revolution, set up a restaurant in Houston. At 21, Chan came to Las Vegas where he worked as a Glitter Gulch fry cook on Fremont Street. He frequently played poker after his shift was over, sometimes still wearing his white apron while sitting at the table. Chan eventually made enough money to quit his minimum wage job and became a full-time poker player.

He rotated between the biggest games in Las Vegas and Houston for a decade before winning his first world championship in 1987. The following year, Chan won the title again. In 1989, Chan was shooting for his third consecutive world championship, which would have been an unprecedented feat. However, he finished second to a young first-timer named Phil Hellmuth, Jr. Since then, Chan primarily plays only in the biggest games, although he made an appearance in the 1998 poker movie, *Rounders*, starring actor Matt Damon.

Phil Hellmuth, Jr.

The self-described "poker brat" is one of poker's most intriguing, yet contro-versial players. At times, he demonstrates a level of ingenuity that is rare, even among high-stakes poker players. On other occasions, Hellmuth admit-tedly plays so poorly he probably couldn't beat a small-stakes game. Originally from Madison, Wisconsin, Hellmuth is the son of a university dean. He started playing poker seriously while enrolled at the University of Wisconsin and soon discovered he was far more interested in playing poker than studying.

At age 24, Hellmuth played in his first World Series of Poker. He shocked the poker world by upsetting two-time defending champion Johnny Chan and became the youngest winner in the history of Binion's annual classic. Hellmuth is famous for terrorizing the poker circuit with devastating hot streaks. In 1991, he finished in the top five in all Hall of Fame events at the Horseshoe. Two years later, he won an unprecedented three World Series of Poker events, in the same year! He also won the Hall of Fame championship in 1995.

Incredibly, all of Hellmuth's big wins have been in Texas Hold'em events, although he normally plays all games. Today, Hellmuth lives in the San Francisco Bay area. He continues to play high-stakes poker and can be seen at most major tournaments.

Scotty Nguyen

The tale of Thuan "Scotty" Nguyen is truly a rags to riches story. Nguyen (pronounced "win") fled South Vietnam in 1979 on a small boat that was stranded in the South Pacific. He was picked up with his family by a U.S. naval vessel and brought to the United States. Nguyen arrived virtually penni-less and eventually settled down in Chicago.

At age 21, Nguyen moved to Las Vegas and began working as a poker dealer. In his spare time, Nguyen started playing for low stakes and entered small, daily tournaments that were common in Las Vegas (and remain so). Over the next decade, Nguyen's skills gradually improved and he quit dealing to play poker full-time. Nguyen's first big break came when he won the Omaha High-Low Split event at the 1997 World Series of Poker. He returned the following year at age 35, and won poker's world championship, defeating a then-record 350 opponents.

Chris Moneymaker

Chris Moneymaker — yes that's his real name — turned the poker world upside down and on its ear by winning the 2003 World Series of Poker. Poker had a different look in 2003, and "Money" as his friends know Chris, is emblematic of it all.

2003 was the year Internet poker took hold, and many of the crowds that swelled the fields for the World Series of Poker events won their way in by playing online. That's how Moneymaker did it. He entered a $40 buy-in satellite event on `pokerstars.com`, a leading online poker site, won his event, and with it an entry into poker's big kahuna. Moneymaker's win isn't only symbolic of Internet poker's coming of age, but also it means that anyone can become a top-notch poker player in the comfort of his or her own living room.

Moneymaker can play poker with the best of them. His victory in a grueling event lasting five days proved that. But he's no grizzled Vegas pro; in fact the World Series of Poker marked the first poker tournament he ever played in a brick-and-mortar casino.

As past champions, big-money pros, and other players were eliminated over the tournament's five-day run, two players were finally left standing: Moneymaker and Sammy Farha of Houston. With his friends cheering "Go Money," he won the event with a full house consisting of three fives and two fours. Farha had a jack and a 10, ending up with a pair of jacks.

Moneymaker's win helps revolutionize poker and boost the game's popularity. "I got lucky along the way. I bluffed a lot during the tournament, but somehow I got away with it," said Moneymaker, who only began playing poker three years ago.

Back in the real world, far from Las Vegas's glitz and glamour, Moneymaker is an unassuming 27-year-old accountant from Tennessee who was working two jobs to support his wife and three-month old daughter when he won poker's premier event and a first prize of $2.5 million. When he burst in from the complete anonymity of Internet play to win poker's most prestigious event, he really tore down the walls. For his efforts, he no longer has to work two jobs, and his young daughter now has her college tuition paid for — and, oh yes, he's no longer anonymous.

Moneymaker, who donated $25,000 of his winnings to cancer research, said, "I was a little underestimated because no one knew who I was. If I can win it, anybody can."

Honorable Mentions

Some other poker legends who at least deserve honorable mentions include:

- **T. J. Cloutier:** One of the greatest tournament players ever.

- **Mike Caro:** The "Mad Genius of Poker" and founder of the Mike Caro Poker University.

- **Susie Isaacs:** A two-time Women's World Champion.

- **Barbara Enright:** A great tournament poker player.

- **Bill Boyd:** Known as the "Father of Modern Poker" for his extensive contributions to cardroom management and methodology.

- **David "Chip" Reese:** Once regarded as the best all-around poker player in the world.

- **"Puggy" Pearson:** Well known for his folksy philosophies, trademark cigars and 1973 World Championship.

- **Tom McEvoy:** A former World Champion and author of leading tournament poker books.

- **Robert "Harpo" Burton:** One of the greatest amateur and most dangerous players to ever play the game.

(This chapter was primarily prepared by Nolan Dalla, a columnist for Card Player Magazine. His connections to the world of high-stakes poker have given him unique insights into the personalities of many of the world's top players. Using a mathematical points system he devised, Dalla has awarded poker's "Player of the Year" annually since 1997. Dalla has also written a critically acclaimed book on the life of perhaps the greatest poker player in history, Behind the Shades: The Life and Times of Stu Ungar, the World's Greatest Gambler.)

Chapter 19

Ten Keys to Success

· ·

*B*ookstores are filled with self-help books. Seminars galore promise to teach you how to be a winner in business, in love, and in your personal life. Some of these same principles can make you a winner at the poker table. Here are ten you may want to think about.

Be Aware of Your Strengths and Weaknesses

An outrageous image at the table may work for some people but not for others. Some players are better suited to tournaments, others to ring games (cardrooms). Play your best game and play within the confines of your own comfort zone. In other words, know yourself, and do what you do well.

Act Responsibly

What you achieve in poker will be the product of your own play. Yes, luck is a factor in the game, at least in the short run. Over the long haul, it generally evens out. But until you acknowledge your own accountability for the results you achieve, you won't be able to exercise enough control over your skills and abilities to ensure success.

Think

Don't just play poker — you have to think about it. Unless you're consistent about doing your poker homework, you'll simply find yourself marking time. You need to keep up with the current poker literature, and you need to think about the game. Think about it while you're at the table and when you're away from it. Analyze hands you've seen. Decide whether you would have played them differently — and if so, why? Learning about poker, like learning about most other things, is a recursive process. Think, analyze, and modify your game. Then, repeat as needed.

Have a Plan

What is your goal as a poker player? Do you want to have fun and just break even? Do you want to be a top tournament player? Or do you want to be the best $15–$30 player around? How much are you willing to risk? You need a definite plan for your poker play. Without a plan to guide you, you're likely to wind up as a pawn in someone else's game!

Set Deadlines

If your goal is to play an average of 30 hours per week, then do it. If you plan to reread *Poker For Dummies* until you know it cold, then set a deadline for yourself and do that too. If you've lost all your poker money and need to rebuild your bankroll before venturing back into a casino, plan on how long it will take until you are back in action. Once you have a plan, go out and get the money you need to enable you to start playing again.

Be Realistic

If your goal is to win the World Series of Poker next year but you've never played a big limit game in your life, don't expect to achieve that simply by virtue of having read this book. Let's get real here. While your authors are terrific teachers (who are now learning to walk on water) they haven't quite mastered it yet.

Instead of indulging your fantasies, start with a challenging but reachable goal. Once you make it, you can set the next, more difficult, goal. Perhaps you want to set a goal of playing in one or two inexpensive tournaments per week, or playing in satellites that are usually part of the format surrounding major tournaments. If you don't do well there, keep trying. But save your money. You're probably not ready yet to invest big bucks in entry fees to major events.

Expect Difficulties

You will succumb to all of your flaws as a poker player during the period you are struggling, growing, and reaching for a higher level of skill. Just because you've read all the books by all the experts, don't deceive yourself into believing that you're going to play as well as they do. Every top-notch player struggled to reach the level of success they've achieved. You're going to have to do the same. Golf videos won't turn you into Tiger Woods, chess monographs won't turn you into Gary Kasparov, and *Poker For Dummies* will not turn you into Doyle Brunson. The best poker books will teach you how to *talk the talk*. You'll have to *walk the walk* on your own!

Build on Small Accomplishments

If you're not a winning player today but you study hard, put into practice what you read, and integrate these strategies into your own style of play, you'll find yourself improving. You may not be able to make your living from the game, but at least you'll no longer be a contributor. Keep doing what works for you, and you'll find that success builds upon itself.

Don't let small setbacks put you on tilt. You've already taught yourself to expect difficulties. If you play poorly, correct it next time. However, if you find yourself saying, "Just this once won't hurt me," you're wrong. It can hurt you, and it will. You've got to focus on what produces accomplishments. Playing a weak hand or taking the worst of it on a hunch — or just for the fun of it — is nothing more than premeditated backsliding. Do it, and you have only yourself to blame.

Persist

You must sustain. The saying, "Ninety percent of success is just showing up" has a lot of truth to it. You need to keep playing, keep practicing, and keep building on small successes. Each time you reach one of your goals, savor the moment. Then quickly set another goal.

Try visualizing. Golfers visualize their putts dropping; baseball players visualize the bat connecting with the ball; basketball players visualize the hoop growing and the ball dropping through, hitting nothing but net. In your mind, watch yourself make the right plays at the poker table. When you're able to visualize strategies in action, you'll see your winnings accrue in the process. Keep showing up, play your best game, and keep moving forward. Remember that some of your opponents will be improving too. If you do not consistently move forward with your own game, you are probably moving backwards in relation to your opponents.

Have Fun

Enjoy yourself while you are playing. Time spent playing poker is discretionary. No one has a gun at your head. If poker is not enjoyable, don't play. While there are lots of bitter pills we all have to swallow in life, we ought to enjoy what we *choose* to do. If you cannot enjoy yourself when you play, perhaps you should find another outlet for your time and money.

Some players are constantly griping when they play. Some of them have done this for years. It seems they are never happy. Why do they bother to play when they get no enjoyment from it? Questions like that can take a lifetime to answer. But unhappy players generally represent profit to you. So have fun when you play, or find something more enjoyable to do. You won't succeed as a poker player if you have to fight yourself as well as your opponents.

The information in this chapter is simple stuff, and it's as true in life as in poker. Look inward, look outward, set goals, deal with the inevitable setbacks, show up, have fun, and succeed. Sometimes it's that easy.

Chapter 20

(Almost) Ten Things to Consider Before Going Pro

· ·

*T*o most recreational poker players the idea of playing professionally seems like a dream. Get up when you want to, work when and where you choose, and ply your trade almost anywhere. From London to Las Vegas and California to Costa Rica, casino poker awaits you there. So what's stopping you? Only the answer to this critical question, "Can I make a living as a poker player?"

Poker Isn't Like Most Jobs

For one thing, if you're a poker player, you won't have a steady salary coming in. Even commissioned salespeople don't *lose* money if they fail to make a sale. But poker players do lose money whenever they have a bad day. It's one of the few jobs where you can go to work and lose money. Imagine that. An entire day of poker — under stressful conditions — and all you've got to show for it is less money than you started out with. Not a pretty picture, is it?

Still, people take up poker as a profession every day. Some do so after years of deliberation. A few do it on a whim. Others pursue it as a second career — after retirement — when they have alternative sources of income to steady the ship in a storm. How successful are they? There are no statistics handy — but we'd be willing to venture a guess that the majority of newly hatched professional poker players go broke, and probably do so within a year.

So how do you know if you can make a living playing poker? For a relatively unstable profession, there seem to be quite a few indices available to the seasoned player who's thinking about earning his living at the tables. Here are a few we'd recommend:

Considering Your Own Results

Anyone seriously considering poker as a career needs to keep his or her poker diary up-to-date, and do it assiduously. Never mind that you were tired, just had a fight at home, were stuck in horrible traffic on the way to the casino, and didn't play your best. When you're playing for a living, no excuses are allowed. Only reality counts, and wouldda, shouldda, couldda doesn't mean a thing.

Playing When You're Not at Your Best

Part of being a professional player is how well you play when you're not at your best — and you won't be at your best all the time. But professional poker players need to play their best game every time they walk into a casino. If you don't feel you can, you shouldn't play. Remember that playing poker frees you from a time clock. You don't *have to* play. And if you're not up to par, it will cost you far less to go see a movie than it will to visit the tables.

Keeping Good Records

If you haven't been keeping good records, you are not ready to play professionally. Oh, you can give it a go. No one's going to stop you. But without a foundation in data of your results, you might be deceiving yourself about your ability, and that can cost you more than money. If you have a career, a family, or other responsibilities, then going broke playing poker will take its toll on them all. If you don't believe us, just look around. Casinos are littered with broken souls.

Deciding Where to Play

Let's look at the bright side. Suppose you have been keeping good records, and furthermore, you're a winning player. What should you do now? That's easy. You need to decide where you want to play for a living. Perhaps you are living in an area where there are only small limit games — too small to provide the kind of livelihood you want — and you decide to move to California, or Las Vegas, or Atlantic City, or even Europe for that matter. Before you make the leap, do yourself a favor. Take the time to go there for at least a month to six weeks.

There might be a big difference between the games where you'd like to live and those in your own backyard. And if you're moving up to bigger limits because you can't earn enough money in small limit games, you can be assured of this: As you move up the ladder, the players get better. Part of becoming a professional poker player is finding your rung on the ladder. It's a question of striking a balance between the betting limits, which have a major impact on how much money you *can* earn, and the quality of your opponents, which will have a huge impact on how much you *will* earn.

Smaller games are more easily beaten, but lower betting limits constrain the amount of money you can expect to win. Big limit games usually have tougher players in the lineup. But if you are good enough, there's a limit you can beat that offers the best balance between your theoretical earning power and your actual win rate. When you've found that limit, you've arrived. That's not to say you can't move up. But that's where you belong now.

Using Statistics to Predict Your Expectations

If you think you can beat the games you intend to play in for a living but aren't certain, you can use statistics to help you assess what you might expect to win over the long haul. This involves calculating your standard deviation (see Chapter 9) and using it to assess the kind of results you might achieve.

Let's say that after 900 hours of playing $20–$40 Hold'em, your standard deviation is 20 small bets per hour, which is equivalent to $400. Everyone's standard deviation is different. Yours will depend on a number of factors, including your playing style, your opponents', and how aggressive or passive the game is.

Once you become familiar with the concept of standard deviation, you'll begin to see it as a useful tool for *qualifying* and *describing* your hourly winning average. You'll also realize that poker strategy frequently involves walking a fine line between playing aggressively so as to maximize your win rate, and not taking unnecessary risks in order to minimize the variance or swings you experience.

Assessing Your Risk Tolerance

The answers to so many "How should I play this hand?" questions really depend on your own risk tolerance. And you're free to choose your playing style; there's no right or wrong answer. You might be comfortable adopting a playing style designed to yield the highest possible win rate — and along with it, a much higher variance. Or you could win just as much money by playing cautiously, but you'd have to put in more hours at the table to achieve it.

If this seems like an anomaly, it's not. It's also the reason why very aggressive, top-notch players — those who take advantage of every edge, no matter how slight, in order to maximize their win rate — run a greater risk of going broke than work-a-day, grind-it-out professionals.

No Licensing Required

No credentials are required to be a professional poker player. No licensing or certification is needed. Anyone can do it. You can jump in if you dare, and who knows, you might succeed beyond your wildest dreams. But if you'd rather take a calculated risk before you give it a go, our advice is to be scrupulous about your recordkeeping and track your standard deviation to provide some perspective on your win rate. And give yourself a fair tryout in your venue of choice before scorching the earth behind you.

Following Good Examples

Playing poker for a living can be a solitary and sometimes lonely experience, and it helps to build relationships you can trust and to find other successful players who can serve as role models. Look at players whose results you admire and try to find out what they do and how they do it. See if you can learn the secrets of their discipline. Find out how they resist the temptation to play marginal hands in bad positions. Learn how they keep from going on tilt, and discover how they exploit the table when they have the best of it.

You'll find plenty of people you can talk to in any cardroom, but few you can absolutely trust to speak openly, honestly, and truthfully with you. When you find these people, keep those friendships. You can discuss your play and problems with them. You will each improve as a result of reinforcing one another. But you have to be willing to give more than you get in any relationship, and cardroom relationships are no exceptions.

Asking the Right Questions

Some players persist in asking the wrong questions. If you persist in asking, Why can't I win? Why do I always get the bad beats? Why does the idiot in seat five always win with aces and I always lose with them? You're asking the wrong questions too. Questions like these are self-defeating because they are based on the paradigm that life at the poker table is beyond your control.

If you change that paradigm to acknowledge that you are responsible for your actions at the card table, you might ask instead: How can I keep applying the winning strategies I've learned? What can I do to continue to prepare to win? How can I increase my winnings by recognizing and eliminating the "leaks" in my game?

If you ask the right questions your mind will direct itself to positive suggestions. Once you tell your mind that you do exercise control over your actions, it will suggest strategies based on this assertion. Successful people, and that includes successful poker players, do this routinely.

There's an old cliché that says, "Poker is a hard way to make easy money." And it's true. To be a successful professional poker player you need skill, discipline, strength of character, and the willingness to persevere when everything seems to be going against you and the light at the end of that proverbial tunnel seems to be receding like the view from the back end of a telescope.

But if you have the right stuff you can overcome this. Professional poker can be fun, rewarding, and social; and not many jobs let you set your own hours. You can even promote yourself to bigger games whenever you think you're ready for the challenge.

Playing poker for a living is not easy. But if you're realistic about assessing your chances, you might just be able to pull it off.

Chapter 21

Ten Ways to Improve Your Poker Today

● ●

Do you want to become a better poker player today? Right now? Here are ten specific things you can do today, and each one of them will improve your game.

Know Your Numbers

If you don't learn, understand, and use poker's mathematical parameters, it will prove difficult to be a consistent winner in the long run. For example, if you're playing Hold'em and flop four cards to a flush but don't know the odds against completing that hand, what will you do when it's your turn to act?

How will you ever know whether calling, raising, or folding is a play with a *positive expectation?* Finding positive expectations is the essence of winning poker, and it's no more complex than recognizing those situations that will show a profit if they could be replayed time and again.

Knowing when a positive expectation is associated with a given play is a big part of winning. Imagine you're faced with a $20 call into a $100 pot, but the odds against making your hand are only 3-to-1. That's a positive expectation. Repeated 100 times, you'd expect to lose $20 on 75 of those occasions, for a loss of $1,500, but on 25 occasions, you'll win $100, for a total of $2,500. Your net win of $1,000 ($2,500–$1,500) is what's important — not whether you won or lost on any particular hand. Divide your $1,000 win by the 100 times this situation occurred, and you'll see that in the long run, each correct decision was worth $10 to you.

Applying mathematics, statistics, and probability to poker can be an incredibly involving subject. But if you want to find out more about poker mathematics, read *Hold'em's Odds Book,* by Mike Petriv; *Getting the Best of It,* by David Sklansky; or *Gambling Theory and Other Topics,* by Mason Malmuth.

Know Your Opponents

How many times have you made a strategic move that's doomed to fail because you chose the wrong opponent? Ever tried to bluff against someone who's a veritable *calling station*? It won't work. We all know that, but far too often we do it in spite of our better judgment.

If mathematics was the only skill required for winning, the best players would all be mathematicians — and they're not. Knowing your opponents is equally important. Observe their actions at the table. Analyze their decisions and the choices they make. Are they in every hand? Do they raise with hands that don't warrant it? Are they rock-tight? You'll find it fairly easy to get a read on most players within an hour. The best time to do this is when you're *not* in a hand. If you find yourself waiting for a game, watch your opponents-to-be, so you can adjust and temper your game strategies to their play before you sit down at the table.

Keep Your Ego Out of the Game

Never, never let your ego control your play. Like they said in *The Godfather*, "This is business, not personal." Never personalize it if an opponent wins a big pot from you, not even if he looks you right in the eye and laughs like a loon as he rakes in the chips. The minute you decide to " . . . get him," you're sure to miss other opportunities and probably squander some chips chasing him down. If the old adage, "Living well is the best revenge" holds true, then playing well — and walking away with a few racks of chips — is a giant step in that direction.

Keep Records — Even When It Hurts

If you don't keep records how will you know whether you're winning or losing in the long run? Players who fail to keep records deceive themselves. Most players, when asked, will say they're life-long winners. But we both know that's not true. The next time someone tells you he's a life-long winner, ask about his records. If he doesn't assiduously record wins and losses, he's seeing only what he wants to — and more often than not, it's an illusion.

While few things are more painful than recording a big loss in your notebook, records are critical because the human mind is blessed with an endless capacity for self-deception.

Choose the Best Game

Much as we'd like to believe otherwise, the truth is that most of our winnings come not from our own brilliance but from our opponents' poor play. Choose the game with the weakest opponents. A game full of weak players who call too often but are reluctant to raise with strong hands will do fine. After all, if you can't beat players who call too much, who can you beat?

Commit to Excellence

Want to be a great poker player? Commit to greatness. Declare your excellence tonight, starting with the next hand you play. Visualize yourself as the greatest poker player ever — and act accordingly. You can reach excellence in a heartbeat, and you can do it today. If you want to be a winning, excellent player, go ahead and commit to it. Achieving change takes no time at all, but it will take forever to maintain it. Committing to excellence is that simple, but it requires every bit of your willpower.

Practice with Computerized Software

No matter how many hands you play at the table, using software like Wilson Software's *Turbo Texas Hold'em* to practice against lifelike opponents and run simulations that will test your own theories will help you make rapid progress in your development as a poker player.

Computers can do things humans don't have the time to accomplish. We've run experiments that simulated a *lifetime* of poker. We could have tested that same hypothesis by playing eight hours a day, five days a week, for 30 years, but what could we accomplish with that knowledge once we finished our research? It might be helpful if poker is played in the afterlife, but we're more concerned with earthly uses for our know-how.

Read the Newsgroup

If you don't have a computer, now is the time to go out and buy one. When you get that box home, connect to the Internet and read the discussions and poker news on the Internet newsgroup, `rec.gambling.poker` (RGP). While you'll find lots of social chatter, the Internet is often the source of some incredibly creative ideas about poker.

These ideas, for the most part, are not circulated outside the newsgroup. It's not out of secrecy, mind you, it's just that RGP attracts very bright, creative, and insightful folks who enjoy talking poker. As a result, it's fertile ground for new ideas and concepts. Ideas are posted, and comments swiftly feed back to the author. Information at warp speed: that's what the Internet is all about. You can follow the growth and development of ideas as they are molded and shaped by some of the poker community's brightest thinkers and theorists. The Internet is a medium you cannot ignore if you are serious about keeping up with the game's most current thinking and concepts.

Analyze Your Game — and Your Opponents'

Think when you're at the table, away from the table, and whenever you're not involved in a hand. Watch your opponents. Remember what kinds of hands they are willing to enter pots with in early, middle, and late position. See if they call too often or whether they are susceptible to bluffing. Learn their proclivities and patterns, and plan your strategy accordingly. You won't be very successful bluffing someone who calls all the time, and you only hurt yourself if you fail to bet for value against someone who calls far to often with weak hands.

Think about your own play too. Review hands you've won and lost. Determine whether there were alternative plays that would have resulted in a bigger win, or saved a bet or two if you lost. The line between winning or losing can be a fine one, and concentration may make all the difference between winning and losing in the long run.

Concentrate on Things That Matter

If you pay attention to the wrong things, the very best you can hope for is to get lucky. Asking for a deck change won't help you win. It won't cause you to lose either, but why concentrate on something that is of absolutely no value at all?

Poker tables are full of bad beat stories, and it won't take long until you've heard all of them. Why waste time grousing about the fact that your opponent got lucky? We all take turns getting lucky. That's not the point. Instead, think about what you might have done to knock him out of the pot so he wouldn't have had a chance to draw out on you. That matters!

Focus on how you played, and think about what you might have done differently to influence the outcome. Thinking about luck, or a deck change, or a dealer who's always bad news for you is unproductive. It's just like howling at the moon. It may feel good to do it, but ultimately it's silly and self-indulgent, and it won't help you win.

Face it. Nothing will make you an expert overnight. But there are a number of shortcuts along the road to poker excellence. Some of them, like computers, software, and books, require investments. But you will lose much more than you would ever invest in your own skill-building and development if you fail to invest in these tools. If poker matters to you — if you really want to become a winning player — then you owe it to yourself to take the steps that matter.

Read All the Books

We hear players eschew books all the time at the poker table. "I've played 20 years," they grumble, "and I don't need books to teach me about the game." Yet it's these very players who think a deck change is going to improve their luck, or that a certain dealer has it in for them. Sheeesh! These guys have been making the same mistakes for years, and their know-nothing attitude ensures that they will repeat this unproductive, mindless behavior for the next two decades.

There are lots of good poker books out there and we suggest you read them all. If you get just one good idea from a book, it will return the cost of its purchase many times over. Poker books are not an expense, they are an investment — one that's absolutely critical for improving your game. Check out Chapter 16 for our recommended list of poker books.

Chapter 22

Ten Real-Life Poker Lessons

● ●

*I*s there a player out there who hasn't observed that poker is a metaphor for life? That metaphor is probably one reason why poker is so popular. Not only does it frequently mirror life, poker models it. Poker is life in a nutshell. The entirety of our existence compressed into a single hand of poker is a compelling thought.

A metaphor and a model for life! If true, there should be important life lessons everyone can take away from the poker table. When learned and applied, these lessons should make it much easier for a poker player to survive in a world where most people haven't been force-fed these life-lessons across the poker table.

Being Selective and Aggressive

In the real world you do have to pick your battles, just as you must in poker. Sometimes you have to draw your proverbial line in the sand ("You've gotta know when to hold 'em"); other times you have to carefully choose when to retreat ("Know when to fold 'em").

History is replete with examples. General Robert E. Lee, confronting overwhelming supremacy in men, munitions, and technology, was able to keep the Confederacy's cause alive as long as he did because he picked his battles carefully. He did not engage the Union Army at every opportunity; he selected opportunities only when he believed he could negate the Union's inherent advantages and overcome them.

Safety at All Costs Can Be Costly

During the early stages of the U.S. Civil War, Union General George McClellan was unwilling to commit his troops, even when the odds were strongly in his favor. McClellan behaved like a player who is overly weak and overly tight, and General Lee consistently ran him off the best hand. McClellan ultimately suffered the military equivalent of a really bad beat. President Lincoln, who realized that his man held most of the big cards — and wondered why he wouldn't play a hand and therefore couldn't win — sacked him!

You can't wait for a royal flush in cards or in life. When you have an overwhelming advantage, it's usually time to engage your opponent.

Knowing Your Opponent

If you can pick up tells in a poker game — where players take great pains not to broadcast them — think how easy reading people away from the table can be. Yet seemingly few of us really take the time to know our opponents. Is your boss in a nasty, irritable mood? Maybe you'd be better off feigning an emergency and postponing your annual performance review until next week. You have a bad hand, and rather than risk losing even more money, the smart move is to fold and wait for a better opportunity.

There's undoubtedly something romantic about the fatalistic approach of marching into the jaws of death or some more civilized equivalent, but it's not a strategy that will help you win at either poker or life. But you needn't take our word for it. General George Patton said much the same thing in his celebrated quote, "The idea of war is not to die for your country; it's to make the other guy die for his."

Timing Can Be Everything

Is that boss of yours still in a foul mood? Wouldn't you stand a better chance of winning if you held a stronger hand? Tackle a tough project now. Close that sale and make some customer so happy that he calls your boss and tells him how valuable you are. Once you've been able to accomplish that, you're holding strong cards — strong enough to stand up to your annual performance review.

This situation is like so many that occur in poker. Someone bets, another player raises, and you throw your marginal hand away, preferring to wait for a much stronger hand before engaging your opponent.

Timing is important in your social life too. You don't have to be an expert on body language to realize that you're not making a great impression on your date, who has legs crossed, arms folded, and is leaning away from you with a bored, indifferent facial expression. It's time to try a new strategy, or be selective, fold your hand, and wait for some new cards to be dealt.

Deciding If the Prize Is Worth the Game

Winning poker players usually won't draw to a flush when the odds against making it are 3-to-1 or more, but the pot promises a payoff of only two dollars for each dollar invested. They'll wait until the pot promises a bigger payoff before risking their money.

The analogy is also true away from the table. While real-life payoffs can vary widely, your investments are usually time, money, or both. Is it worth your time to spend half a day trying to make a small sale without the promise of greater rewards down the road, or are you better off courting one of your bigger, better customers?

Whenever you analyze situations like this, the answers often seem obvious. Still, many people fritter away large amounts of time, not realizing that they are being horribly unproductive in the process. Office workers spend hours dealing with problems and issues that may be urgent, but are often neither significant nor important.

Better time management frees you from dealing with issues that have small payoffs associated with them. If you aspire to success, you'll look for chances to *capitalize on opportunity*, rather than spend your time fighting small, insignificant brush fires.

Reaching for Objectives

If you have no standards to guide you in selecting the hands you choose to play and adopt an any-two-cards-can-win philosophy, it probably won't be long until you lose all your poker money. Knowing in advance which cards you're going to play, what position you'll play them from, and how you'll handle different opponents are key factors to success at the poker table. The real world is no different. If you don't plan, you're just a leaf in the wind. While traveling in a random direction does get you somewhere, it's probably not where you hoped to go.

Poker teaches you to plan, to have an agenda, and to pursue it aggressively. In the real world, if you don't have your own agenda, you'll soon be part of someone else's. In fact, it's probably safe to assume that if you examined every person foolish enough to join a cult, you'd find very few of them with a plan or a set of governing values to guide them.

Being Responsible

Everyone, it seems, has a favorite *bad beat* story. It won't take long until you've heard them all and grow weary of them. Whenever someone launches a misery-laden tale in the direction of poker author Lee Jones, he announces that he charges a $1 fee to listen to each bad beat story. Some people are so bent on sharing their woeful tales that they toss him a chip and go right on talking.

No one wants to hear you whine at the poker table. So you lost in a way that defied all imaginable logic and odds. Enough, already. It doesn't change anything. You'll never be a successful poker player until you accept full and complete responsibility for the results you achieve.

Real life is much the same. Success in any field demands a willingness to be held accountable for your actions. Don't expect sympathy because you weren't born with Rockefeller's money, Einstein's brains, or Tom Cruise's looks. Neither were most folks. Get up. Get on your feet. Play the cards you were dealt — in poker and in life — and go on from there. Like successful poker players, those who are successful in real life are willing to place the blame for their failures right where it belongs — squarely on their shoulders.

Painting Yourself into a Corner

When Lou Krieger was 12 years old, his archenemy was Zimp, an overgrown, overweight 13-year-old. Zimp was always threatening to beat the daylights out of Krieger, who had no doubt he could do it. But Krieger had an out. Zimp was big and strong, but he was slow. Since Krieger could outrun him, outride him on a bicycle, and outclimb him over garage roofs and trees, he easily escaped every time Zimp took a run at him. As long as he was never cornered in a blind alley, he knew he could survive childhood.

Skinny Vinny didn't care for Krieger any more than Zimp did. Krieger could take Vinny, although Vinny was faster. Had Vinny and Zimp been card players, they would have known that even though Krieger was a favorite against each of them individually (he could outfight Vinny and outrun Zimp) if they ever teamed up, he was dead meat. All it would have taken was for Vinny to run Krieger down and keep him engaged until the ponderous but powerful Zimp arrived. But neither Zimp nor Vinny were fledgling rocket scientists; they weren't friends anyway, and never got together to conspire about how to take out their mutual enemy.

Next time you're holding a pair of kings or aces and thinking about just calling instead of raising to limit the field, remember Zimp and Vinny. They never got the better of Krieger because each chose to face him individually — and

Krieger was a big favorite heads up. If they took him on together, Krieger would have gone from a favorite individually to an underdog against their collective efforts.

Thinking Outside the Box

In the early 1970s, George Foreman was not the cute, funny, larger-than-life, genial grandfather he appears today. Back then many experts considered him the most punishing force boxing had ever seen.

On his road to a fight with Muhammad Ali, Foreman destroyed Ken Norton and Smokin' Joe Frazier — two fighters who gave Ali a very tough time. Foreman was so strong and his punching power so punishing that he literally walked through the best his opponents could offer and annihilated them with his stinging jab and devastating right hand. Foreman hit Joe Frazier so hard with a right hand to the body that Smokin' Joe was lifted about four inches off the ground. When he landed, Ali's toughest opponent collapsed like a sack of potatoes in the center of the ring.

That was enough for Ali, who realized that if Norton and Frazier couldn't stand up to Foreman, neither could he. He needed a new strategy, and to devise one he hand to think outside the box.

When the *Rumble in the Jungle*, as the fight was called, finally got under way in Zaire, it began as the pundits predicted. Big George Foreman was relentless, throwing punch after punch at full force in the direction of Ali, who covered up while leaning back against the ropes.

Ali offered little resistance. Outside of a few seemingly futile jabs, he looked as if he wasn't even trying to fight back.

But that was Ali's strategy. After a few rounds, the heavily muscled Foreman grew tired. He had punched himself out and was spent. Ali, by comparison, was fresh. He was also unhurt. Ali then began a counterattack. He came off the ropes and danced in the center of the ring. Ali, who was faster, peppered Foreman with jabs and stinging overhand right hands. Now it was Foreman who had nothing to offer. "What's the matter, George," Ali said as Foreman launched a slow, tepid punch in his direction, "Is that all you got?"

"Yeah," Foreman recalled saying to himself as he related the tale years later, "that's all I had."

Ali, who — like any good poker player — was selective and very aggressive once he had the best of it, won the fight. Like many good poker players, he also managed to get inside his opponent's head by dint of his guile, style, and image. But ultimately it was Muhammad Ali's creativity and ability to think outside the box that allowed him to beat George Foreman in a fight only he thought he could win.

Realizing When Discretion Is the Better Part of Valor

Sometimes life's lessons don't have to be transported from the card table and applied elsewhere; they are learned right on the spot. At Hollywood Park Casino players can bet on the horse races without leaving the card table. Bet runners take the bets and return with pari-mutuel tickets.

One of the players in a $20–$40 Hold'em game was particularly animated whenever it was race time. He would get up from the table yelling and shrieking at the top of his lungs as each race was run.

Whenever his horse won he would laud it over the table. "I win, I win, I win," he would shout, "and all the rest of you are losers."

Whenever he lost he would yell even louder, often directing his remarks to different players at the table. Once, when he had a particularly large wager on a horse that finished out of the money by a nose, he noticed a player at the other end of the table who was smiling at him. "What are you looking at, loser," he screamed. "I'll kill you."

The player just sank further down in his seat, as if to avoid any confrontation with the manic horseplayer. This only encouraged the horseplayer's aggressive tendencies. "Are you laughing at me?" he shouted. "No one laughs at me. I'll rip your head off," the horseplayer continued, as he stood up next to his seat.

"I don't think so," the player at the other end of the table said softly, as he stood up, still smiling.

As soon as his adversary stood up, the horseplayer quickly realized the error of his ways. The player he was threatening to kill was a former professional football player (an All-Pro lineman, to be exact) who had spent 13 years in the NFL. The horseplayer was of average height and weight. The former football player was about 8 inches taller and 120 pounds heavier.

The former football player smiled at the horseplayer and said, "Just sit down, shut up, and start over. Only this time, be nice."

Just to show you how rapidly some of life's lessons are learned, the suddenly conciliatory horseplayer sat back down immediately. This time he was the one who seemed to slide all the way down in his chair. And all he said was, "Yes, sir."

Index

• D •

• E •

Notes

Notes

Notes

Notes

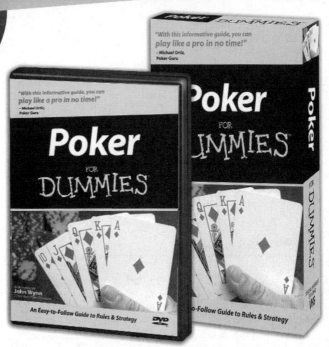